SOMALI NATIONALISM

INTERNATIONAL POLITICS AND THE DRIVE FOR UNITY IN THE HORN OF AFRICA

SAADIA TOUVAL

HARVARD UNIVERSITY PRESS
CAMBRIDGE, MASSACHUSETTS · 1963

Distributed in Great Britain by Oxford University Press · London

Library of Congress Catalog Card Number: 63–13817
Printed in the United States of America

Foreword

BY RUPERT EMERSON

AFRICA is a continent rich in nationalisms but poor in nations. At the two extremes of the continent at least a reasonable approximation of nations can be found in the Mediterranean countries of North Africa and among the Afrikaners in South Africa, although in the latter instance it is evident that the nation embraces only a fraction of the people of the country. Elsewhere in Africa, in the vast stretches south of the Sahara, many states have sprung into existence but few among them can lay claim to a people which has been welded together in national solidarity. Although the demand for independence and equality is posed in the name of the nation, the task of imposing national coherence and of leading a variegated and divided people to a sense of communal identity is for the most part still to be accomplished.

One of the distinctive attributes of the Somalis, whose political existence Saadia Touval surveys in this book, is that they possess a good measure of the elements, derived from the example of the classic Western European prototypes, which have in the past been assumed to be the essential ingredients of the nation. In contrast to most other African peoples, the Somalis are united in language, although there are dialectical differences and there is no written language. They are also united in the Muslim religion and in the belief of a common descent and heritage. In addition they regard as their rightful patrimony a great expanse of territory, part of which they inhabit only in nomadic fashion. It is here that trouble enters in, since a large part of the claimed territory is outside the frontiers of the Somali Republic and is embraced within Ethiopia, Kenya, and French Somaliland. The dimensions of the problem may be seen in the estimate that Ethiopia and Kenya would each be called upon to surrender one fifth of its territory, and French Somaliland might well be faced with total extinction though Somalis make up less than half its population.

The demand of the Somali Republic that there should be a "restoration of *Somalia irredenta*" is an authentic successor to the similar nationalist claims which have been advanced in almost every part of the world. It is a central tenet of the nationalist creed that the proper role of the state is to serve as the vehicle of political expression for the nation. Hence when nation and state fail to coincide, as in the case of the Somalis, the state system must be reshaped to bring it into harmony with the national foundations on which it should rest.

No less in the Horn of Africa than elsewhere, however, such an opposition of state and nation inescapably produces a head-on collision between two conflicting rights derived from different orders of legality. The Somali position is sustained by the rights gathered under the rubric of self-determination which have had the blessing not only of all nationalists but also of the United Nations Charter and, repeatedly, of the General Assembly, which in 1952 laid it down that the Covenant on Human Rights must contain the provision that "all peoples shall have the right of self-determination." This inherently revolutionary doctrine runs afoul of the juridical and political reality of the existing state structure, which rests upon the proposition that the sovereignty and integrity of the political units composing it is to be respected. The normative postulates of national self-determination challenge the positive law which safeguards the maintenance of the established order.

This is an issue which has been, and presumably will continue to be, of peculiar concern to Africa because the independent states which are now coming to compose it are the arbitrary creations of the imperial powers which lumped disparate tribes together within the colonial boundaries and often drew those boundaries in such fashion as to divide a single tribe between two or more European countries. Thus the Bakongo people found themselves parceled out to the French and Belgian Congos and Portuguese Angola, the Ewe were divided between the Gold Coast and the two Togolands, and the Yoruba between Nigeria and Dahomey. The Somalis themselves, already internally divided on tribal lines, were broken up into a number of segments under Italian, French, Ethiopian, and two types of British rule. For the Somalis as for others these colonial divisions meant not only the formal fact of a frontier cutting across a people but also that on the two sides of the frontier different languages were taught and different political, legal, and economic systems imposed.

In this colonial setting it was a reasonable expectation that the frontiers which the imperial powers had created would be swept away as the newly independent peoples redrew the map of Africa to meet their own needs and conceptions. Instead, with the rarest of exceptions, the colonially established frontiers have remained and the African states which have taken their place in the international society are the precise heirs of the colonial regimes. Far from seeking to overturn the existing boundaries, almost all the ruling groups in the new countries have committed themselves to the proposition that the political and territorial integrity of the colonially defined states should be preserved. Even President Nkrumah of Ghana, who, on grounds of tribal affiliation, had voiced claims to Togo and a slice of the Ivory Coast, appears to have receded from active advocacy of a program of reshaping states to achieve greater ethnic unity. The earlier doctrine came to the fore again, however, in a communiqué issued in October 1961 when President Aden Abdulla Osman of the Somali Republic visited Nkrumah. The two presidents took the position that although African frontier problems, inherited from colonial days, would be made obsolete by the achievement of a union of African states, they "recognized the imperative need to remove the existing frontiers artificially demarcated by the Colonialists without respect for ethnic, cultural or economic links." This objective, they maintained, could be achieved "by adherence to the principle of self-determination."

Because of the Somali Republic's broader national base, its claims have a somewhat different bearing from those of other African countries where what is immediately at stake is the joining together of tribal communities, forming only part of the larger state-nation, which have been severed in the course of the colonial scramble for Africa. But the Somalis are a part of Africa, and the kind of solution which is found for their problems cannot help having an effect on other peoples and territories in the continent.

With skill and objectivity Dr. Touval has given us a book which sketches the history and composition of the Somali people, depicts their emergence into the modern world, and indicates the major issues which lie before them.

Center for International Affairs
Harvard University

Author's Preface

THIS IS a study of one of the more complex and little-known problems of contemporary Africa—the Somali claims for national self-determination and unification, and their effect upon regional and international politics. My purpose is to present a balanced and useful survey of the problem and the many issues involved, not to make a "study in depth" of particular aspects such as the history of the region, Somali society and politics, or the politics of Ethiopia and Kenya.

The writing of this book, which grew out of a Ph.D. thesis presented at Harvard University, was made possible through the most generous assistance rendered by Harvard's Center for International Affairs. Special thanks are due Mr. Robert R. Bowie, Director of the Center, who has shown an interest in this study from its early stage. The Center enabled me to travel and study in the Horn of Africa and then to spend several months as a Research Fellow on the Center's premises while working on the book.

It would be infeasible to list all those from whose advice and assistance I benefited in this work. Yet, the book would be incomplete if I failed to mention certain persons without whose advice and assistance the book would have been much poorer. Foremost among them is Professor Rupert Emerson of Harvard University whose teaching first aroused my interest in the phenomenon of nationalism in general, and in its African variety in particular. I have also greatly profited from the teaching and advice of Professor Stanley Hoffmann, also of Harvard, and from the helpful criticisms of Dr. Jo W. Saxe, former Adviser to the Fellows at the Center for International Affairs. I wish also to mention the late Reuven Shiloah of the Israel Foreign Ministry who first suggested that I write about Somali nationalism. I should like to avail myself of this opportunity to thank the many knowledgeable and helpful people—government ministers, scholars, political leaders, soldiers, civil servants, and plain citizens, in the United States, England, France, Italy, Ethiopia, French Somaliland, the Somali Republic, and Kenya—whose hospitality and assistance greatly contributed to this book.

Finally, my thanks to Mr. Max Hall, the Center's Editor of Publications, for his dedicated and thorough work in improving the manuscript.

The responsibility for the book, of course, is solely mine.

Saadia Touval (Weltmann)

Jerusalem, January 1963

Contents

1. Introduction: Local Conflict and World Involvement 1
2. The Land and the People 5
3. The Somali Nation 23
4. The Partition of the Horn 30
5. Two Heroes of Somali Nationalism 49
6. The Development of National Consciousness 61
7. Nationalism and Politics in the Trust Territory of Somalia 85
8. Nationalism and Politics in British Somaliland 101
9. The Problems and Politics of Unification 109
10. The Politics of French Somaliland 123
11. The Problem of the Ethiopian Somalis 132
12. The Problem of the Kenya Somalis 147
13. A Question of Boundary Lines 154
14. The International Environment 164
15. Possibilities 181

Party Abbreviations 184
Notes 185
Index 207

CHARTS

Map of the Horn of Africa 7
An Outline of Somali Genealogy 17

TABLES

1. Territorial Distribution of the Somali People 12
2. Economic Activity, 1953, in Somalia 14
3. Election Results in Somalia, 1954–1959 88
4. Results of 1958 Municipal Elections in Benadir, Upper Juba, and Lower Juba Provinces 94
5. Results of February 1960 General Elections in British Somaliland 106
6. Tribal Composition of Somalia, British Somaliland, and the Somali Republic 118

SOMALI NATIONALISM

A NOTE ON THE NAME "SOMALIA"

The name "Somalia" commonly has more than one meaning. It is often used to designate the particular strip of territory which was formerly known as Italian Somaliland and which, after the Second World War, became a United Nations trust territory administered by Italy. The trust territory became independent on July 1, 1960, and that same day united with British Somaliland to form the Somali Republic. Thus, what had become widely known as "Somalia" became the Southern Region of the new state. At the same time, however, the term "Somalia" began to be used by many as a synonym of "Somali Republic," embracing both the Southern and Northern Regions.

In this book, to avoid confusion, whenever we mean the Somali Republic we shall say "Somali Republic." When we mean the Southern Region, we shall say "Southern Region." When we mean the trust territory under Italian administration between 1950 and 1960 we shall say "Somalia." When we mean the same piece of real estate before 1950, we shall say "Italian Somaliland."

The term "Greater Somalia," of course, is a concept rather than a reality, and its meaning will be evident.

Chapter 1

Introduction: Local Conflict and World Involvement

AMONG the most far-reaching consequences of colonialism in Africa has been the partition of the continent into political units whose borders were determined largely on the basis of European rivalries and interests. Now that colonies are becoming independent, the borders established by the colonial powers are being called into question.

Europe itself, after the emergence of modern nationalism there, underwent considerable shuffling of boundaries in order to make *states* conform to *nations*. A similar process may take place in Africa. The peoples grouped into political units in Africa, whether colonies or independent states, often do not constitute communities which can be readily recognized as nations. In newly independent African states where the sense of national cohesion is weak, powerful centrifugal forces, tribal and regional, are at work. Where ethnic groups are divided by an international border, there are pressures for territorial revisions with the object of achieving unity within the borders of one state.

Such pressures are at the root of the political problems of the Horn of Africa, the easternmost part of the continent. As a result of the territorial delimitations which took place at the end of the last century, the Somalis were divided among five different political entities: Italian Somaliland (later called Somalia), British Somaliland, French Somaliland, Ethiopia, and Kenya. For about fifty years, the division of the Horn did not create a major political problem. With the emergence of Somali nationalism, this division ceased to be generally acceptable to the people of the area, who began claiming the right to form a Somali nation state, a "Greater Somalia." Somali nationalists aimed at establishing this "Greater Somalia" through the unification of Somalia, British Somaliland, French Somaliland, and the Somali-inhabited portions of Ethiopia and Kenya. The establishment in 1960 of the Somali Republic through the unification of Somalia and British Somaliland is viewed by the nationalists as a step toward the realization of "Greater Somalia."

Somali nationalist aspirations raise a number of vexing international problems. Some of these problems bear similarity to the "nationalities question" which bedeviled European politics for generations, and they are likely to cause much bitter conflict in the Horn of Africa for years to come.

In French Somaliland, Somali claims have brought into the open the conflicting interests of the two major ethnic groups in the territory—the Somalis and the Danakils. Like any conflict between ethnic groups within the political boundaries of one territory, the issue is likely to be intractable. Moreover, Somali claims have spurred the interest of outside powers in this strategically located territory.

Somali irredentism with respect to Ethiopia is another source of bitter conflict. The territory claimed by the Somalis is sizable, amounting to one fifth of Ethiopia. Bitter as the conflict is, it perhaps would have been negotiable if no more than a territorial issue were involved. But much more is at stake. The problem is explosive because the Somali aspirations implicitly question the polyethnic foundations of the Ethiopian state.

The Somalis also claim a large chunk of Kenya. With the development of nationalism among Kenya Africans, a voluntary cession of territory by Kenya to the neighboring Somali Republic seems highly improbable. Thus, a conflict between the Somalis and the Kenya Africans seems to be in prospect as well.

How are these issues to be solved? A peaceful solution would require compromises and an accommodation of different points of view. Such a solution seems unlikely in present circumstances. The highly emotional nationalist attitudes and claims are viewed as challenges to the political and territorial integrity of states. A change in the political attitudes of the peoples involved, making a compromise possible, might take place in the course of time. But such a change is likely to occur only if the existing disputes are restrained from erupting into violent conflicts that would aggravate regional tensions.

Perhaps, if the Horn of Africa could be kept effectively isolated from the cold war and other outside tensions, a gradual change in political attitudes would be possible. Unfortunately, the region is being swept into the maelstrom of world politics. The region's strategic location has attracted the attention of outside powers. Britain and Italy are involved in the affairs of the region because of their connections as former administering powers. Britain still retains responsibility over Kenya, and France remains in possession of French Somaliland. Egypt has lent consistent support to Somali nationalism, and seems eager to establish Egyptian influence in the area. The Soviet Union has offered economic aid both to Ethiopia and the Somali Republic. China has entered the game by supporting certain opposition groups in the Somali Republic. The United States is a major source of economic aid to the region and has a military assistance agreement with Ethiopia.

The stage seems to be set for an inevitable conflict, involving not merely the local protagonists but outside powers. Yet it would be foolish to predict that such an outcome is bound to occur. African politics today has an extraordinary element about it. Political developments are not determined solely by conventional considerations of interest, namely the enhancement of one's power and influence. It is not uncommon in contemporary Africa, although the reverse is also known to happen, that tribal leaders give up their privileged positions for the sake of realizing broader nationalist goals. The precipitate unification of Somalia and British Somaliland is an illustration of this. In the present state of ferment in Africa and given the great appeal of Pan-Africanist sentiments, it is not altogether outside the realm of possibility that the problems raised by Somali nationalism will ultimately find a solution on a federal basis, and that a bloody conflict will be avoided.

In any event, the present task is not to predict war or peace, but to analyze the major factors in this complicated situation.

Chapter 2

The Land and the People

THE Horn of Africa can be thought of as a triangle, whose up-tilted eastern point extends so far into the Indian Ocean that it is approximately due south of Tehran. The "Horn," of course, is not a definite territorial jurisdiction, but for the purposes of this book we define it arbitrarily (but conveniently) as the region inhabited mainly by Somalis. More specifically, we give it 374,200 square miles, covering the whole of the Somali Republic, about one third of French Somaliland, about one fifth of Ethiopia, and about one fifth of Kenya. One side of the triangle extends along the Indian Ocean for more than a thousand miles, southwest and northeast, from the vicinity of the mouth of the Tana river in Kenya to Cape Guardafui at the eastern tip of the Horn. The northern side of the triangle, running approximately east-west, is the coast of the Gulf of Aden. The third side is an irregular north-south line from the Gulf of Tajura in the north to the Tana river in the south.

THE LAND[1]

The greater part of the Horn of Africa is extremely arid, meagerly supporting a population that is primarily nomadic. The territory is largely high ground. A mountain range extends along the northern leg, facing the Gulf of Aden and leaving room for a very narrow maritime plain. These mountains, which rise above 8,000 feet in some places, are dissected by a series of river beds and valleys running in the general direction of south to north and draining into the Gulf of Aden. Toward the west, where the coast curves northward to the French Somaliland city of Jibuti, the mountains continue inland and connect with an easterly arm of the loftier Ethiopian mountains, home of the Ethiopian city of Harar. South and southeast of this Ethiopian range lies the great Ogaden plateau, covering the whole eastern part of Ethiopia and named after the Ogaden tribes of Somalis that inhabit it. Starting at an elevation of about 6,000 feet, the Ogaden slopes gently toward the Indian Ocean. In the Southern Region of the Somali Republic—formerly Somalia—the plateau gives way to a maritime plain, which is a hundred miles wide in the south, below the coastal city of Mogadishu, but gradually narrows until it hardly exceeds five miles near the eastern tip of the Horn.

Only two watercourses within the Horn of Africa contain water throughout the year. These are the Juba and Webi Shebeli rivers. Both rise in Ethiopia and flow southeast through the Southern Region of the Somali Republic toward the Indian Ocean. Of the two rivers only the Juba reaches the sea. The waters of the Webi Shebeli are lost in swamps southwest of Mogadishu. Both rivers are used extensively for irrigation, and agricultural settlements have developed in their vicinity. The Tana, part of which forms the southern edge of the Horn as defined here, also runs the year round, and some Somali tribes use it to water their stock during the dry season. Other watercourses run only seasonally. Most of their waters are lost without being used for irrigation; but their valleys often provide good pasture after the rains.

Although the region is arid, it is not a desert, but rather savanna. Rains are meager, and the precipitation fluctuates considerably from year to year and is therefore not only small but unreliable. Precipitation averages a mere two inches annually in the northern maritime plain facing the Gulf of Aden. In the mountains, it reaches up to twenty inches, and farther south, in the plateau, it tapers off gradually; the northern part of the Ogaden sometimes receives up to

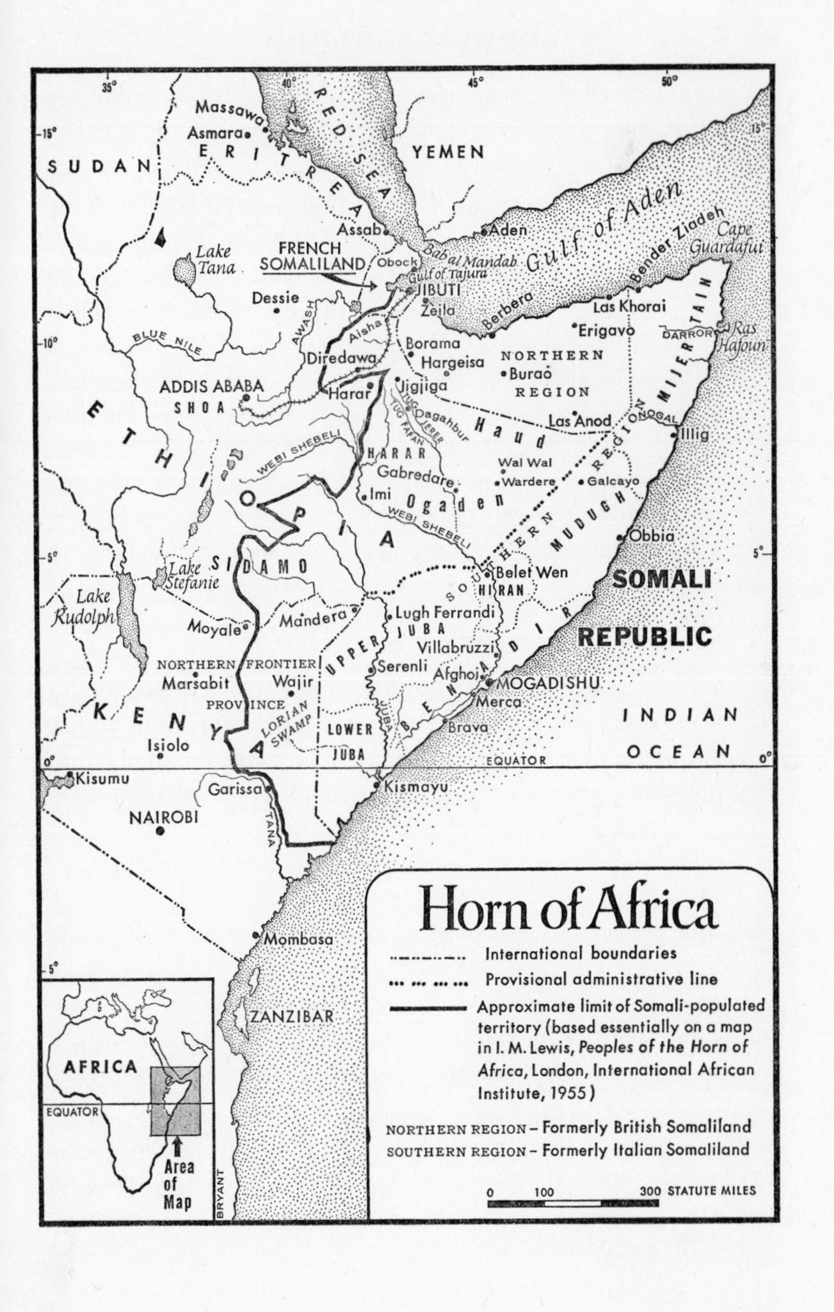

Horn of Africa
International boundaries
Provisional administrative line
Approximate limit of Somali-populated territory (based essentially on a map in I. M. Lewis, *Peoples of the Horn of Africa*, London, International African Institute, 1955)
NORTHERN REGION – Formerly British Somaliland
SOUTHERN REGION – Formerly Italian Somaliland
0 100 300 STATUTE MILES
SUDAN
ERITREA
Massawa
Asmara
RED SEA
YEMEN
Aden
Gulf of Aden
Assab
FRENCH SOMALILAND
Obock
Bab al Mandab
Gulf of Tajura
JIBUTI
Zeila
Lake Tana
Dessie
BLUE NILE
AWASH
Aisha
ADDIS ABABA
SHOA
ETHIOPIA
Diredawa
Harar
Jigjiga
Borama
Hargeisa
Berbera
Bender Ziadeh
Cape Guardafui
Las Khorai
Erigavo
MIJERTAIN
DARROR
Ras Hafoun
NORTHERN REGION
Burao
Las Anod
NOGAL
Illig
Haud
TUG JERER
TUG FAFAN
Dagahbur
HARAR
WEBI SHEBELI
Gabredare
Imi
Ogaden
Wal Wal
Wardere
Galcayo
SOUTHERN REGION
MUDUGH
Obbia
SIDAMO
Lake Stefanie
Lake Rudolph
Belet Wen
HIRAN
SOMALI REPUBLIC
Moyale
Mandera
Lugh Ferrandi
UPPER JUBA
Villabruzzi
BENADIR
Serenli
Afghoi
MOGADISHU
Merca
Brava
NORTHERN FRONTIER PROVINCE
Marsabit
Wajir
LORIAN SWAMP
LOWER JUBA
JUBA
KENYA
Isiolo
INDIAN OCEAN
EQUATOR
Kisumu
Garissa
Kismayu
TANA
NAIROBI
Mombasa
ZANZIBAR
AFRICA
Area of Map
BRYANT

fifteen inches, whereas the southern section ordinarily gets only two inches. In the Mijertain and Mudugh provinces of the Southern Region the average annual rainfall is negligible—around four and six inches respectively. In the south of the Southern Region, and in most of northern Kenya, the rainfall is somewhat heavier, though extremely variable from area to area. For example, in Kenya it has averaged as high as thirty inches at Moyale and as low as five inches at Mandera.[2]

There are two rainy seasons and two dry seasons. In the north, the heavy rains commence in April and taper off by June. The light rains fall between August and October. The other months are exceedingly dry, but the worst dry period hits the north between December and February. The south experiences similar weather, but the seasons begin and end there about a month later than in the north.

The Horn in Early History

Archaeological evidence found at several locations throughout the Horn indicates that the region was inhabited in prehistoric times. The earliest culture found has been assigned to the beginning of the last pluvial age, roughly 100,000 years ago. Several successive stone-age cultures have been identified.[3]

Earliest historical records relating to what is now the Somali coast were found in ancient Egyptian inscriptions. It is known that the ancient Egyptians visited that coast in search of incense and aromatic spices. It is even possible that some of the expeditions sent by various Egyptian rulers established trading settlements there. There is reason to believe that the Jews and the Phoenicians also traded with the coastal peoples. The land of Ophir mentioned in the Bible was probably situated somewhere along the eastern shore of Africa. Records of later contacts between the area and the Mediterranean civilizations are found in the writings of Greek Alexandrine geographers.[4]

For the period following the spread of Islam in the seventh century, information about the Horn is more abundant. Local chronicles, in addition to reports of travelers and explorers, provide valuable data about the coastal settlements, though information about the interior remains rather scanty.[5] It is known that an Arab sultanate was established in the seventh century at Zeila on the Red Sea coast, and that by the thirteenth century it had developed into the powerful "Adal Empire." In the sixteenth century the capital was moved to Harar, but the Empire gradually disintegrated and the coast became a dependency of Yemen, thus falling under the nominal suzerainty of the Ottoman Empire.[6]

The towns along the coast of the Indian Ocean were inhabited mainly by Arabs who immigrated at different times from Arabia. Prosperous local Arab sultanates had existed at Mogadishu, Brava, and other localities until the fifteenth century, when pressure from the nomadic people of the interior (probably Somali) increased, interfering with trade. In the sixteenth century the coastal towns were conquered by the Portuguese. They, in turn, were driven out in the seventeenth century by the Imam of Muscat. In the middle of the nineteenth century the coastal towns were occupied by the Sultan of Zanzibar, from whose hands they passed later to Italy.[7]

The Somalis

The inhabitants of the Horn were known by a variety of names throughout history. The ancient Greeks and Romans called them Berbers. The name survives today in the town of Berbera in the Northern Region of the Somali Republic. Some of the tribal names mentioned by Arab geographers in the Middle Ages (e.g., Hawiya) are clearly traceable today to individual Somali tribes. The collective name Somali is, however, of more recent origin. Apparently it first appears in an Ethiopic hymn eulogizing Negus Yeshaq (1414–1429) for his victory against the neighboring Moslem sultanate of Ifat. The name appears quite frequently in the *Futuh al Habasha,* a chronicle written sometime between 1540 and 1550.[8]

The etymology of the name Somali has not been authoritatively established. According to one version, it is a combination of *so* (go) and *mal* (milk), referring to the words the wandering stranger would hear upon his arrival in a Somali encampment when his host sent one of the women or children to fetch some milk. According to another version, the name is derived from "soumahe," an Abyssinian word for "heathen." The Somalis' own view is that the name derives from the name of one of their ancestors. This ancestor, an heir to a rich trader, was nicknamed "Zumal," which in Arabic means "the wealthy."[9]

When did the Somali people begin to figure in the history of the region? Unfortunately, little is known. Folk traditions and archaeological evidence indicate that the Somalis arrived in the Horn of Africa during the Middle Ages and therefore are relative newcomers. Earlier, the region had probably been inhabited by Negroid people, who had been pushed southward and replaced by Hamitic invaders. There is evidence that the early Hamitic inhabitants of the Horn were Galla tribes. They were succeeded by the Somalis.[10]

The origin of the Somali tribes is unknown. One possibility is that they are descendants of a distinct wave of Hamitic people who arrived in the area after the Gallas. Another theory is that the Somalis are actually Semiticized Gallas. That is, they are descendants of the Galla tribes which inhabited portions of what is now the Northern Region of the Somali Republic and which were subject to influences emanating from Arabia, both through a certain degree of intermarriage and through the adoption of Islam. Supporting evidence for this theory can be found in many Somali traditions and folk tales.[11] In any case, the Somalis, from their probable original habitat in what is now the Northern Region, spread throughout the Horn.

The Somalis' expansion from the relatively small area they occupied in the north is believed to have begun in the fourteenth century and to have particularly intensified in the sixteenth. It continues to this day. The present migration southward is caused mainly by the increase in population and stocks and the search for better grazing areas. Most likely, similar pressures had been the cause of past Somali migrations as well, though in some periods, and notably in the sixteenth century, the economic necessity was apparently supplemented by religious zeal for the spread of Islam. The history of the migrations of the last sixty years suggests that the expansion was carried out by the dual methods of assimilation and war. Some of the Gallas who inhabited the Horn before the Somali expansion were Islamized and assimilated into the Somali tribal structure; others were defeated in war and forced to vacate their lands. Among the first Somalis to move southward were the Hawiya tribe who took the coastal route and occupied around the fourteenth century their present habitat north of Mogadishu. From there, they expanded gradually westward and by the seventeenth century occupied areas between the Webi Shebeli and Juba, though Gallas remained to live among them. The Rahanwein Somalis made their appearance in the south about the same time, settling on the fertile lands along the rivers. A portion of the Darod tribe moved southward along the same coastal route, pushing the Hawiya farther south, and another branch moved westward into the Ogaden, driving the Issa and Ishaq Somalis northward toward the Gulf of Tajura. Some of the Ogaden Darod descended along the Juba river, displacing the Gallas and forcing them to move south and west into what is now Kenya. The Somalis first crossed the Juba sometime in the middle of the nineteenth century, and their expansion into northern Kenya has occurred within the last sixty years.[12]

Thus it came about that the Somalis inhabit today the area of approximately 374,000 square miles stretching from Jibuti in the north to the river Tana in the south, and from the Indian Ocean in the east to the Ethiopian highlands in the west. They number some 2,850,000. Estimates of population and territory are set forth in Table 1.

Ethnic Minorities in the Horn

The ethnic composition of the population of the Horn of Africa—except for cosmopolitan Jibuti—is homogeneous: almost the entire

TABLE 1 Territorial Distribution of the Somali People

Country	Somali-inhabited area in square miles	Somali-inhabited area as percentage of total area	Estimated Somali population	Somali population as percentage of total population
Somali Republic, total	246,000	100	1,880,000	99
Southern Region . .	*178,000*[a]	*100*	*1,230,000*[a]	97
Northern Region .	*68,000*[b]	*100*	*650,000*[b]	99
French Somaliland . .	3,200[c]	36	29,000[d]	43
Ethiopia[e]	80,000	20	850,000	4
Kenya	45,000[f]	20	94,000[g]	1
Totals	374,200		2,853,000	

[a] Source: Italy, Ministry of Foreign Affairs, *Rapport du Gouvernement Italien à l'Assemblée Générale des Nations Unies sur l'Administration de Tutelle de la Somalie, 1959* (Rome, 1960), p. 211. Population estimate is for 1953. European, Arab, and Indo-Pakistani minorities are excluded; Negroid agricultural communities are included.

[b] Source: Great Britain, Colonial Office, *Somaliland Protectorate,* Report for the Years 1956 and 1957 (London, 1959), pp. 9, 46.

[c] Estimate based on data gathered by the author in Jibuti.

[d] Estimate based on *Guide Annuaire de la Côte Française des Somalis, 1959* (Jibuti), p. 36. Figure includes immigrant Somalis.

[e] Estimates are based on data gathered by the author in Ethiopia. Population estimate is for 1960; total population of Ethiopia is assumed to be 20 million.

[f] Excludes Somali-occupied area in Isiolo district.

[g] 1958 estimate based on data gathered by the author in Kenya. It excludes the Somalis of Isiolo district and those living outside the Northern Frontier Province.

population is Somali. There are, however, several minority groups. From the point of view of their cultural impact, the most important minority are the Arabs. There are close to 35,000 Arabs scattered throughout the Horn—30,000 of them in the Southern Region of the Somali Republic. They are traders living in separate communities, mainly in the coastal towns, with a few dispersed groups in the interior. Some of these communities have been established for centuries, their ancestors having come from Yemen and the Hadramaut; others are more recent immigrants.[13]

There are also scattered Negroid groups in the Southern Region estimated in 1948 at 44,000.[14] Their origins are unknown and are the subject of various hypotheses. It is believed that they are remnants of pre-Hamitic inhabitants of the region and that their ranks were reinforced through intermarriage with large numbers of free slaves. They live in segregated communities along the Webi Shebeli and Juba, as well as in the area between them. The Somalis look upon them as an inferior race; yet in many respects these communities form "an integral part of the total Somali social structure." They are mainly agriculturists and hunters and live in a symbiotic relationship with the neighboring Somali tribes.[15]

In the Southern Region there are also several smaller minorities. Two very small groups of mixed and unknown origins are the Amaranis and the Bajunis. The Amaranis are merchants and sailors, and speak a Swahili dialect. They are concentrated mainly in Brava, though smaller communities are to be found in Merca, Mogadishu, and Afghoi. The Bajunis are mainly fishermen and live in Kismayu and the islands near it.[16]

There is also a small Indo-Pakistani population. Approximately 1200 Indians and Pakistanis, mainly traders, live in the Southern Region of the Somali Republic. In the Northern Region and in the Somali-inhabited portions of Kenya there are scattered Indian and Pakistani traders and government employees.[17]

The Europeans in the Horn are few in number. In December 1958 there were in Somalia approximately 3,000 Italians. Of these, 2,330 were permanent residents engaged in commerce and employed by various foreign-owned enterprises, and 536 were employed by the administration. After the attainment of independence in 1960—and even before—many of the Italian civil servants left the country. The rest of the European population in the Horn is largely British and does not exceed a few hundred.[18]

Somali Society and Way of Life

The presence of minority groups does not diminish Somali predominance in the Horn, nor detract from its ethnic homogeneity. The social and political cleavages in the region do not stem from the presence of minority groups, but have their roots in the traditional structure of Somali society.

The majority of the Somalis, approximately 80 percent, are nomads who migrate according to the season to places where water and grazing are available. The nomadic tribesmen make their living by raising cattle and camels, and in some areas sheep and goats. The animals provide food and transport, as well as the means of exchange for other necessary transactions, such as bride money and blood compensation. Occupational statistics are available only for Somalia, at a time before it became the Southern Region of the Somali Republic; this is the only territory with a sizable sedentary population. The figures are given in Table 2.

TABLE 2 Economic Activity, 1953, in Somalia
(Now Southern Region of Somali Republic)

Source of livelihood	Number of people	Percent of total population
Nomads	542,000	42.9
Semi-nomads (engaged partly in agriculture)	356,000	28.1
Agriculture	240,000	19.0
Marine and fishing	13,000	1.0
Trade and commerce	40,000	3.2
Artisans	12,000	1.0
Other	61,000	4.8
Totals	1,264,000	100.0

Source: Italy, Ministry of Foreign Affairs, *Rapport du Gouvernement Italien à l'Assemblée Générale des Nations Unies sur l'Administration de Tutelle de la Somalie, 1959* (Rome, 1960), p. 212.

Permanent settlements in the Horn are relatively few. The largest are the coastal towns, which have served as ports and trading centers for many centuries. The most important of these is Mogadishu, capital of the Somali Republic and principal city of the Southern Region, with a population of 90,000. The second largest town is nearby Merca, with 62,000 inhabitants. Hargeisa, the administrative center of the Northern Region, is situated on high ground some distance from the Gulf of Aden, and has a population of 45,000. Berbera, the principal seaport of the Northern Region, has 15,000 during the hot season and 30,000 during the cooler months. In the interior of the Horn a number of small settlements have developed around religious schools and near wells and watering places.

In Western terms the Somalis have not been greatly affected by urbanization, but in the African framework their urbanization is moderately high. Mogadishu is the only place in the Horn that approaches a population of 100,000 but there are twenty-two with more than 5,000 inhabitants. The rate of urbanization is highest in the Southern Region (Somalia) where approximately 325,000 people, or about one fourth of the population, live in towns of more than 5,000 inhabitants. The comparable figure for the remainder of the Somali-inhabited territories is 85,000, or 5.6 percent of the population. Thus the total for the Horn is approximately 410,000 people, or 14 percent of the population. This figure includes semi-nomadic people who settle within townships during the dry season. These cannot be considered "urbanized" in the sense of having adopted a city or town way of life. Nevertheless they are to some extent influenced by urban attitudes.[19]

The two most significant facts concerning Somali society are the Somalis' belief in common ancestry and their segmentation. Their belief in common ancestry is at the root of Somali national solidarity. Their segmentation into lineage groups provides the key to the understanding of their politics.

The traditional genealogies of Somali tribes trace their origins to the Quraysh, the lineage of the Prophet Mohamed. The claim reflects the historical contact with Arabia and with Islam. Most probably small groups of Arab immigrants settled among the Somalis and intermarried with them. It is not surprising that the Somalis, being Moslem, developed a tradition of having descended from these immigrants, and ultimately, from the Prophet himself.[20]

From their common ancestor the Somali people branch off into lineage groups, referred to here as "tribes." The term "tribe" is here used loosely to denote an intermediate group—larger than the clan, yet smaller than the nation. There is no ethnic difference among

Somali tribes. The Somalis' view of their tribal relationships is analogous to the Old Testament version of the tribal segmentation of the Children of Israel.[21]

As the chart shows, there is a primary division in Somali society between Sab and Samaale. This differentiation not only is sociological, but also is reflected in politics. The chart is primarily a genealogy, in the sense that all names on it are names of people who are considered ancestors of important Somali groups. The chart also shows present-day tribal divisions, since tribal names usually derive from the person who started the line. Names underlined twice represent the principal Somali tribes, and names underlined once represent their most important divisions.

Generally speaking, the Sab are cultivators, living mainly in the south, between the Juba and Webi Shebeli. They are descendants of formerly nomadic tribes, the first Somalis to migrate into that area and conquer the country from its previous Negroid and Galla inhabitants. The victorious Somalis were much influenced by the vanquished; Negroid and Galla physical and cultural features are noticeable among the Sab. The social organization of the Sab is much more hierarchical and formal than that of the Samaale. The Sab are considered "less warlike, less individualistic, more cooperative and more biddable" than their Samaale brethren.[22]

The Samaale are largely nomadic. They are the dominant element throughout the Horn, except in the fertile lands between the rivers. They are warlike people living in small, temporary hamlets, dismantling their huts and loading them on burden camels as they migrate. Because of the nomadic way of life, their social units are smaller and more self-sufficient than those of the Sab. The Samaale do not recognize clearly defined territorial units, and often families and clans of different tribes are interspersed in the same area. But the tribes do have "home wells" and traditional grazing areas which they inhabit according to the season. Thus, wells and grazing areas might be associated with particular tribes, but not to the exclusion of other tribes or clans which might use the same wells or graze their livestock in the same territory.[23]

An Outline of Somali Genealogy

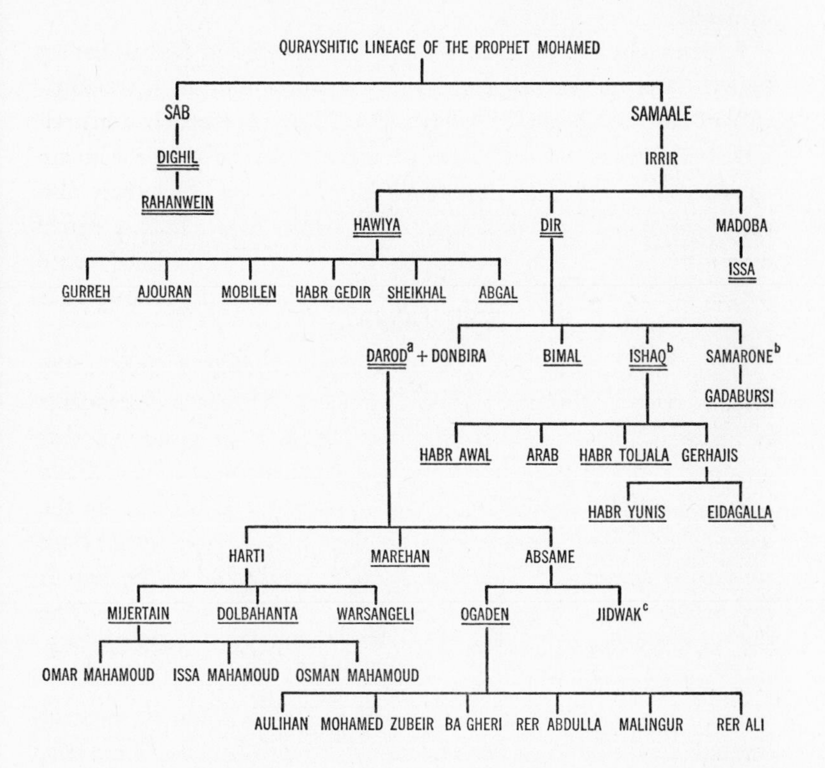

[a] Darod, who was of Arabian stock, married Dir's daughter.

[b] Ishaq and Samarone were immigrants from Arabia at first protected by the Dir. Their marriage relationship to the Dir was more indirect and distant than Darod's.

[c] Agricultural people in the Harar area (includes such groups as Abaskul, Bartire, Geri Jarso, Geri Babile).

NOTE: The chart, of course, is not intended to be a detailed genealogy—only to point to groups with political significance. It is based on: R. E. Drake-Brockman, *British Somaliland* (London: Hurst & Blackett, 1912), pp. 71, 272–273; J. A. Hunt, *A General Survey of the Somaliland Protectorate, 1944–50* (London: Crown Agents for the Colonies, 1951), pp. 125–151; I. M. Lewis, *Peoples of the Horn of Africa* (London: International African Institute, 1955), pp. 15, 18–40; and additional information collected by the author.

Between the Samaale and the Sab there is some antipathy. I. M. Lewis relates that

> to the nomad, the Sab are *masaakiin,* poor not so much in material wealth as in spirit. Their greater respect for authority and Government, founded in their agricultural economy, is at complete variance with the nomadic ideal of the independence of the warrior. Equally their interest in cultivation provides strong grounds for despisal. Even those westernized Somalis of nomadic origin, who recognize the contribution made by the Sab to the conquest of clanship and to the development of Somali nationalism in Somalia still seem to have a lingering feeling of superiority to the Sab.[24]

A third group, the outcaste *sab,* must also be mentioned.* The term *sab* denotes low caste and is used to designate three main groups: the Tumal, the Yibir, and the Midgan. The Tumal are blacksmiths making spears, arrows, horse bits, and other such articles. The Yibir are leather workers and the Midgan are hunters. All three groups have a reputation for witchcraft and magic. They are dispersed among the other Somali tribes and are attached to them in a client-patron relationship, the *sab* performing certain services for the "noble" tribes. There is no mixing or intermarriage between the *sab* and the patron tribes. The *sab* seem to accept their inferior status, a disposition reflected in the absence of traditions claiming "noble" ancestry. When questioned, the *sab* usually answer that their ancestor was found in the bush by the Somali patron tribe.[25]

Traditional political organization among Somali tribes is limited both in scope and in effect.

Among the Sab there often, though not always, exists a formal hierarchical organization of councils and headmen. Where these exist, they are charged with judging disputes, representing the tribe in its relations with other tribes, and organizing and supervising certain public works projects.

* Following Lewis's practice, we use *sab* when referring to these scattered outcaste peoples, and Sab when referring to the settled Dighil and Rahanwein tribes of the Southern Region.

As for the nomadic Samaale, their political organization is less formal. Some tribes, though not all, have titular chiefs called *suldaan* (sultan), *garad, boqor,* or *ugaas.* The chief represents his tribe in dealings with other tribes, and often aids in the settlement of disputes among the clans. The individual's loyalty extends beyond his family to the "dia-paying group," that is, the group which jointly pays and receives compensation for murder and other personal injury. These are fairly stable units, varying in size from a few hundred to a few thousand men. With the exception of the "dia-paying groups" there are among the Samaale no permanent and stable traditional political units and no traditional formal political organizations. The absence of formal political organizations is probably the consequence of the nomadic way of life, characterized not only by mobility but also by the extreme fragmentation of tribes and clans.[26]

Somali Personality and Physical Features

The conditions of life had their effect also on the molding of the Somali character. Generalizations on "national character" are ordinarily of questionable validity. However, the attention paid to the subject by a number of observers, and certain similarities in their descriptions, perhaps justify a few references to the subject. The Somali is invariably described as independent in nature, temperamental, and strikingly intelligent. R. E. Drake-Brockman, who studied the Somalis at the beginning of this century, told how he encountered a caravan in Kenya escorted by natives whom he could not identify. He queried the Muganda police corporal in his own entourage. The corporal replied: "Somalis, *Bwana,* they no good; each man his own Sultan."[27] The traits of independence and reluctance to submit to authority have been ascribed to the living conditions, which are not conducive to the development of large social units with the hierarchy and interdependence that they entail. These living conditions tend rather to reward individual initiative and resourcefulness.[28]

By their physical characteristics, the Somalis are classified with the Ethiopic peoples. They are tall, with long legs, shortish arms, curly hair, and "complexion varying from intense pigmentation to very dark." The Somalis are not as dark as the Negroes and differ from them also in their facial characteristics, having a "narrow, fairly sharp" face, long thin nose, and lips that are "rarely very thick."[29] The Somalis, however, are not all racially uniform. Among the southern agricultural people one frequently encounters individuals with Negroid characteristics. In the coastal towns, there is a considerable admixture of Arab and Persian stock. These variations notwithstanding, the Somalis are clearly distinguishable by their physical features from their Bantu and Nilo-Hamitic neighbors to the south. On the other hand, it is difficult to distinguish them by their physical features from their Galla and Danakil neighbors to the west and north.

Religion, Language, and Customs

Culturally, there is much cohesion among the Somali people, distinguishing them from the neighboring tribes. They differ from their neighbors in their religion, their language, and to some extent in their customs and way of life.

The practice of Islam differentiates the Somalis from the Christian peoples of Ethiopia, and from the Christian and pagan peoples of Kenya. The Gallas who border on the Somalis in the southwest are mainly pagan. The distinction among the Somalis, the Danakils, and certain Galla tribes near Harar is less clear, since Islam is the religion of all these. Nevertheless there are some variations among the three groups in their practice of Islam.[30]

Religious practice, for that matter, is not entirely uniform among the Somalis. The settled Somalis in the south are often more orthodox than the nomads. The nomadic Somalis are less regular in their prayers, yet perform certain formal duties of Islam and particularly enjoy certain social aspects of religion, such as celebrations of saints' days. The religious practice of the nomads has been greatly influenced by Sufism (Moslem mysticism). Four Sufi orders are especially influential among the Somalis: the Qadiriyah, Ahmadiyah, Salihiyah, and Rifaiyah. The orders have established schools throughout the region, usually associated with the burial place of a saint. At times, the influence of an order and its leader can assume considerable proportions and may have political significance, as in the case of the Mullah Mohamed ibn Abdullah Hassan.[31]

The Somali language has been classified as Cushitic. It is related to Afar (spoken by the Danakils), the Galla languages, and other languages spoken along an arc encircling the eastern part of Ethiopia. There are numerous Somali dialects. Linguistically, they can be grouped into three main divisions: one, the dialects spoken by the Samaale nomads; the second, dialects spoken by the Sab agriculturists; the third, the dialects spoken by the inhabitants of the coastal towns of the Southern Region.[32] The dialects differ markedly both in pronunciation and in vocabulary. Nevertheless, Somalis speaking different dialects comprehend each other, and there is no language barrier to oral communications between individuals who may normally live a thousand miles apart.

A great obstacle to communications is the fact that Somali is only a spoken language. Various attempts to adapt an alphabet to Somali have been suspended because of the political controversy they aroused. Three alternative alphabets have been considered: Latin, Arabic, and a specially devised alphabet called Osmaniya (after its inventor Yusuf Kenadid Osman).[33] Sooner or later the political deadlock over this question will be resolved. In the meantime, the absence of an acceptable way of writing Somali creates great difficulties in administration and everyday life, and is a barrier to cultural and literary development.

Besides the Somali language, Arabic, Italian, English, French, and Amharic are used throughout the area. Arabic is known by religious teachers and by a portion of the educated Somalis. It is widely used as a scholarly written language, and most newspapers have an Arabic section in addition to the Italian, English, or French text. The use of Italian, English, French, and Amharic is generally limited to official and administrative purposes.

Customs and the way of life are not uniform among all Somalis. As already noted, there is a significant differentiation between settled and nomadic tribes. Moreover, customs often vary from place to place and tribe to tribe. The extent of the differentiation between the Somalis and the neighboring peoples is a subject requiring further study. In some cases the distinction is pronounced. Whereas the Somali tribes of northern Kenya are nomadic, some of their Nilo-Hamitic and Bantu neighbors are settled cultivators. Nomadism distinguishes the Somalis also from the settled Amhara and Galla peoples of the Ethiopian highlands. Again the differences between the Somalis and the nomadic Gallas and Danakils are less clear. As a generalization, it might be said that the Somalis are not as warlike as the Danakils and some of the Galla tribes, and place less importance on killing; but it is often hard to distinguish the Somalis by custom and way of life from neighboring Gallas and Danakils. This is particularly the case in border zones, where there are considerable cross-influences. There are similarities between some Issa and Danakil clans. Settled Somalis in the Harar area bear close resemblance to the local agricultural people known as Kotu, who probably derive from the amalgamation of Somalis and Gallas centuries ago. And in northern Kenya, cultural distinctions between neighboring Galla and Somali clans are not readily recognizable.

Yet, on the whole, the nature of the country inhabited by the Somalis and some of their cultural and physical traits impose upon them certain characteristics distinguishing them from the neighboring peoples. Does the existence of such characteristics mean that the Somalis ought to be regarded as a distinct and separate nation? The question is important, for the Somali claim to nationhood is at the core of the turbulent politics of the Horn of Africa.

Chapter 3

The Somali Nation

THE political problems of the Horn of Africa revolve around the Somali claim for "national" unification and the establishment of an independent Somali "nation state." The underlying assumption of these claims is that the Somali people constitute a distinct "nation" entitled to a separate existence and to rights and duties similar to those of other nations in the world. This assumption requires examination. Surely, it would make little sense to discuss Somali nationalism if there were nothing approaching a Somali nation to sustain it. Moreover, the assessment of the prospects of Somali nationalism depends, among other factors, upon the cohesion and sense of purpose of the nation it claims to represent.

In setting out to discuss Somali nationhood one encounters a basic difficulty regarding the criteria to be applied. The question of whether the Somalis can properly be regarded as a nation hinges necessarily upon the question of what is a nation. The problem of nationality has been discussed by numerous writers. No rigid definition of a nation seems possible. There are, however, a number of attributes usually associated with nationhood. These have been variously defined, and their essentials may be restated briefly. Nations normally are supposed to have a common language, to be associated with a certain territory, and to have a common culture, history, and tradition. Often nations are also bound by common racial origins, and practice the same religion.[1] If these criteria are used, there seems to be a strong case for considering the Somalis a nation.

The first criterion—a common language—is clearly met in the Somali case. To be sure, there are differences in dialect, but these do not prevent Somalis from understanding one another. Their common language not only facilitates communication among them but also differentiates Somalis from their neighbors who speak different languages.

The Somalis meet also the second criterion—association with a certain territory. The Somalis have lived throughout their recorded history in the Horn of Africa. The exact limits or boundaries of Somali territory are subject to dispute, and are indeed difficult to establish because of the Somalis' historical expansion. Their claims to portions of northern Kenya are frequently countered by the argument that Somali occupation of the area began only sixty years ago. Yet, although the limits of Somali territory are uncertain, their association with the region of the Horn is not questioned.

The nomadic way of life and the pastoral economy are common to most Somalis with the exception of the Sab agriculturists. Other cultural traits and customs are shared by all, including the Sab. Moreover, there is a rich literature transmitted orally which, significantly, does not display sharp regional characteristics. For example, many of the poems composed by the Mullah Mohamed ibn Abdullah Hassan are well-known throughout the territory.

Common traditions and history are a strong unifying force among the Somalis. Their belief in common descent and their traditional genealogies foster a sense of unity. They also share traditions about their history, in which the wars against the common enemies, Christian Ethiopia and pagan Galla tribes, play a prominent part.

The fact that the Somalis are of one race and differ racially from some of their neighbors also tends to foster a sense of unity among them. Indeed, the Somalis can be termed race conscious and affected by a sense of racial superiority, directed mainly toward Negroid Africans. This attitude stems probably from the fact that when the Somali tribes migrated southward, they encountered many Negroid agricultural communities which became subject to the conquering Somali tribes. Furthermore, Somalis were slave owners until the early part of this century, and their slaves were generally Negroid people.[2]

Until recently Somalis have generally objected to being regarded as "Africans," because the term to them implied subject Negroid peoples. Their sentiments on this point are illustrated by the 1944 mutiny in the Somaliland Camel Corps, which was a locally raised force in British Somaliland. The uprising was caused by dissatisfaction at the unit's being treated as an African rather than an Asian unit. Another illustration is the campaign of Somali immigrants in Kenya towns in the 1950's to be classified as Asians rather than Africans.[3] Only recently, with the growing political importance of Africa, have there appeared signs of a change in this attitude, though the feeling remains strong in north Kenya where Somalis border upon Bantu and Nilo-Hamitic tribes.

Another bond unifying the Somalis, which at the same time differentiates them from their neighbors, is the Somalis' practice of Islam. Moreover, various religious authorities and Sufi (mystic) orders have traditionally endeavored to eradicate tribal divisions prevalent among the Somalis, by emphasizing the common religious link. The tribal barriers remain; but the sense of Islamic unity is nevertheless pervasive.

Although according to the aforementioned criteria there would seem to be a sound basis for regarding the Somalis as a nation, it is nevertheless difficult to conclude, solely on the grounds set forth above, that the Somalis are actually such. A nation is not merely a group of people who possess certain characteristics in common. In addition, it is a group of people who constitute a society and communicate with one another on matters of common interest. The common characteristics outlined above are merely general conditions facilitating national integration and the spread of national solidarity. A useful indicator of whether integration is taking place, or whether it is possible at all, is the state of communications within the society. The extent and character of communications among the Somalis is a subject requiring further research. But a few general observations are in order.[4]

The flow of information among the people is obstructed by the large size of the territories inhabited by the Somalis and the relatively undeveloped state of technical means of communications.

The distance from Kenya to Cape Guardafui is over 1100 miles. The air distance (over Ethiopian territory) between Mogadishu and Hargeisa is 530 miles, and by land the trip takes three days. Roads are generally bad, and during the rainy seasons are often impassable. Air communications are infrequent; at the end of 1960 there were only two scheduled flights per week connecting Mogadishu and Hargeisa. Telephone and telegraph facilities are not widespread. The exchange of letters is hampered by the low literacy rate and the absence of a commonly accepted Somali script. The circulation of newspapers and other printed matter is limited for the same reasons. The number of radio receivers in proportion to the population is low in comparison to Western countries. Furthermore, the structure of the economy is such that it does not require extensive communications. The great majority of the population are largely self-sufficient, and require only a very limited range of outside products, such as cloth, coffee, and sugar. Their participation in the market economy, mainly through the sale of cattle, is still very limited. Services, such as skilled craftsmanship, are performed by associated *sab* tribes and do not require wide intercourse with distant centers.

Yet this description of the state of communications is incomplete. Any conclusions drawn on the basis of the normal indicators of communications, such as statistics on mail, telephone, telegraph, the number of radio sets or motor vehicles per capita, implying a very low incidence of communications, are misleading. The Somali way of life and social habits provide alternative avenues of communication, the effectiveness of which is indeed surprising.

The real state of communications is reflected in the similarity of interests and responses that can be encountered among Somalis throughout the Horn. They are aware of developments in the neighboring Somali territories, and like to discuss them. Events in the world at large are also a subject of interest. The relatively high degree of political sophistication in the otherwise primitive environment stems in part from the Somalis' fondness of foreign travel and adventure. It is not uncommon to encounter Somalis who have seen much of Europe and America traveling as seamen, and have lived in Marseilles, London, or New York for a few years before returning to their tribes in the interior. The stories of returning travelers undoubtedly have a certain educational effect, and tend to arouse interest in the world at large.

How is current information communicated through this large and underdeveloped territory? The relatively high degree (by African standards) of urbanization among the Somalis may provide a partial explanation; for communications within urban societies are normally intensive. Political activity takes place mainly in the towns, and as we have seen, 14 percent of the Somalis live in towns of 5,000 inhabitants or more. Besides, close links are maintained between individuals in towns and their tribesmen in the interior. Most Somalis are illiterate, but the word is passed orally by traveling relatives and tribesmen.

The functioning of communications among the non-urban population could provide the subject of a fascinating study. Some of the elements of this communication network seem quite evident and can be outlined here. The fact that Somali society is largely nomadic is a very significant factor. The nomadic way of life requires seasonal migrations which sometimes extend over considerable distances. Tribes often move a hundred miles in search of grazing.[5] Wells and grazing areas are not under exclusive ownership or control of individual tribes, but are normally shared by clans from different tribes. They provide convenient meeting places and an opportunity for exchange of news and gossip for people who during certain seasons live hundreds of miles apart.

The relative scarcity of radio receivers in relation to the population may also be deceptive. A radio receiver serves a much larger group of people than it normally does in Western countries. Moreover, battery-operated radios, which can be used even in the bush, are increasingly becoming available.

There are, nevertheless, obstacles inhibiting the cohesive forces of national integration. Foremost among them are tribal rivalries and antagonisms. These vary with time and place, and are not always politically significant. They stem in part from traditional attitudes, and in part from the realities of the struggle to survive through the dry seasons. The most profound cleavage in Somali society, between the Samaale and the Sab—between the nomadic and the settled agricultural tribes—has found political expression in the party structure. The agricultural tribes have largely confined themselves to the support of their own party, the Hizbia Dastur Mustaqil. Rivalry between Darod and Hawiya in the Southern Region of the Somali Republic and feuding among the tribes of the Northern Region are also fraught with political implications. The political parties recognize this obstacle to their nationalist goals and have engaged in a sustained effort to help settle disputes peacefully and stop tribal feuding.[6] In this they have been partly successful. Despite rivalries, feuding, and tensions, the tribes have supported the nationalist aims of their leaders, and although tribal tensions inhibit the spread of national solidarity, they do not constitute an insurmountable obstacle to it.

A definitive evaluation of the relative weight of the divisive elements as compared to the unifying forces operating in Somali society does not seem possible. Intangibles such as "will" and feeling of "common destiny" seem crucial to such an evaluation. Tribal antagonisms do not preclude a will to unite or a feeling of common destiny. Perhaps some indication of the degree of cohesiveness and unity is reflected by the fact that all tribes and segments consider themselves ultimately "Somali." If nothing else, then tribal genealogy reminds them of it. The individual's primary loyalty is to his "dia-paying group"; but when relating himself to a wider grouping, it is the tribe and ultimately the rest of the Somalis to which he feels attachment.

Admittedly, the process of national integration has hardly begun, and a great deal remains to be accomplished before the Somalis constitute a nation in the Western sense. However, in the African context, the Somalis are a rare case of a homogeneous ethnic group, inhabiting a large territory, and united by culture, religion, and tradition. Their sense of unity was not effaced even by the divisive impact of alien rule.

Although their claim to nationhood may be open to challenge, the political movement claiming to represent Somali rights, aspirations, and interests—in other words "Somali Nationalism"—is unquestionably important enough to deserve careful study.

Chapter 4

The Partition of the Horn

EUROPEAN contacts with the Horn of Africa were limited until 1869, when the opening of the Suez Canal focused attention upon the area's strategic importance. The heightened interest in the area and the wave of European imperialist expansion in Africa led to the establishment of the European colonies and protectorates in the 1880's. This coincided with the consolidation of power in Ethiopia under Menelik II, and the extension of Ethiopian authority into areas which were previously under only nominal Ethiopian suzerainty. By the end of the century the Horn had been partitioned among Britain, France, Italy, and Ethiopia.

EXPLORATION

The colonial administrations were preceded (as elsewhere in Africa) by explorers and adventurers. In modern times the exploration of the East African coasts—Somali and Eritrean—was first undertaken by the Portuguese in the sixteenth century; but their activity soon subsided. British, Portuguese, French, and Dutch merchantmen en route to or from India visited the area occasionally, but no really systematic explorations were undertaken until the 1830's.

With the growth of trade among India, Arabia, and Zanzibar there occurred a number of shipwrecks along the Somali coasts in which the survivors were badly mistreated by the native tribes. These incidents drew the attention of British authorities in India.[1] When the British occupied Aden in 1839 they initiated systematic exploration of the nearby coastal areas. Lieutenant W. C. Barker of the Indian Navy, a member of the British mission to the Ethiopian Kingdom of Shoa, visited the Somali coast along the Gulf of Aden in 1840. Lieutenant W. Christopher, commanding the East India Company's brig-of-war *Tigris,* visited the coast along the Indian Ocean in 1843. Of particular value were the explorations of Lieutenant C. J. Cruttenden of the Indian Navy, who was Assistant Political Agent in Aden and who familiarized himself with the Somali coastal plain facing the Gulf of Aden.[2] The French too sent several expeditions, starting with Charles Guillain in 1848 commanding the corvette *Ducouëdic.*[3]

The interior beyond the coastal plain, however, remained inaccessible to Europeans for many years. The first European to penetrate any distance into the interior was Richard F. Burton. In 1854, after his celebrated visit to Mecca disguised as a Moslem, he undertook to visit Harar. The center of a fertile region in the highlands, some 200 miles from the coast, Harar was ruled at the time by a local Amir whose reputation for savage fanaticism deterred Europeans from exploring the area. The town acquired a certain mystique, which attracted Burton:

> Harar, moreover, had never been visited, and few are the cities of the world which in the present age, when men hurry about the earth, have not opened their gates to European adventure. The ancient metropolis of a once mighty race, the only permanent settlement in Eastern Africa, the reported seat of Moslem learning, a walled city of stone houses, possessing its independent chief, its peculiar population, its unknown language, and its own coinage, the emporium of the coffee trade, the head-quarters of slavery, the birth-place of the Kat plant, and the great manufactory of cotton-cloths, amply, it appeared, deserved the trouble of exploration.

Burton chose again to travel in disguise and completed the expedition successfully, returning with much valuable information. Shortly thereafter Burton set out on another African expedition, but his camp at Berbera was attacked by Somalis and he was forced to return to Aden. This was in 1855.[4]

In the preceding year John H. Speke, who was Burton's associate and protégé, and who later discovered the sources of the Nile, had started out from the coast near Las Khorai, near the eastern end of what later became British Somaliland, in an attempt to reach the Nogal valley far to the south. He became the first European to visit the Dolbahanta and Warsangeli areas, but was obliged to return without reaching the Nogal.[5] There was a lull in the explorations during the 1860's, but activity was renewed in the 1870's and 1880's. Among the more successful explorers during this period were the Germans Hildebrandt and Paulitschke, both of whom visited Harar, and the Frenchman Georges Révoil, who penetrated to the valley of the Darror near the tip of the Horn.[6]

The great wastes of the Ogaden remained, however, *terra incognita* until 1885. Attempts by Italian, Greek, and French traders to reach the interior of the Ogaden in the 1880's met with disaster; the adventurous Europeans were killed before they got far. For example, this was the fate of an Italian expedition led by Count Porro in April 1885. More fortunate was the British explorer F. L. James. In that same year he traveled from Berbera to the Webi Shebeli and returned with an abundance of valuable information, marking the first successful European expedition into the Ogaden.[7]

The Establishment of the British Somaliland Protectorate

British interest in the Somali coast was at first motivated mainly by concern for the security of trade and communications with India. The looting of wrecked ships prompted the British government to conclude treaties with Somali tribes, providing for the protection of crews and cargoes of storm-wrecked vessels. The first of these treaties, concluded in 1827 between Captain Bremer of H.M.S. *Tamar* and the sheiks of the Habr Awal tribe, was occasioned by the plunder of the brig *Marianne* and the murder of her crew near Berbera in 1825. The treaty declared that "hence-forth there shall be peace and friendship between the subjects of his Majesty the King of England and the Sheiks of the Habr Owul [Habr Awal] tribe and their men." It included an agreement for the protection of commerce and provided compensation for lives and property lost in the *Marianne* incident.[8]

The 1839 establishment of the protectorate over Aden brought an increase not only of British exploration but also of British diplomatic activity in the area. The following year, Captain Robert Moresby, on behalf of the East India Company, concluded treaties with the Sultan of Tajura and the Governor of Zeila, territories nominally under Turkish suzerainty. Under these treaties the company acquired title to two small islands off the coast; the Sultan of Tajura sold the island of Mussa to the British for the price of "10 bags of rice," and the island of Aubad was ceded by the Governor of Zeila without compensation. The same two personages undertook "not to enter into any Treaty or Bond with any other European nation or person," without bringing the subject "to the notice" of the British authorities at Aden. Subsequent contacts with the Somalis led to an agreement in 1855 between the Governor of Aden and the Habr Toljala tribe for the suppression of the slave trade. British relations with the Somalis were not always peaceful. The raid on Burton's party in Berbera in 1855 resulted in a blockade of the coast and led finally to a new treaty with the Habr Awal in 1856.[9]

A great change in the geopolitical evaluation of the region occurred with the opening of the Suez Canal in 1869. As the Red Sea became a major avenue of trade and other traffic with India and the Far East, its shores acquired considerable strategic importance. Coinciding with this geopolitical transformation, there was a revival of Egyptian activity directed at acquiring control of the sources of the Nile. Egypt's expansion-minded ruler, Khedive Ismail, sent expeditions into the Sudan and Equatorial Africa, made war on

Ethiopia, and dispatched forces to occupy certain sections of the east coast of Africa as far south as Kismayu, near the equator.[10]

The Red Sea coast was subject to the nominal suzerainty of Turkey but was actually governed by local potentates. In 1865 the Sultan of Turkey had assigned the administration of the Red Sea towns of Suakin, Massawa, and their dependencies to the Egyptian Khedive. Consequently, in 1870, when ships were plying through the great canal, an Egyptian governor was appointed over the whole coast from Suez to Cape Guardafui, and Egyptian posts were established in the Gulf of Aden ports of Zeila and Berbera, and in other locations in the area. A further force was dispatched inland in 1875 and took possession of Harar.

These measures provoked the opposition of the British government, which repeatedly stated that it did not recognize the Turkish Sultan's claims to sovereignty over the Somali tribes between Zeila, near the western end of the Gulf of Aden, and Ras Hafoun, on the Indian Ocean just around the tip of the Horn.[11] British objections to the Egyptian and Turkish claims led to protracted negotiations between the British and Egyptian governments. In September 1877 an agreement was finally reached, whereby the British government recognized Egyptian "jurisdiction, under the suzerainty of the Sublime Porte, over the Somali Coast as far as Ras Hafoun." Britain's concern lest the region come under the domination of a rival European power jeopardizing the safety of British sea-communications is reflected in the terms of the agreement. It included a pledge by the Khedive "for himself and his successors, that no portion of the territory, to be thus formally incorporated with Egypt under his hereditary rule, shall ever be ceded to any foreign Power." The treaty was, however, conditional upon formal assurance by the Turkish government, which also exercised nominal suzerainty over Egypt itself, "that no portion of the Somali Coast, . . . shall more than any other portion of Egypt . . . be ceded on any pretence whatever to any foreign power." [12] Since the Turkish government did not grant such an assurance, the agreement remained inoperative.

Though the British acquiesced in the Egyptian occupation of the Somali coast facing the Gulf of Aden, they strongly objected to the Khedive's claims to sovereignty over the coast facing the Indian Ocean, between Ras Hafoun and the Juba river. Instead, the British government supported the claim of the Sultan of Zanzibar to suzerainty over this area. In 1875 the Khedive sent a force which occupied the towns of Brava and Kismayu, as a prelude to a push from the coast to Lake Victoria and the sources of the Nile. But, largely as a result of British pressure, the project was given up and the troops withdrawn.[13]

The coast facing the Gulf of Aden and the town of Harar in the interior remained under Egyptian rule until 1885. As a result of the pressure of the Mahdist revolt in the Sudan, the Egyptian government had decided to curtail its commitments and to withdraw from Harar and from the entire Somali coast. Harar was evacuated in May 1885, and control was transferred to Amir Abdullahi Ali, the son of the former despot. The town remained under Ali's inept rule until its conquest by Menelik of Ethiopia in January 1887.[14] As for the Somali coast, past which paraded the Suez Canal traffic of all nations, the Egyptian decision to withdraw did not pass unnoticed in European capitals. The European powers were engaged at the time in the "scramble for Africa." Among them Great Britain was the most vitally interested in the Gulf of Aden, because a hostile power in possession of the Somali coast at Bab al Mandab, the waterway between the Gulf and the Red Sea, could easily disrupt imperial communications with India and other British possessions in Asia and the Pacific.

As the Egyptians were about to withdraw, it gradually became clear to the British that they would have to occupy the area themselves if they intended to prevent other European powers from establishing themselves on the Somali shore. To the British the only acceptable alternative seemed to be the establishment of effective Turkish authority over the area. The reversion of the coastal towns to their local rulers was not considered a practical alternative at that time, because the avid eyes of Europe were fixed on Africa, and the independence of the local potentates was likely to be rather short-lived.

Thus, during July 1884 the British undertook a series of diplomatic moves to prepare a legal basis for occupying the Somali coast. They reiterated their earlier reservations about the validity of Turkish claims for the coast between Zeila and Ras Hafoun. They also notified Turkey that Britain would be ready to recognize the Sultan's authority over the coast as far as Zeila, provided Turkey took steps to maintain its authority after the Egyptian withdrawal and pledged itself not to cede the territory to any foreign power. In August, while the Turks were considering the situation, the British notified them that in view of information regarding the imminent outbreak of disturbances in the area, British forces would be sent there at once to maintain order, unless the Turks themselves were ready to take immediate steps for the occupation of Zeila. As the British had probably foreseen, the Turks were slow in reacting to this challenge. Since no clear reply was received from the Turkish government, the British put a force into Zeila and took the position that they "will continue to occupy Zeila until measures have been taken by the Porte for relieving them of this duty."[15]

In December the French took possession of Tajura, and Italy extended its holdings around Assab near the lower end of the Red Sea. Turkey was in no position to undertake any positive steps. It contented itself with protesting against Italian expansion and reiterating its claim to the entire coast as far as Ras Hafoun.[16]

Meanwhile the British busied themselves during the last half of 1884 making a new crop of treaties with the Somali tribes east of Zeila. Since there was still some uncertainty about the ultimate disposition of the region, and about Turkey's role, these treaties stopped short of extending British protection to the tribes. But the treaties with the Habr Awal, Gadabursi, Habr Toljala, Habr Gerhajis, and Issa, concluded between July 1884 and January 1885, all contained pledges by the tribes "never to cede, sell, mortgage or otherwise give for occupation, save to the British Government, any portion of the territory presently inhabited by them or being under their control."[17]

During 1885 it became clear that the Turkish government was not in a position to maintain its sovereignty over the coast; so the British government proceeded to extend formal protection. In the early months of 1886, supplementary treaties were concluded with the Habr Awal, Habr Toljala, Habr Gerhajis, and Warsangeli tribes. The British government undertook to extend to the tribes and their respective territories "the gracious favour and protection of Her Majesty the Queen-Empress." On their part, the tribes promised "to refrain from entering into any correspondence, Agreement, or Treaty with any foreign nation or Power, except with the knowledge and sanction of Her Majesty's Government."[18]

On July 20, 1887, the European powers were officially notified in pursuance of the General Act of the Berlin Conference that a British Protectorate had been established on the Somali coast from Jibuti eastward to and including Bender Ziadeh on the 49th meridian of longitude.[19]

The Founding of French Somaliland

French actions along the Somali coast, unlike British policy, tended to be from the outset somewhat haphazard and inconsistent. British policy was guided by the strategic necessity of securing imperial communications, and all British actions were directed to that end. Britain was not particularly interested in the commerce of the area, her only concern in this respect being supplies for Aden. France, on the other hand, had three principal motives: her need for a base and coaling station along the long route to Madagascar and Indochina, her desire to develop trade, and later, the exigencies of the competition among the powers. These factors brought about periodic spurts of activity, subsiding after a while and then reviving again, until they led in 1885 to the formal establishment of the French colony and protectorate.

Early indications of French interest in the area date back to the 1830's and 1840's, when several French scientific expeditions visited the Red Sea and its coasts. One of them, led by C. E. X. Rochet d'Hericourt, visited the Kingdom of Shoa in 1839 and 1840 and helped stimulate interest in that mysterious country. The same man, sent on a second mission in 1842 and 1843, signed on behalf of France a "political and Commercial Treaty" with Sahle-Selassie, the King of Shoa.[20]

A period of inactivity set in and lasted until 1858 when Henri Lambert, French consular agent at Aden, entered into negotiations with Ibrahim Abu-Bekr, a local potentate on the Gulf of Tajura, regarding the cession of a port on that little body of water. The interest of the French probably had been reawakened by the Suez Canal project and by their operations in China and Indochina in 1857 and 1858, indicating the desirability of maintaining a coaling station in the general vicinity of the Gulf of Aden. Lambert's negotiations ended in tragedy when he was assassinated on one of his trips to Tajura. But the relation he had established with Abu-Bekr ultimately proved to be useful, as did the on-the-spot investigations of Comte Stanislas Russel, heading another French mission in 1858. Captain (later Admiral) Fleuriot de Langle took a force to Tajura in 1859, looked into Lambert's death, brought the culprits to justice, and restored French prestige in the area.[21] Then he reopened negotiations with Abu-Bekr and other Danakil chieftains regarding the cession of a port in the Gulf of Tajura.

These negotiations were successful and the chiefs delegated one of the members of the Abu-Bekr family to go to Paris, where a treaty was ceremoniously signed on March 11, 1862. It provided for the cession of Obock, situated on the north shore of the Gulf of Tajura, and the adjoining coastal plain. Moreover, the chiefs pledged themselves to report to the French every proposal for cession of territory made to them by a foreign power and to reject any such overture which had not first received the assent of the French government. Two months later, the French flag was hoisted at Obock, and France officially took possession of the place.[22]

For nearly twenty years Obock lay forgotten by France. This neglect can perhaps be explained by France's other preoccupations during this period. Italian affairs required continued alertness and attention during the 1860's. The Mexican adventure of Napoleon III was another distraction. Then came the preparations for the inevitable conflict with Prussia and that disastrous war itself. During the 1870's France was greatly preoccupied with internal affairs, and her principal foreign ambitions were directed toward regaining her lost western provinces. Indochina remained relatively peaceful during these two decades, and French communications through the new Suez route did not appear in danger. A campaign waged by the author and traveler Denis de Rivoyre for the establishment of French enterprises and a supply depot at Obock met with general apathy and was not encouraged by the government.

The 1880's, however, saw a general revival of French interest in colonial affairs. In 1881, de Rivoyre's efforts were rewarded with partial success. The French established two companies, which proceeded with the construction of installations at Obock—the "Compagnie Franco-Ethiopienne" and the "Société Française d'Obock." At the same time Obock became the base for French commercial enterprise in Abyssinia.[23]

The 1882-1883 insurrection in Indochina and the 1883 outbreak of war in Madagascar demonstrated again to the French government the necessity of establishing a naval station and a supply base along the Suez route to the east. There was no French base between the Mediterranean and Madagascar or India, and the French navy was dependent upon the British facilities at Aden. In view of the colonial rivalry between Britain and France at the time, this dependence was considered by the French as extremely unsatisfactory; therefore they decided on the military development of Obock, which was ideally situated for the purpose. The man chosen to carry out the new policy was Leonce Lagarde, a man of vision as well as action, who immediately proceeded to extend and fortify the French foothold there.

During 1884 and 1885 a series of treaties were concluded with the Sultans of Gobad and Tajura providing for the cession of their territories to France, in return for which French protection was extended to the Sultans and their peoples. A similar treaty was signed with the Issa Somalis in March 1885. French Somaliland was fast taking shape. Through these treaties France acquired the coastline from Ras Dumeira to Ambado as well as undetermined portions of the interior. The limits of the French possession were extended eastward by a treaty with Britain in 1888. Subsequently, commercial activities were transferred from Obock to Jibuti, where conditions were considered favorable. The government of the territory also moved to Jibuti in 1892.[24]

The Establishment of Italian Somaliland

Italian interest in East Africa was motivated by aspirations for imperial grandeur and was a by-product of the rise of Italian nationalism. Concurrently with the struggle for domestic unification, interest was displayed in the establishment of overseas colonies. One of the individuals active in this movement was Cristoforo Negri, an historian, economist, and diplomat, who started investigating various possibilities for imperial expansion as early as the 1850's. The government under Cavour was receptive to the idea, and several expeditions to African and Asian waters received official support. Although the quest for a colony did not limit itself to any one region, there was a marked interest in Africa. Negri himself repeatedly wrote about the possibilities in the Red Sea area and along the East African coast nominally under Zanzibar suzerainty. Because of domestic preoccupations nothing came of the colonial drive until 1869, when a station was established at Assab. The principal object was to provide a coaling station in the Red Sea, but the acquisition nevertheless stimulated the drive for the exploitation of the fabled riches of Abyssinia.[25]

Italian interest in Ethiopia and the neighboring areas persisted through the 1870's and resulted in pronounced activity in Eritrea and along the Red Sea coast. However, it was only in the 1880's that

Italians were attracted to the Somali coast facing the Indian Ocean, part of the domain of the Sultan of Zanzibar at the time. The impetus came from commercial interests. An Italian trader, Vincenzo Filonardi, living in Zanzibar and witnessing the growing German and British activity on the East African coast, repeatedly called the attention of the Italian government to the trade opportunities there. His memoranda took several years to bear fruit, but in 1884 the Italian government decided to send an exploratory mission to Zanzibar and to the Benadir region on the mainland.[26]

The mission, headed by Captain Antonio Cecchi, left on the frigate *Barbarigo* early in 1885 and, after surveying the mouth of the Juba river, reached Zanzibar in April. Its main accomplishment was a commercial treaty and the establishment of an Italian consulate in Zanzibar. The Italians, after waiting a few months, also raised the question of acquiring sections of the mainland coast, but the Sultan's reaction appears to have been firmly negative. Then, in October 1886 the Sultan unexpectedly offered to cede to Italy the port of Kismayu and "the region of the Juba." The offer seems to have been a diplomatic ruse, perhaps intended to thwart the signing of an Anglo-German agreement delimiting the boundaries of the Sultan's domain and partitioning it into British and German spheres of influence. Soon after the offer was made, it was withdrawn, resulting in a sharp protest by the offended Vincenzo Filonardi, who had become the Italian consul. Another incident occurred in the spring of 1888, when, after the death of Sultan Barghash and the accession of his brother Sultan Khalifa, Filonardi again demanded the cession of Kismayu and the mouth of the Juba. The demand was refused—according to the Italians in an offensive manner—and the Italians broke off relations in protest.[27]

The crisis was soon resolved with the help of the British government. The British proposed that the Italians try to negotiate for the coveted concessions on the Benadir coast through the friendly services of Sir William Mackinnon, Director of the British East Africa Company. The Italians proceeded upon this suggestion, and in

August 1888 arrived at a preliminary agreement with the company for the transfer to Italy of a concession which the company expected to acquire over certain territories on the East African coast. The Sultan gave his assent to the deal in January 1889, and an agreement between the Italian government and the British East Africa Company was signed on August 3 of that year. Finally, on November 18, the territories concerned were transferred to Italy, the Italians acquiring control over the towns of Brava, Merca, Mogadishu, and Warsheikh. The port of Kismayu was placed under joint occupation of the British East Africa Company and the Italian government.

Italy acquired its rights in Benadir under the terms and conditions of the Sultan's concession to the British East Africa Company. Italy was granted administrative authority over the territories and was obligated in turn to make certain payments to the Sultan's exchequer. The territories in which Italy acquired concessions were rather limited. The authority of the Sultan of Zanzibar over Brava, Merca, and Mogadishu extended landwards only within radii of ten miles, and his authority over Warsheikh only within a radius of five miles. But the Italian government assumed a protectorate over those portions of the coast lying between the aforementioned towns and so notified the European powers on November 19, 1889.[28]

Britain's motives in assisting Italy in the realization of its ambitions with respect to the Somali coast are not entirely clear. The episode may have been connected with the Anglo-Italian rapprochement and with the agreements signed between the two powers in 1887 concerning the Mediterranean and Middle East. Moreover, the British probably hoped that Italy might be helpful in checking the growing German activity in East Africa, and forestalling German claims to Mijertain where the German East Africa Company had concluded a series of treaties with local chiefs in 1884. Indeed, even as the Italians were being handed their concessions in Benadir, they were busy extending their influence to Obbia and Mijertain to the north.

Consul Filonardi negotiated with representatives of the Sultan of Obbia, and on February 8, 1889, signed a treaty with the Sultan himself establishing an Italian protectorate over the area. For the next two months, Filonardi visited various locations along the coast in an effort to cement relations with local chieftains and to persuade the recalcitrant Sultan of the Mijertain Somalis to sign a similar treaty. The Sultan finally consented, and on April 7 signed a treaty placing his domains under an Italian protectorate. The Germans at first objected on account of the earlier treaties between the German East Africa Company and local chiefs. However, as Germany had not claimed a protectorate and had not notified the powers in pursuance of Article 34 of the General Act of the Berlin Conference, its objections did not rest upon a solid legal basis. In negotiations between the two countries the mattter was soon settled in Italy's favor, and the Italian Protectorate in Mijertain became recognized by the European powers.[29]

Thus, by 1889, Italy had established her influence over the Somali coast from Bender Ziadeh, on the Gulf of Aden in the north, to Kismayu on the Indian Ocean in the south. The legal status of the territories underwent several modifications during the next two decades, and the extension of effective Italian authority over the area was slow. In 1892, following the establishment of a British protectorate over Zanzibar in 1890, the title over the Benadir towns that Italy hitherto held through the British East Africa Company was transferred directly to Italy. In 1905, in agreement with Britain as the protecting power, Italy purchased the territory from the Sultan of Zanzibar, and the nominal suzerainty of the Sultan over the Benadir coast thus came to an end. At the same time, Italy's trading and storage rights at Kismayu, first acquired by agreement with the British East Africa Company in 1889, were put on a new legal basis by an exchange of notes with the British government.[30]

The administration of the territory also underwent changes in its early years. By an agreement concluded in 1893 between the Italian government and "V. Filonardi and Co.," a commercial company under the directorship of the same Vincenzo Filonardi who had been the Italian consul in Zanzibar, the company became responsible for the administration of the Benadir concession. But the venture proved to be a commercial failure, and in 1896 the Italian government assumed provisionally the administration of the territory, pending the organization of a new firm.

The "Commercial Company of Benadir" was soon formed, and assumed the administration of the territory in accordance with a convention between the Italian government and the company, signed on May 25, 1898. The new company was hampered by difficult local conditions, insecurity, and lack of capital; moreover it came under severe criticism at home. The compulsory labor the company recruited was described by its critics as slave labor, which it indeed resembled. The criticism led the company in 1903 to dispatch a commission of inquiry consisting of Gustavo Chiesi and Ernesto Travelli. Their report criticized severely not only the local officials, but also the Italian government and its representatives in the area. Partly because of the pressure of public opinion, and partly because of deteriorating security conditions resulting from the activities of the rebel Mullah Mohamed ibn Abdullah Hassan, the Italian government resumed direct administration on May 1, 1905.

The Italian protectorates in the north, Obbia and Mijertain, which were the responsibility of the Italian Consulate General in Aden, were the scene of considerable unrest during the early years of the new century. At times the Mullah controlled sizable portions of the area. Attempts at military repression being unsuccessful and agreements with the Mullah failing to last, it was deemed necessary to place the entire Somali area under an integrated military and administrative control. Thus, in April 1908, Benadir in the south and the protectorates in the north were unified to form Italian Somaliland.

Effective Italian authority was extended inland very gradually. Besides the difficulties of terrain and communications, the Italians often encountered a hostile native population, and in some cases incurred heavy losses of life. The most serious incident of that kind occurred in 1896 when Captain Cecchi and thirteen other Italians were killed by Bimal tribesmen, near Lafole. The activities of the Mullah were another obstacle to the extension of Italian administration. Consequently, it was not until 1914 that effective Italian administration reached all parts of the territory. Still, the Mullah continued to disturb the peace, and only with his final defeat and death in 1920 was the country at last pacified.[31]

We must return to this remarkable man in the next chapter in order to relate him to the tradition of Somali nationalism.

British East Africa

The history of the British involvement in East Africa and of the acquisition of Kenya and Uganda is of only marginal concern for us here. Most of the area lies outside the Horn of Africa, and at the time when Britain acquired it, the Somalis occupied only its fringes. Later these Somalis moved deeper into the territory, and their numbers were augmented by new arrivals from the Italian and Ethiopian territories in the north.

Britain's interest in territorial acquisitions in East Africa was aroused mainly by German activities in the region. Until the 1880's the British government did not wish to assume direct responsibilities in the area but preferred to exercise its influence indirectly through the Sultan of Zanzibar. As late as 1877, London apparently discouraged a scheme of Sir William Mackinnon, then Chairman of the British India Steam Navigation Company, to acquire a concession over portions of the east coast of Africa nominally under the suzerainty of the Sultan of Zanzibar. But the British position changed in 1885 after the German Emperor granted a charter of protection to the Society for German Colonization, which had previously concluded a number of treaties with tribes in the interior.[32]

In order to prevent further German encroachments the British government supported the establishment of a company for the purpose of administering, under a concession from the Sultan of Zanzibar, those portions of his domain which were recognized by an Anglo-German agreement as the British sphere of influence. It was also intended that the company acquire territories from the native chiefs within the British sphere. This was how the Imperial British East Africa Company got its start in 1888. The official encouragement for its activities is embodied in a royal charter granted to the company in the same year.[33]

From the outset the company encountered financial difficulties. It was gradually compelled to relinquish its responsibilities for the administration of the territory, and the functions were taken over by the British government. The company's difficulties finally led to its dissolution and to the extension of a British protectorate over British East Africa in 1895.[34]

With the growth of Britain's involvement in Egypt, British attention turned to the sources of the Nile, and in particular to the Lake Victoria region in Uganda. At the same time the troubles that missionaries were having in Uganda caused concern in England. Interest in that territory was heightened, too, by reports about possibilities for the agricultural development of fertile areas there. Since the best access to Lake Victoria and Uganda led from the Indian Ocean coast, rather than up the Nile, the value of the newly acquired sphere of influence, including Kenya, greatly increased in British eyes.[35]

The border between the British sphere and the Italian territories to the north of it, established by the Anglo-Italian protocol of 1891, was the Juba river. The river was apparently considered a convenient reference point; but it did not represent an ethnic boundary, since both sides of the border were populated by Somali tribes. A similar situation exists along the boundary between the British territories and Ethiopia, established in 1907. There the border cuts across Somali and Boran Galla tribes.[36]

Though the Somali population in British East Africa was relatively small when that protectorate was established in 1895, it grew considerably thereafter as the Somali tribes continued to migrate southward from Italian Somaliland and Ethiopia. With the establishment of British authority in what is now the Northern Frontier Province of Kenya, the Somali expansion southward was halted. But, by then, the Somalis occupied approximately one fifth of the total territory of Kenya—almost half the Northern Frontier Province.

Ethiopia and the Somalis

The scramble for Africa coincided with the resurgence and extension of central authority in Ethiopia under Menelik. Already, as King of Shoa and one of the vassals of Emperor John IV, Menelik displayed great energy and skill in consolidating his position and extending his power into the neighboring Somali and Galla territories. The extension of Ethiopian authority was pursued even more vigorously after his accession to the imperial throne as Emperor Menelik II in 1889.

Ethiopian expansion was motivated by two principal factors.

One was the desire to redeem all territories which according to Ethiopian traditions were once part of their empire. According to Menelik, Ethiopian domains extended as far as the Nile city of Khartoum in the north, Lake Victoria in the west, and the ocean in the south and east.[37] The historical basis of these claims is rather shaky. As far as the Horn of Africa is concerned there is evidence that in the third century A.D. an Ethiopian king conquered much of the Ogaden, but his possession of the region was apparently short-lived. In the tenth century, Ethiopia conquered Zeila on the Gulf of Aden and the neighboring coastal sultanates but lost them by the beginning of the next century. However ill-founded historically, Menelik's territorial claims reflected a national myth which by itself was a powerful driving force.

The second factor motivating Menelik's expansionist policy was a defensive reaction to the establishment of European colonies in the vicinity. Italy, Britain, and France were pushing inland from their respective coastal possessions, and Menelik endeavored to keep them as far as possible from the center of his power in the highlands, through the expedient of extending his own frontiers. In this, he was moderately successful. Menelik also greatly desired an outlet to the sea. Such an outlet was required not only for purely commercial reasons, but also for the free importation of armaments, upon which Ethiopia's military strength depended. However, this ambition was frustrated at the time.[38]

Menelik's expansion into Somali-inhabited territories began in 1886 soon after the Egyptian withdrawal from Harar. The departing Egyptians, with British support, had set up the son of the previous ruler as the independent head of a Harar principality. The new ruler was easily defeated by Menelik's forces, which occupied Harar in January 1887. Ras Makonnen, Menelik's able general, was appointed governor of the area and placed in charge of the Ethiopian drive eastward toward the French and British possessions, and southward into the Ogaden. In the autumn of 1891, Ras Makonnen took Imi on the Webi Shebeli, and then continued to press toward the Indian Ocean. Meanwhile the Italians were advancing inland. A serious clash in this area was averted at the time by the outbreak of hostilities in the north and the Italian defeat at Adowa in 1896.[39]

Ethiopia's expansion into Somali-inhabited territories brought into the open the traditional antagonisms between Ethiopians and Somalis. The Ethiopians forced the Somali tribes to pay tribute and to provide cattle and beasts of burden for Ethiopian garrisons, and there were frequent clashes between Ethiopian forces and the tribesmen.[40] For many years the Ethiopians' occupation of the Ogaden remained incomplete, for their authority did not extend far beyond the scattered military posts established throughout the region. The continuing friction with the tribesmen was instrumental in stimulating Somali self-consciousness and reviving the memories of past conflicts with Ethiopia.

The biggest and most dramatic of those conflicts had taken place in the sixteenth century. That war has not been forgotten by either side. To politically minded Somalis it is a nationalist inspiration, to the Ethiopians a reminder of a lingering danger.

Chapter 5

Two Heroes of Somali Nationalism

A CENTRAL figure in Somali traditions of conflict with Ethiopia is Ahmed Gran, the leader of the Moslem armies during the great war of the sixteenth century. With the development of modern Somali nationalism Ahmed Gran has come to be viewed by the Somalis as a national hero. He shares a place of honor among Somali national heroes with the Mullah Mohamed ibn Abdullah Hassan, whose struggle in the early part of the twentieth century is still fresh in Somali memories.

AHMED GRAN

The sixteenth century was a period of intense unrest among the people of Adal, a Moslem sultanate between the Gulf of Aden and the present Ethiopian city of Harar. The Sultanate was a loosely integrated state and consisted of a number of small principalities populated by Somali, Galla, Danakil and other tribes. The unrest was probably caused by population growth, resulting in tribal pressures to expand, and by a simultaneous upsurge in religious fanaticism. A number of leaders appeared on the scene during this period and launched a series of "holy wars" against Christian Ethiopia.

The Imam Ahmed ibn Ibrahim al Ghazi (1506–1543), whom the Ethiopians nicknamed Gran—"the left-handed"—was according to tradition a Darod Somali. Little is known about his early life. He married a daughter of the Imam Mahfuz of Zeila, a prominent Moslem leader in the campaigns against Ethiopia. After a period of struggle against rival chieftains, Ahmed succeeded in establishing his predominance and then turned to the prosecution of the *jihad* ("holy war").

In the fighting which followed, the Somalis played a prominent part, but the Moslem armies included many other tribes and peoples as well. For a while, Ahmed was successful in winning a series of victories against the Ethiopians. Between 1528 and 1535 the Moslems succeeded in overrunning considerable portions of the Ethiopian Empire and penetrated far north, reaching Kassala in 1535. Ethiopian power appeared to be completely broken, and the Emperor Lebna Dengel had to take refuge in the mountains. Many of the people were converted to Islam, and according to an Ethiopian chronicler, "hardly one in ten retained his religion."

In their hour of danger the Ethiopians appealed for assistance to Portugal (the only Christian country with which they had contact at the time). The arrival of the Portuguese forces in 1541 encouraged the Ethiopians to rally, and jointly they succeeded in inflicting a series of defeats upon Ahmed. The tides of war fluctuated for a while, as the Moslems obtained muskets and cannons from the Turks. Ahmed was wounded in one of the early encounters with the Portuguese, but succeeded in escaping and regrouping his defeated army. Later, in 1542, the Portuguese commander, Cristovão da Gama, was killed in battle. But the decisive encounter took place near Lake Tana in 1543 and resulted in the defeat and the death of Ahmed.

The Moslem armies now disintegrated and Galawdewos, son of Lebna Dengel, reestablished Ethiopian authority over the country. The threat of the Moslem conquest was over, though wars between the Ethiopians and neighboring Moslem peoples continued on a smaller scale for many years.[1]

The sixteenth-century wars have left an imprint upon the consciousness of successive generations of Amharas and Somalis. The

Christian Amharas have remained fearful of a possible recurrence of a Moslem invasion. Their neighbors, both in the Sudan to the north and in the Somalilands to the east, are Moslem. Moreover, a sizable minority of Ethiopians, estimated at nearly 40 percent of the population, adheres to Islam. Any time that Moslem minorities receive political inspiration from neighboring Moslem states, as the Somalis do today, Ethiopia feels seriously threatened.

Among the Somalis, the memory of Ahmed Gran as a folk hero has lingered on for generations, and is emphasized today in the context of Somali nationalism. One cannot be certain whether Ahmed Gran was really a Darod Somali, as widely claimed, or the offspring of a Somali woman and an Abyssinian priest, as related by another tradition.[2] Historical facts are, however, sometimes less important than popular beliefs in shaping the attitudes of peoples. The significant point here is the revival of Ahmed Gran's memory as a Somali national hero and leader in the wars against Ethiopia.

The Mullah

Another historical figure who has come to be regarded a national hero is the Mullah Mohamed ibn Abdullah Hassan. The Somali attitude toward the Mullah is still somewhat ambivalent. He is remembered as a great leader who wanted to unite the Somalis in a struggle against foreign influences. At the same time, his religious fanaticism, his despotic rule over his followers, and his bloody massacres of fellow Somalis have not been forgotten. During his lifetime he made many irreconcilable enemies, and his cruel methods earned him the epithet of "Mad Mullah." Today, this title is considered by many Somalis to be in bad taste, and he is usually referred to more respectfully as Sayid Mohamed ibn Abdullah Hassan.

Sayid Mohamed was born in the early 1870's. He was a Darod Somali. Very little is known about his early life beyond the fact that he traveled extensively and made several pilgrimages to Mecca. There he became a disciple of Mohamed Salih, the founder of the Salihiyah. This order, one of several mystic orders in Islam, is notable for its puritanical precepts. Mohamed ibn Abdullah Hassan, during one of his visits to Mecca, was apparently appointed by the founder of the order as his deputy and charged with its propagation among the Somalis.[3]

In 1895, Sayid Mohamed settled in Berbera, then the main center of the British Somaliland Protectorate; there he started preaching the doctrines of the Salihiyah and reproaching the people for their irreligious mode of life. His drive did not meet with much success in Berbera, and he gained only few adherents to his order. Soon he retired to the interior and settled among the Dolbahanta, a Darod tribe in the southeastern section of the Protectorate. There, his preaching found more acceptance. People recognized his authority not only in purely religious questions but also in various tribal affairs. His exercise of authority was welcomed by the British, as they were not in a position to extend their administration into the interior and preferred to rule indirectly through tribal notables. During this period, Mohamed was in regular communication with the British authorities in Berbera, and there was nothing in his activities, either at Berbera or later among the Dolbahanta, to which the government could take exception.[4]

The Rebellion

By late 1898 and early 1899, Mohamed's letters to the authorities in Berbera became truculent. At the same time, rumors began to circulate that he was arming his followers and was forcing the neighboring tribes to submit to his authority. According to some reports, Mohamed was preparing for a war against the Ethiopians. In August 1899 he and his followers occupied Burao, in the center of British Somaliland, and through this move established control over the watering places of two Ishaq tribes, the Habr Yunis and Habr Toljala. There he declared himself the Mahdi and proclaimed holy war against infidels. All Somalis were called upon to join him, and those who failed to acknowledge his authority were denounced as infidels. Shortly thereafter he raided a settlement of the

Qadiriyah (a rival order) at Sheikh, massacred its inhabitants and razed it.

Only after these incidents and the panic that spread in Berbera did the British become seriously alarmed. The authorities at Berbera called upon the home government in London to undertake an expedition against the Mullah. But the latter part of 1899 saw the outbreak of the Boer War and the early British reversals in that conflict. While the British were preoccupied with those events, conditions in the Protectorate continued to deteriorate. Trade with the interior came to a standstill because the caravans were attacked and looted. But more serious was the plight of the tribes that refused to cooperate with the Mullah. They suffered great losses in stock from repeated raids and, as the disturbances spread across the border, they had to abandon their regular summer grazing grounds on the Ethiopian side.

The authorities in Berbera continued to urge the government in London to take action, and finally received permission to raise a local levy of troops which would attempt to suppress the Mullah in coordination with Ethiopian troops.[5]

Four expeditions were undertaken by the British against the Mullah in the next four years. The forces employed in the first two expeditions (1901–1902) consisted mainly of locally recruited levies. In the third and fourth expeditions (1903–1904), principal reliance was put on regular troops of the Indian army and the King's African Rifles. Somalis were employed too, but only in mixed units or as scouts—a policy which was decided upon after panic and demoralization had occurred among the Somali levies at Erigo in the final battle of the second expedition. In that incident the Somalis' morale collapsed because of superstitious fear of the Mullah.[6]

The results of these operations were inconclusive. The Mullah's power was not completely broken, but he suffered heavy losses, resulting in a decline of his influence and prestige. For a while he ceased to be a menace.[7]

Needing a respite, Mohamed entered into negotiations with the

Italian authorities, and in March 1905 an agreement was reached at Illig by the terms of which the Mullah was assigned a territory of his own under Italian protection. He was guaranteed access to grazing areas within the British Protectorate and given freedom to trade, except in slaves and firearms. Lastly, Mohamed's authority over his followers was recognized. To this agreement between the Mullah and the Italians the British gave their assent, and for four years relative peace reigned in the area.[8]

By 1908 it appeared, however, that Mohamed was preparing to resume his harassment of the Protectorate tribes. This threat forced the British to choose among the following courses of action: a new expedition; a defensive policy through temporary military occupation of the interior; withdrawal from the interior and concentration at the coast; complete evacuation of the Protectorate.

After extensive deliberations, the government finally resolved in November 1909 to withdraw from the interior and to concentrate at the coast—the least costly policy short of complete abandonment of the British position in Somaliland. Arms were distributed among the friendly Ishaq tribes, and it was hoped that they would be able to hold their own against the Mullah's forces. Soon after the withdrawal, however, the interior was seized by complete anarchy. The tribes took advantage of the opportunity to settle old accounts and to raid one another's stocks, instead of uniting to face the Mullah. The Mullah's followers were active too, trying to coerce the tribes to accept his authority. It is estimated that one third of the Protectorate's male population perished in these disorders.[9]

Emboldened by his successes against the tribes, the Mullah threatened to attack the coastal towns. The deteriorating situation persuaded the government to authorize in 1912 the establishment of a Somali Camel Constabulary, a small striking force, some 150 strong. Its task was to patrol the hinterland behind Berbera and thereby to discourage the Mullah from attacking the town, and at the same time to promote peace among the friendly tribes. The Constabulary was placed under the command of Richard Corfield, a former political officer in Somaliland. This man, who enjoyed some popularity among the Somalis, was successful in improving security in the interior and encouraging the friendly tribes to face the Mullah. But in August 1913 his force was ambushed while pursuing one of the Mullah's raiding parties. The Constabulary was almost annihilated and Corfield himself was killed.[10]

In his fateful decision to pursue the Mullah's raiders Corfield contravened orders. But, ironically, the disaster which overtook him and the Constabulary had the effect of persuading the British government that it could not escape involvement if it wished to maintain Britain's position in Somaliland. Consequently, measures were taken to strengthen the military, and the government gradually proceeded to reoccupy certain strategic locations in the interior. Intermittent fighting with the Mullah continued throughout the period of the First World War.

At the end of that war, in response to urgent representations by the Protectorate officials, the British government decided to launch another offensive against the Mullah. In this operation, the final one, the Somaliland Camel Corps, along with an irregular Somali tribal levy, played a prominent part. In addition to Somali troops, detachments of Indian troops and King's African Rifles took part, along with six airplanes. The operations were successful, except for their failure to capture the Mullah. His forces were beaten and dispersed and Mohamed fled into Ethiopian territory with a small group of followers. There, near Imi, in the Arussi country, he died of influenza in November 1920. A small tomb with a dome, like the tombs over the burial places of other Moslem saints, was erected over his grave. After his death, his remaining followers scattered, and thus ended the rebellion which for twenty-one years Britain, assisted by Italy and Ethiopia, was unable to suppress.[11]

Nationalism or Religious Fanaticism?

No clear-cut classification of the Mullah's rebellion as "religious" or "nationalist" is possible. It was motivated primarily by religious fanaticism and had as its ultimate objective the imposition of the Salihiyah precepts and way of life upon the population. But, to attain that objective, political means were necessary. The political struggle inevitably had nationalist ingredients, and the ultimate religious objectives of the movement had certain nationalistic aims as their corollaries. It would seem, therefore, that characterizing the Mullah's movement as primarily a religious one, coupled with nationalistic corollaries, would be more appropriate than attempting to constrain it into a purely "religious" or "nationalist" mold.

Mohamed ibn Abdullah Hassan's failure to gain many adherents to his order during his activity as "holy man" in Berbera is believed to have instilled in him a sense of frustration and a conviction that foreigners were to blame. The work of a French Roman Catholic mission which maintained an orphanage and a school in Berbera was particularly repugnant to him. At the beginning of his uprising, in July 1899, he wrote to the Eidagalla tribe seeking their support: "Do you not see that the infidels have destroyed our religion and made our children their children?" His proclamation, upon his arrival at Burao in August, calling on the tribes to accept his authority, was religious in character; he declared himself the Mahdi and proclaimed a holy war against the infidels.[12]

Though denounced for his misdeeds in 1909 by Mohamed Salih, the founder of the order, the Mullah continued to believe in his religious mission. In 1913 he wrote to one of the tribes: "I also inform you that I am a pilgrim and a holy fighter, and have no wish to gain power and greatness in this world . . . I am a Dervish, hoping for God's mercy and consent and forgiveness and guidance, and I desire that all the country and the Moslems may be victorious by God's grace."[13]

Among his followers, there certainly were many who joined for the sake of loot. Mohamed was well aware of this and often apologized to the victims of his undisciplined followers. In one letter to the British authorities at the end of 1912, he said that "most of the Dervishes have got beyond my control and frequently raid the people without my orders." But the Dervishes behaved in battle like religious fanatics rather than common outlaws interested only in loot. Moreover, they evidently believed in the Mullah's supernatural power, such as his ability to turn bullets into water. Defeat was attributed to failure to adhere to his religious injunctions. To ascribe to the Mullah's followers mere avarice and desire for a life of licentious raiding seems unjustified.[14] Those who were impelled to raid and loot their neighbors could have continued to do so in the traditional tribal framework and manner, as indeed the majority of Somalis have done for centuries.

When this religion-motivated movement assumed the form of a political struggle, its nationalistic elements were what impressed the tribes—friend and foe, near and distant. Significantly, these features of his movement have had the most lasting and influential effect in molding Mohamed's image in tribal traditions.

Mohamed's primary political objective was to attain independence from foreign rule. Like modern nationalists, he viewed foreign domination as disrupting the way of life of his people and inhibiting the development of their spiritual well-being. Foreign rule was responsible for the superficiality of his countrymen's adherence to Islam. The foreigners were trying to divert his people from the just path of Islam and even established a mission attempting to convert them to Christianity. Various rival religious orders were operating in the country and, being less austere in their demands than the Salihiyah, were more successful in gaining adherents. This too was attributed partly to the foreigners. In any event, it seemed to Mohamed that the attainment of his religious objectives was contingent upon the expulsion of the foreigners and the establishment of his own temporal authority over the tribes.[15]

Thus, in his view of foreign rule as a barrier to the well-being of the population, and in his desire to rid the country of that rule, Mohamed ibn Abdullah Hassan bears close resemblance to modern nationalist leaders. However, the resemblance cannot be stretched much further, for modern nationalism is essentially a secular movement. Its strictures against foreign rule usually emphasize the inhibitive effect of colonialism upon the social and material development of the population. The spiritual well-being of the people is also a matter of concern to modern nationalists, but it is spiritual well-being in this world, rather than the next. Modern nationalists are concerned with social and racial equality. The Mullah's concern was the institution of an austere and devout way of life, so as to gain admission to Heaven. The modern nationalists' case for independence is stated in terms of a Western ideology, involving principles of democracy and self-determination. The Mullah did not justify his demands by such arguments, and indeed there is no evidence that he was aware of the existence of this Western ideology.

The Mullah and the moderns do agree, however, in their opposition to tribalism—tribalism in the sense of activity directed toward maximizing the political influence of a lineage group. Somali nationalists, like other African nationalists, have put very considerable emphasis upon the elimination of tribal political activities. The same can be said about the Mullah, as well as about other Moslem religious orders active among the Somalis. Tribalism had always hindered the propagation of the orders, just as today it hinders the spread of national unity. The orders, on their part, propagated the doctrine of Moslem unity and brotherhood and attempted to combat tribal divisiveness. The same policy was followed by the Mullah. He attempted to abolish tribal distinctions and affiliations among his followers. Instead of identifying themselves by the names of their tribes, they all assumed the unifying title of Dervish. In this respect, the Mullah's movement, along with other religious orders, helped prepare the way for the emergence of modern nationalism.[16]

It is significant that the Mullah's followers not only avoided tribal names but also the name "Somali." The Mullah always used terms such as "Dervishes" and "Moslems." Some of his letters indeed give the impression that he regarded the Somalis as his enemies. For example, in 1908, at the end of his truce with the government, he wrote to the British authorities complaining about the harassment by the tribes:

I beg to inform you that I am in peace with the British Government, and I shall never attempt to tell you lies. All that I mentioned to you in my letters is true, but most of the people who talk to you about me are telling lies, and you must know that all the Somalis are talking and dealing against me, and no doubt always they tell you that the Dervishes have done so-and-so . . . Although I have been treated as stated above by the Somalis, yet I am considered by them and called a bad man, such as "old singer," "killer," "looter," "disturber of peace," "thief" . . . My request from you now is for *aman* [truce] and peace, and I also request you to put out your hand and make peace between me and the other Somalis.[17]

This style and language contrast rather sharply with modern expressions of nationalism. Modern nationalists claim to speak for their people whom they normally call by the name of the nation (Somalis, Arabs, Hungarians, and so on). Similarly, modern Somali nationalists claim to speak for their nation and strive to counter tribalism by calling themselves Somalis.

The Influence of the Mullah

The attitude of the Somali tribes toward the Mullah varied from enthusiastic support to implacable hostility. Most of the Mullah's support came from the Darod tribes, but only a few of these were unwavering in their loyalty to him. The Ishaq and Dir tribes were for the most part hostile to his movement, and at times actively fought against him.

Mohamed's rising caused a great deal of unrest throughout the region. Word of his movement spread far, and his struggle against foreign infidel authority aroused sympathy. As far south as Benadir, restless tribes, encouraged by the Mullah's example, and sometimes invoking his name, caused trouble for the Italian authorities.[18]

What inspired the Somalis—his friends and foes alike—was his defiance of alien authority. Douglas Jardine, whose account of the Mullah is by no means a sympathetic one, wrote in 1923: "Intensely as the Somalis feared and loathed the man whose followers had looted their stock, robbed them of their all, raped their wives, and murdered their children, they could not but admire and respect one who, being the embodiment of their idea of Freedom and Liberty, never admitted allegiance to any man, Moslem or infidel."[19]

The question whether Mohamed ibn Abdullah Hassan was a nationalist, or merely a religious fanatic, seems less important than the fact that his example was widely admired. Today, he is regarded throughout the Somali area as a great national hero and fighter for independence. Modern Somali nationalism probably would have developed without his example. However, every nation has its historical heroes who symbolize and inspire its national struggle. Mohamed ibn Abdullah Hassan is the Somali symbol.

Chapter 6

The Development of National Consciousness

HISTORICAL figures become national heroes only in nationalistically charged environments. With the growth of Somali national consciousness in the course of the fifty years preceding the Second World War, such an environment gradually took shape in the Horn of Africa. National consciousness was essentially the Somalis' feeling of solidarity, an awareness of their own identity, a "we" versus "they" attitude. It was not an awakening of intellectual or romantic pride in the qualities of the nation, such as had been associated with some European nationalisms. The rise and spread of national consciousness prepared the ground for the emergence of modern nationalism after the Second World War.

Three factors contributed to the development of national consciousness among the Somalis.

The most important factor was resentment against their governments. Before the partition of the Horn of Africa, the Somalis had never been subject to an institutionalized government, though they had been subject to the authority of the elders and to the consensus of the *shir* (the assembly of all male members of the clan). The actions of the alien governments were sometimes incomprehensible, and tended to interfere with the traditional way of life. Tribal interests often conflicted with government regulations. Furthermore, some of the colonial practices prior to the Second World War were harsh and oppressive, especially those of the Italians, who instituted forced labor and a humiliating racial policy. The very notion of international boundaries ran counter to the requirements of the Somalis' nomadic existence. True, Somalis, continuing their seasonal migrations after the fashion of their forefathers, paid (and still pay) little attention to the existence of frontiers. Even so, the movement from one political jurisdiction to another could have unsettling effects, and occasionally the governments went so far as to interfere in these migrations by attempting to prevent or regulate them. All in all, the confrontation of the nomadic, individualistic, and independent Somalis with organized government inevitably led to resentment and conflicts.

A second factor responsible for the development of national consciousness was religious antagonism. The alien governments represented Christian "infidel" rule. Islam fosters the belief in its superiority over other religions, a superiority not only spiritual, but to be attested in the field of battle as well. In Islam there is no separation between religious and secular matters, as there is in Christianity. It is therefore exceedingly difficult and humiliating for a Moslem society to accept non-Moslem rule.[1]

A third factor was the deliberate encouragement of Somali national feelings by various governments from time to time. Such encouragement was usually given with the purpose of undermining the authority of a neighboring government. Yet agitation or subversion in one country tended to cause ripples of unrest which spread throughout the Horn.

These three factors, leading toward the later emergence of nationalism, operated in the relations between the Somali population and the government of each territory.

British Somaliland

With the Mullah's death in 1920, relative peace was restored to British Somaliland. Tribal feuds continued as before, and there occurred occasional clashes between the Somalis and the administration; but, compared to the disorders of the century's first two decades, the country attained tranquility. Life flowed on as it had for centuries, with only minimal government activity to disturb it. Somaliland being a protectorate, rather than a colony, the British government had a convenient legal justification for leaving things as they were. In their protectorates, the British have usually attempted to leave the indigenous political institutions intact and have sought to limit their own interference in local affairs to measures absolutely essential for the protection of British interests.[2] Their policy in Somaliland was probably the closest approach to this "ideal."

Despite the government's desire not to interfere in the traditional way of life, the few measures it introduced were regarded by the Somalis as a disturbing imposition. The most disturbing measure of all had been the establishment of an international border cutting across the traditional grazing grounds of many of the Protectorate tribes. An attempt had been made to minimize its impact upon the Somalis by a provision in the Anglo-Ethiopian border agreement of 1897, stipulating that the tribes "occupying either side of the line shall have the right to use the grazing grounds on the other side." [3] The tribes continued their seasonal migrations after the establishment of the border as they had always done. But occasional interference by the authorities inevitably caused resentment.

Since at first the boundary was not demarcated on the ground, one found it sometimes difficult to determine whether tribes were under British or Ethiopian jurisdiction. The Ethiopians, in attempting to assert their authority near the frontier, used to send military expeditions on tax-collecting missions. These often resulted in armed clashes between Ethiopian troops and Somali tribes. To avoid disputes caused by the uncertainty about the exact location, the border was demarcated on the ground by an Anglo-Ethiopian commission between 1932 and 1934. The Somalis, suspecting that the boundary implied restrictions on their grazing, destroyed many of the pillars marking the border. This resulted in the imposition of fines by the Protectorate government upon the tribes responsible.[4]

The translation into modern political terms of the resentment against the impositions of alien government is a task normally performed by an articulate, educated elite. Such an elite was barely beginning to develop in British Somaliland in the interwar period. The slowness of its emergence was largely due to the equally slow development of an educational system in the Protectorate. Prior to the introduction of Western education by the French Catholic mission in 1891, only Koranic schools existed in the area. The Catholic missionary schools were closed at the request of the British in 1910, as a result of pressure by the Moslem religious authorities. By then, there were a few government schools in operation, the first having been established in 1898 at Berbera. Very few Somalis attended those schools, however, and for many years the pupils were mainly children of Indian and Arab merchants. After the First World War, Somali interest in Western education increased somewhat, but educational facilities remained pathetically insufficient. Indeed, in 1934 only one government elementary school existed in the Protectorate. It had 120 students. The total government expenditure on education amounted to £500 a year. The maintenance of the elementary school cost the government £100; a further £100 went for subsidies to Koranic schools; and £300 was spent on the education of a small number of students from the Protectorate at Gordon College in Khartoum.[5]

The British government's lack of initiative was the main reason why modern education came so slowly to the territory. But Somali resistance to the imposition of taxation to finance education was also to blame. This resistance culminated in a riot at Burao in 1922, in the course of which the District Commissioner was shot and killed. No new vigorous steps were taken by the government until 1935, when an education scheme for the Protectorate was drawn up. This was followed by the establishment of an Education Department in 1938. However, the implementation of the scheme was delayed because of opposition of religious leaders who feared that a new educated class might question their authority, and that the schools might be an instrument for Christian missionary activity. The opposition reached a climax in another riot at Burao in May 1939, resulting in the death of three Somalis.[6]

The small elite that had received a Western education and been exposed to Western ideas consisted almost entirely of civil servants. It was not possible, however, for government servants to engage in politics, and least of all, to be in the forefront of nationalist agitation. Only upon leaving the civil service did individuals feel free to undertake political activity.

One of the first modern politicians to emerge in the Protectorate was a former civil servant by the name of Haji Farah Omar, who became active around 1920. His political agitation did not find favor with the authorities and he was exiled to Aden. There, he participated in the establishment of the Somali Islamic Association. Although not a political organization, this association took an active interest in developments in the Protectorate, and frequently petitioned the British government on Somali affairs. Haji Farah Omar kept up his own activity as well. This consisted mainly of collecting information about Somali affairs and publicizing grievances through letters to British newspapers and Members of Parliament. Significantly, he did not limit his activity to matters concerning British Somaliland, but also took a wide interest in Somali affairs outside the Protectorate.[7]

There were also attempts at political organization. Through the initiative of local merchants, political clubs were established in 1935 in Berbera, Hargeisa, and Burao. The clubs did not attempt any large-scale organization, but were limited instead to a select membership, drawn principally from among the Ishaq. In 1937, growing discontent among the civil servants regarding their status and their opportunities for advancement led to the establishment of the Somali Officials' Union. Inevitably, the promotion of the officials' interests could not be entirely divorced from political matters. The Somali officials felt particularly aggrieved by the practice of appointing

Somalis only to the lowest ranks of the civil service and reserving middle and senior positions to British and expatriate Indian personnel.[8]

These were merely the beginnings of political grumblings. They reflected not only the existence of discontent, but also the growing political consciousness among the population and their gropings to express their grievances in modern political terms. A nationalist movement did not emerge, however, until after the Second World War.

Kenya

Until the 1940's the Somalis of the Northern Frontier Province of Kenya lived relatively unaffected by government measures or by modern economic or political influences. But the small number of Kenya Somalis living outside the Northern Frontier Province, including those in Nairobi, were earlier exposed to Western influences, and to the effects of the economic, social, and political developments in the territory. In the interwar period they undoubtedly took notice of the growing political fermentation among the Africans of Kenya. Some information about these developments probably reached the tribes with which urban Somalis maintain contact. But no political or nationalist awakening occurred among the Kenya Somalis.

The Kenya government's attempts to impose its authority caused some resentment among the Somalis and encouraged group consciousness. The most serious troubles occurred in Jubaland (the territory immediately adjacent to the Juba river) prior to its transfer to Italian jurisdiction in 1925 as a consequence of an undertaking made by Britain during the First World War. The troubles in Jubaland when it was still part of Kenya involved the unruly Marehan and Aulihan tribes (sections of the Ogaden Darod). The incidents usually grew out of Somali reluctance to submit to British administration and out of the government's attempts to stop intertribal raids. The personal ambitions of tribal leaders who wanted to extend their authority also played a role. The most notable of these leaders was Abdurrahman Mursaal, of the Aulihan. He visited Nairobi in 1915 and returned to Jubaland "with a heightened sense of his own importance and a wholly unfounded claim that the government had given him all the country between Serenli and Wajir."[9] He raided the government post at Serenli, killing its British commander. Finally his force was defeated and he had to flee.

Yet the strife never assumed the form of a Somali rebellion against the government. The tribes were usually divided—some sections rebelling, some supporting the government, others taking advantage of a rival group's conflict with the authorities in order to raid the rivals and loot their livestock. In the course of various punitive expeditions, local Somalis served with the King's African Rifles and, in addition, the authorities made use of tribal levies. These Somalis were not considered wholly reliable, and on a few occasions mutinied. Nevertheless, Somali troops continued to be employed and were of great value to the British in their attempts to establish their authority in Jubaland.[10]

As already stated, population pressures in the northern portions of the Horn have caused a persistent trend of migration southward and westward, a migration which has been in process for centuries. Somali penetration into Kenya has taken place only in the last sixty years. A history of this expansion remains yet to be written. Some generalizations about it are, nevertheless, possible.[11]

The Somalis moved into Kenya both by peaceful methods and by conquest.

Peaceful penetration was achieved mainly through the ingenious introduction and application of the widespread custom of clientship. The newly arrived Somali clan or section would attach themselves as clients (*shegat*) to a clan or section inhabiting the area, either Galla or Somali. To consolidate this relationship and ensure their access to wells and grazing grounds occupied by the patron tribe, the newly arrived Somalis would give their daughters in marriage to the patron tribe. The attachment of Somalis as clients to Galla tribes was often accompanied by attempts on the part of the Somalis to Islamize the pagan Gallas. If the Gallas adopted Islam, they would then be assimilated within the Somali society, which was culturally and religiously superior. Such tendencies have normally been encouraged by the client Somalis. The final step in the Somalization of the patron tribe would be their "adoption" of Somali ancestors and their integration into the Somali genealogy.

Sometimes, however, peaceful penetration failed, and was followed by conflict over wells and grazing grounds. In such cases, the newly arrived Somalis often proved stronger and the defeated Gallas were pushed farther westward.

In order to limit Somali expansion into Kenya, which was considered detrimental to the interests of the native Galla population, the Kenya government decided in 1909 to regulate grazing and to restrict the movement of Somali tribes beyond a fixed border, the so-called "Somali line." All clans and sections, both Somali and Galla, have been allocated grazing areas. Trespassing is reported to the authorities by the aggrieved party.

The policy of limiting Somali expansion has been applied consistently and successfully for the last fifty years. The effective enforcement of these provisions depended in large measure upon the administrative officers involved and upon their personal attitudes.

The difficulties which apparently existed in the early years before firm patterns of administration were established were described in a somewhat sarcastic comment by an officer of the King's African Rifles (K.A.R.):

> There has never really been a defined continuous policy in the Northern Frontier District, as owing to its inaccessibility and the absence of regular communications matters have perforce been left largely in the hands of the men on the spot. Up to a point this has worked well, but the wily Somal has been clever enough to spot the weak point, and has always managed to find champions and play them off against the sterner officials, who will not listen to his remarkably ingenious excuses for not carrying out any instructions which do not happen to coincide with his own convenience; and, mark you, owing to the scarcity of water and the

internecine sectional feuds he often puts forward a seemingly very good case. Some officials see the Somal's point of view so thoroughly that, after a little, they almost think as he does, and eventually believe that the Somal can do no wrong. Mr. Somal, by the way, as you have probably gathered by this time, is a clever and adroit flatterer. To such an extent has this sort of thing been carried, that it is rumoured that one official has even gone so far as to order supplies of "Glaxo" from England to nourish the young hopefuls of the noble Somal race. This attitude is generally known as the "Glaxo" policy. On the other hand, the sterner school definitely dislike, and are in their turn disliked by, Somalis, and consider that if they disobey orders they should be properly straffed. This point of view is usually referred to as the Hell-Fire Policy, and as the upholders of these policies are about equally divided and frequently interchanged, you can imagine that things are generally rather in a muddle. We K.A.R. are not supposed to have enough brains to follow the intricacies of tribal politics and are strictly enjoined not to interfere, but you will find yourself inevitably dragged into it, and your aim must be to try and steer between the two.[12]

The presence of the British authorities inevitably produced some friction, and caused resentment. It encouraged group consciousness among the Somalis, and thus provided the basis for the rudimentary nationalist movement which developed among the Kenya Somalis after the Second World War.

French Somaliland

The Somalis of French Somaliland had more contacts with the West and Western ideas than those of any other part of the Horn prior to the Second World War. This is largely because Jibuti was the most developed town and the busiest port in the Horn, and contained a sizable European population. Only a few thousand Somalis lived in Jibuti, but here as elsewhere the townspeople maintained their tribal affiliations and transmitted Western ideas and influences to the nomadic tribes.

During the First World War the contacts of the Somalis of this country with the West assumed massive proportions: thousands of them served with the French Army. Over 2,000 Somalis saw action on the western front in Europe. They must have distinguished themselves; about 1,000 of them received individual citations and 400 were killed.[13]

Some interest in politics was displayed by the Seamen's Union established in Jibuti in 1931. The union's range of interests extended beyond strictly sailors' affairs, and included such matters as the Somalis' representation in government and their share in the territory's economy.

Political awakening was further stimulated by Italy's conquest of Ethiopia in 1935. Italian encroachments upon French Somaliland territory, and the occupation by Italian troops in 1938 of a disputed area, caused great excitement and aroused political interest among the population. The Somalis, along with the rest of the population, declared their loyalty to France and their readiness "to help France in case of war, in order to defend our homeland."[14]

The relatively intensive exposure of the Somalis of French Somaliland to Western influences presumably produced a politically more sophisticated population than existed elsewhere in the Horn of Africa. Still, here as elsewhere, political parties and a nationalist movement did not develop in French Somaliland until after the Second World War.

Italian Somaliland

When nationalist movements did emerge in the Horn the most fully developed one was in Italian Somaliland. To a considerable extent this was due to that country's special status as an ex-Italian colony and the deliberations about its future which took place in the late 1940's. But, part of the reason undoubtedly lies in the territory's prewar experiences.

Again the early development of national consciousness was mainly due to "anti" sentiments. These were directed against the Italian authorities, whose colonial practices aroused resentment, and against the Ethiopians, toward whom the Somalis' traditional animosity was further incited by the Italian government.

Resentment against Italian rule was probably the most important factor behind the awakening of national consciousness. The establishment of government authority and administration throughout the territory was not well received by the tribes. Independence, even with anarchy and insecurity, was preferable to subjection to a Christian government and its imposed peace. Resistance to Italian authority flared up sporadically, and pacification of the country took many years. Only very gradually, through a series of military operations, sometimes coupled by severe repressive measures, did the Italians succeed in establishing their authority.[15]

Resistance to the Italians was usually local or tribal. No attempt was made to organize large-scale territory-wide opposition. Throughout the process of pacification the Italians were able to employ Somali troops, as the British had done in their areas.[16] Significantly, however, the Italians, like the British, never relied solely upon Somali troops in their operations, but used them as part of a mixed force, including units recruited outside the territory. The process of pacification left a residue of resentment, which provided the foundation upon which postwar nationalism has developed.

Similar resentment was aroused by oppressive and humiliating policies instituted by the prewar Italian administration, such as forced labor and racial laws. At the early stage of Italian administration there was great difficulty in inducing the Somalis to work on the Italian farms or on public projects. Regular employment for money wages was a practice totally alien to the local inhabitants. The Italians, therefore, reverted to coercion in the recruitment and maintenance of a labor force.[17] In 1938, Fascist racial laws were put into effect in Italian Somaliland. Although these were not strictly applied, those portions of the population which became cognizant of them were deeply offended.[18]

Italian-Ethiopian tension was also instrumental in awakening Somali national consciousness. As early as 1897, the Italians and the Ethiopians, attempting to extend their authority north and south respectively, were involved in a competition to win the loyalty and good will of the Somali population.[19] Later, during the Fascist era, in an attempt to undermine Ethiopian authority in the Ogaden, the Italians encouraged some of their border tribes to penetrate into Ethiopian territory, and to resist Ethiopian assertions of authority. This Italian policy subsequently led to the famous Wal-Wal incident and to the invasion of Ethiopia in 1935.

During that invasion the Italian policy of inciting the Somalis against the Ethiopians reached a climax. A Somali army was recruited by the Italians and employed in the Ethiopian campaign. In addition to some 6,000 troops incorporated directly into this army, many thousands of irregular fighters (*dubats*), armed and trained by the Italians, participated in the campaign.

The Ethiopians resorted to similar devices and, though probably less successful than the Italians, managed to win over dissatisfied elements among Italy's Somali subjects. The most notable addition to their ranks was one Omar Samantar, who had deserted from service with the Italians in 1925 and had enlisted in Ethiopian service shortly thereafter. During the Italian-Ethiopian war he led a force of irregular Somalis who fought on the Ethiopian side.[20]

It seems that the Somalis, as a "nation," did not take sides in the war. Individuals and tribes fought with both armies. Nevertheless, their involvement in the war resulted in an awakening of Somali national consciousness. The Italian designs on Ethiopia required, as one observer has written, a policy of "nurturing nascent Somali consciousness, without, however, permitting the creation of modern Somali nationalism." [21]

Other developments that played a role in preparing the ground for nationalism were economic and social. Italian economic activity, though modest in size, was instrumental in initiating some social changes. Several agricultural enterprises were launched by Italians, attempting to grow cotton, sugar, and bananas for export. Moreover, some commercial and industrial enterprises were established. These were owned almost exclusively by Italians, Arabs, and Indians. Though relatively few Somalis were employed by the industrial and commercial enterprises, many thousands worked on the farms.[22] The weakening of the traditional social fabric, which usually accompanies economic development, facilitated the postwar growth of nationalism.

A nationalist movement could not develop in the territory in the absence of an educated class. Little was done by the prewar Italian administration to provide the Somalis with a Western education. Many Koranic schools existed throughout the territory, but by 1939 only twelve Western-style elementary schools for Somalis, all run by Catholic missions with the help of government subsidies, had been established. There were 1,776 pupils in these schools, out of a total population of approximately one million. Very few individuals, if any, received secondary education.[23] It would be an exaggeration to claim that by the 1940's, when a nationalist movement began to emerge, an educated elite had developed. Rather, it was the Second World War and its upheavals that produced a body of men, motivated and capable, to lead a nationalist movement.

Ethiopia

The Somalis of Ethiopia, like their brethren elsewhere, were subject to considerable stresses during the fifty years preceding the Second World War. Relations between Ethiopians and Somalis were not always hostile; indeed there were numerous cases of cooperation. But inevitably the establishment of Ethiopian authority in the Somali-inhabited areas, Ethiopian internal politics, and the Italian occupation—all tended to exacerbate the traditional antagonism between the Christian Ethiopians and the Moslem Somalis.

The end of the nineteenth century had seen consolidation of central government in Ethiopia under Emperor Menelik II, as we have related. The Ethiopians asserted their authority over many areas previously only under their nominal suzerainty. Among the areas thus subjected to Ethiopian rule was much of the Somali-inhabited territory between Harar and British Somaliland. The establishment of Ethiopian authority was usually accompanied by military operations against reluctant Somali tribes. Often the Somalis refused to pay taxes to the Ethiopians, whereupon their villages were raided and the tax collected by force. Accounts of travelers who visited the area at the end of the nineteenth century and early in the twentieth abound with references to Somali complaints against raids by Ethiopian tax collectors.[24] The unrest caused among the Somalis by these operations explains in part the support given the Mullah by the Ogaden tribes.

But the sense of national consciousness stimulated by Ethiopian military operations did not result in political consequences. In fact, it did not even prevent the Somalis from entering the Emperor's service and participating in Ethiopian military operations against the Mullah. The Somalis do not seem to have been divided into pro-and-anti-Ethiopian camps. Even those serving with the Ethiopian forces were imbued with hostility toward the Christian Ethiopians. The antagonism was mutual, apparently quite deeply rooted, frequently resulting in bloody incidents—but not followed up by any drastic political consequences.[25]

On one important occasion, during the grave constitutional crisis of 1915–1917, the Somalis played a significant role. After Menelik's death in 1913, his grandson Lij Yasu ascended the throne. Lij Yasu leaned, however, toward Islam and was therefore mistrusted by the Amhara nobility and by the Church. In 1915, he was reported to have adopted Islam and to have been in close contact with Turkish agents. At the same time he also was in collusion with the Mullah. In the summer of 1916, Lij Yasu went to Jigjiga to organize an army from among the Somali and Galla population of the region. The suspicious Rases thereupon staged a *coup d'état* at Addis Ababa, appointing Menelik's daughter Zauditu as Empress, and Ras Tafari (later Emperor Haile Selassie) as regent. An expedition was sent against Lij Yasu and his Moslem supporters. Lij Yasu retreated first to Harar, and when the Ethiopian troops reached the city he fled to the Danakil desert. The fighting was brief but bitter, and ended in the conquest of Harar and massacre of the deposed Emperor's Somali followers.[26]

The Somalis' role in the episode was played by them as Moslems, rather than as members of a Somali nation. Moreover, the Gallas, another Moslem minority, were even more deeply implicated. Nevertheless, the fact remains that at a time of a constitutional crisis, Somali-Ethiopian tensions did have serious political repercussions. The possibility that the Somalis might again be mobilized some day into a political force has affected Ethiopian policy ever since.

The extension of effective Ethiopian authority into the southern Ogaden took place only in the early 1930's. Until then the southernmost military post had been at Dagahbur, on the Tug Jerer.* Farther south, Ethiopian authority had been asserted only through sporadic expeditions. But, as the tension with Italy increased, the Ethiopians, in order to counter the gradual Italian penetration into their territory, established several more outposts. Both the Ethiopians and the Italians sought to occupy the few wells in the area, since possession of the wells meant control over the Somali inhabitants of the region.

A competition for the allegiance of the Somali tribes ensued. It seems that, as on previous occasions, the Somalis did not take a united position. Some threw their lot with the Italians, others actively supported the Ethiopians, and the great majority remained neutral, probably waiting to see which side would prevail before committing themselves. The most important Somali on the Italian side was an Ogaden chieftain, Sultan Olol Dinle. He had entered Italian service as early as the 1920's and had aided the Italian penetration in the 1920's and 1930's. During the Italian-Ethiopian war, he and his followers fought on the Italian side. Other Somalis served the Italians as scouts and spies. Similar services were performed by Somalis for the Ethiopian authorities. Moreover, a Somali force organized by the Ethiopians during the war served as a backbone of the Ogaden defense for many months.[27]

Somali national consciousness in Ethiopia received a powerful

* The Tug Jerer and Tug Fafan are dry river beds running in a north–south direction, and provide the most convenient route between Harar and the Ogaden.

stimulus during the Italian occupation. The Ethiopian Church and the Christian population were imbued with an Ethiopian nationalist spirit. As a counterweight the Italians paid special attention throughout the occupied territory to the Moslem population, and attempted to win their loyalty. The special identities of the ethnic and religious components of the Ethiopian empire were emphasized through the administrative organization of the conquered country, as well as through other measures. Italian East Africa (as Ethiopia and the older Italian colonies of Eritrea and Somaliland came to be known) was divided into six provinces corresponding roughly to ethnic divisions: Shoa, Eritrea, Amhara, Harar, Galla-Sidamo, and Somalia. The new province of Somalia included the old Italian colony and most of the Ogaden. Thus, almost the entire Somali population of Ethiopia was united under the same administration with the Somalis of Somalia; and this circumstance had its effect upon the Somali population. However, when Ethiopia was liberated in 1941, the Ethiopian Somalis' awareness of their national identity still had not transformed itself into a nationalist movement.

The Impact of the Second World War

In many parts of Africa, common factors underlying the rise of nationalism were: social and economic changes, the appearance of an educated elite, and grievances against colonial rule or against a settler minority. These internal factors were found to some extent in the Horn. The Somalis, too, resented colonial rule, and besides, economic and social changes were beginning to disrupt their traditional way of life. But such changes were small compared to those in many another African territory, and their impact was not sufficient to transform the passive feeling of national consciousness into a militant political movement. In the Horn the principal impetus to the emergence of nationalism as the most important political force in the region was external. Somali nationalism, instead of evolving gradually from internal events, sprang mainly from global war and its aftermath.

True, the Second World War, service in the armed forces, the effect of war propaganda, and United Nations ideals influenced developments in most African territories. The Horn, however, underwent experiences unequaled elsewhere in Africa south of the Sahara. The Horn was a theater of operations, and portions of it changed hands more than once. Moreover, after the war, the future disposition of the former Italian colony of Somaliland became a subject of political struggle and extensive debate, in the course of which the opinions of the population were consulted. This solicitation of the wishes of the inhabitants became an especially powerful stimulus to a nationalist movement.

War came to the Horn of Africa four years before it came to Europe. The Italian invasion of Ethiopia began on October 3, 1935, and by May 1936 the Italians had overrun the country; but scattered guerrilla resistance continued for years. In August 1940, after Italy's declaration of war upon the Allies, Italian forces invaded British Somaliland, and less than two weeks later the territory was theirs. For a few months the British and the Italians faced each other uneasily along Kenya's northern border. Then, in January 1941, the British opened their offensive. A month later, on February 25, they took Mogadishu; the rest of Italian Somaliland followed. In March, British Somaliland was reconquered from the Italians. On April 6, Addis Ababa was taken, and on May 5—the anniversary of the Italian occupation of the city five years earlier—Emperor Haile Selassie reentered his capital. French Somaliland, controlled by the Vichy government, came under blockade, and finally surrendered to the Allies in December 1942. Thus the Somalis, with the exception of those living in Kenya, witnessed within a period of a few years the successive collapse of all their masters. If the Somalis ever had a feeling of inferiority toward those who governed them, this feeling was considerably undermined by 1941.[28]

The war brought the Somali population into extensive contact with the West. Thousands of Somalis served with the armed forces of the warring powers, and, however unpleasant the circumstances may have been, were thus exposed to Western influences. Some, after participating in the East African campaign, were sent overseas to India, and thence proceeded to the front in Burma. It was scarcely a sightseeing trip, but inevitably their horizons broadened.[29]

In 1941 came the British Military Administration and the decided boost it gave to the feeling of Somali unity. The area liberated by Allied forces was divided into three parts: British Somaliland, the former Italian Somaliland, and the so-called "Reserved Area" of Ethiopia. The Ogaden, which had been governed as a district of Italian Somaliland during the Italian occupation, continued to be administered as part of that territory under British Military Administration. The Reserved Area, that part of Ethiopia closest to French and British Somaliland, was to remain in British hands until the mid-1950's, as we shall see in later chapters.[30]

Allied war propaganda also had its effect. Like other peoples, the Somalis were subject to exhortations about the justice of the Allied cause and its purpose of securing freedom to oppressed peoples. The urban population was exposed to such propaganda continually. Some of the propaganda reached the Somalis of the interior as well. It is not contended that all this indoctrinated the Somalis with any coherent liberal-democratic ideology. But the propaganda could hardly have failed to raise in their minds the question whether "freedom" and "the right of all peoples to choose the form of government under which they will live" might not have some relevance to their own problems.[31]

The Postwar Period

The question of the future disposition of the former Italian colony of Somaliland, widely debated after the war, aroused keen interest among the Somalis. The negotiations among the powers and the various proposals regarding the future of the territory received publicity. The British proposal known as the "Bevin Plan," made to the Council of Foreign Ministers in 1946, was widely publicized by the British Military Administration and was apparently well received by the Somalis. According to this plan the former Italian Somaliland, British Somaliland, and portions of Ethiopia were to be embodied in a single unit and placed under trusteeship. The proposal was elaborated upon by Foreign Secretary Bevin in the House of Commons on June 4, 1946:

Now may I turn to Eritrea and Somaliland. I think that M. Molotov has been more than unjust in stating that we are trying to expand the British Empire at the expense of Italy and Ethiopia, and to consolidate what he calls the monopolistic position of Great Britain in the Mediterranean and Red Seas. In the latter part of the last century the Horn of Africa was divided between Great Britain, France and Italy. At about the time we occupied our part, the Ethiopians occupied an inland area which is the grazing ground for nearly half the nomads of British Somaliland for six months of the year. Similarly, the nomads of Italian Somaliland must cross the existing frontiers in search of grass. In all innocence, therefore, we proposed that British Somaliland, Italian Somaliland, and the adjacent part of Ethiopia, if Ethiopia agreed, should be lumped together as a trust territory, so that the nomads should lead their frugal existence with the least possible hindrance and there might be a real chance of a decent economic life, as understood in that territory.

But what attracted M. Molotov's criticism was, I am sure, that I suggested that Great Britain should be made the administrating authority. Was this unreasonable? In the first place we were surrendering a Protectorate comparable in size to the area we hoped that Ethiopia would contribute. Secondly, it was a British force, mainly East African and South African, which freed this area; and it was a British, Indian, and South African force which bore the main brunt of restoring the independence of Ethiopia and of putting the Emperor back on his throne after several years' sanctuary in this country. We do not seek gratitude on that account but I think it right to express surprise that our proposals should have met with such unjustified criticism. After all, when we were defeating Italy in East Africa, Britain was open to invasion and we were fighting alone. I hope the deputies at the Paris conference will now consider a greater Somaliland more objectively.

All I want to do in this case is to give those poor nomads a chance to live. I do not want anything else. We are paying nearly £1,000,000 a year out of our Budget to help to support them. We do not ask to save anything. But to have these constant bothers on the frontiers when one can organize the thing decently—well, after all, it is nobody's interest to stop the poor people and cattle there getting a decent living. That is all there is to it. It is like the Englishman's desire to go into Scotland—to get a decent living. We must consider it objectively. If the Conference do not like our proposal we will not be dogmatic about it; we are prepared to see Italian Somaliland put under the United Nations' trusteeship.[32]

The proposal to group the territories in a single unit was the most significant element of the Bevin Plan. Somali demands along similar lines were obviously influenced by the British proposal, as is indicated by the testimony of Haji Mohamed Hussein, the then President of the Somali Youth League, before the Four Power Commission of Investigation for the former Italian Colonies. He was being questioned by the Soviet representative:

M. Feodorov: Does the executive of the Somali Youth League know the opinions of the various Governments regarding the future of the former Italian colonies?

Haji Mohamed Hussein: The Somali Youth League is aware of what has appeared in newspapers.

M. Feodorov: What do they know according to the newspapers?

Haji Mohamed Hussein: One of them is a publication in the newspapers wherein it was stated Mr. Bevin advocates the establishment of a Greater Somalia. That point appeared in English as well as Arabic newspapers. When we saw this being uttered by a Foreign Minister of a Great Power we were very happy indeed because it is one of our great aims.[33]

This Four Power Commission consisted of representatives of Britain, France, the United States, and the Soviet Union. Provision for its establishment was made in annex XI to the treaty of peace with Italy. The Commission was charged with supplying necessary data to the Deputy Foreign Ministers and with ascertaining "the views of the local population" on the political future of the former Italian colonies.[34]

The existence of the Commission gave a great boost to political activity. In preparation for its arrival in 1948, new political organizations were formed and existing parties and organizations intensified their activities. As the Commission was to visit provincial centers, political parties made special efforts to establish branches and organize the presentation of opinion throughout the territory supporting the parties' views. Some eleven Somali organizations presented the Commission with their views about the future of the territory, along with Italian organizations and two minority communities.[35] Only a few of the organizations which testified before the Commission were nationalist in character or can be regarded as political parties. But the significant fact is that the consideration of the future of Italian Somaliland, by stimulating political interest, created conditions favorable to the spread of nationalist ideas and the transformation of nascent nationalist parties into mass organizations.

This effect was not limited to the former Italian territory, but was noticeable, though in a lesser degree, in neighboring territories, especially in British Somaliland.[36]

The placing of former Italian Somaliland under United Nations trusteeship under Italian administration with a target date of independence after ten years had a momentous effect upon the Somalis. It encouraged national feelings among Somalis throughout the Horn. News about the existence of the United Nations Organization spread, and it came to be viewed as a protector and guarantor of Somali aspirations. The emerging nationalist politicians drew further assurance from the presence of the United Nations Advisory Council in Mogadishu.[37]

Moreover, Somalis had heard about the anti-colonial struggle in some Asian territories and the attainment of independence by Indonesia, Burma, India, Pakistan, and other countries. The religious and commercial ties with the Arab world and the presence of Arab and Indo-Pakistani communities throughout the region facilitated the dissemination of news about these developments.

In addition, from outside the Horn has come considerable propaganda designed to stimulate Somali nationalism. Since the 1950's, Egypt in particular has been active in this respect, through radio broadcasts in the Somali language and through the dissemination of propaganda by Egyptian teachers in Somalia and by Pan-Islamic organizations linked with Cairo. Egyptian attacks on "imperialism" have not been aimed at the British and French alone, but at "Ethiopian imperialism" as well. Although Somali attitudes toward Egypt are not always sympathetic, the propaganda emanating from Cairo undoubtedly encouraged nationalist sentiments.[38]

Certain internal developments, though less important than external ones, have contributed to the growth of Somali nationalism. It is true that the nomads are still nomads and that attempts to settle them have not achieved significant results thus far. But, as for the sedentary part of the population, their way of life as well as their social and political concepts has been changing because of the development of commerce and industry, the growth of a government bureaucracy, and the spread of a cash economy. Social dislocations resulting from such changes have been a stimulant to political activity.

A nationalist movement and political organizations could not have emerged without some sort of educated class. Educated persons are the most sensitive to external influences, spreading them among the rest of the population. Moreover, the setting up and management of political organizations requires a body of literate functionaries. We have seen that the emergence of such a class was slow. The process accelerated after the Second World War. For example, the total number of persons attending schools in former Italian Somaliland rose from 1,853 in 1947 to 26,796 in 1956. In British Somaliland the total number of pupils in 1948 was 1,424, of whom 617 were in government schools and 807 in private Koranic schools. By 1957 the number had risen to 6,903, of whom 2,253 were in government schools and 4,650 in Koranic schools.[39] These figures are not very impressive compared with total populations of about 1,300,000 in Italian Somaliland and 650,000 in British Somaliland. They indicate, nevertheless, that change was taking place.

The growth of modern political organizations has encountered many obstacles. Probably the most important have been religious and tribal interests. Religious leaders have viewed with suspicion the rising influence of secular politicians. The politicians on their part have not been in sympathy with the religious orders, which they regarded as divisive forces. The politicians have also fought against clanship and tribal loyalties. But those loyalties and the influence of religious leaders are deeply engrained in Somali society, and will continue to inhibit the spread of national unity for years to come.[40]

The Roots of Somali Nationalism

The demand for Somali unification is sometimes justified by arguments from the arsenal of democratic ideology, claiming for the Somalis of Kenya, Ethiopia, and French Somaliland the right of self-determination. But the mainspring of the demand for unification is not the enlightenment brought about by Western ideas. The nationalist awakening and the espousal of the aim of independence and unification are not the result of Western ideological influence.

In that connection our emphasis upon the crucial role of the educated class in the nationalist movement should not be misunderstood. The educated class is the group in society most aware of the external environment. Its awareness of the world at large acquainted it with the existence of a political framework through which interests can be promoted and within which national consciousness can find its fulfillment. Furthermore, the educated class has provided the leadership and organizational talent essential for modern politics.

On the other side of the continent, in some West African territories, it may be that the emergence of nationalist movements was influenced by Western ideas. A substantial number of West Africans had attended Western universities, and a literate middle class had existed in some of those territories before the development of national movements there. Since West Africa was exposed to Western ideas for an extended period, it is to be expected that these ideas influenced political values and political developments.

Developments in the Horn of Africa were more recent and more rapid. Western education and ideas began effectively to penetrate the area only after the three Somalilands (British, French, and Italian) were already well on the way to self-government.

Somali nationalism stems from a feeling of national consciousness in the sense of "we" as opposed to "they" which has existed among the Somalis for many centuries. It was nurtured by tribal genealogies and traditions, by the Islamic religious ties, and by conflicts with foreign peoples. It ripened and became a political movement as a result of external influences—the establishment of alien governments, the impact of the Second World War, and the example of the struggle for independence in other countries.

Chapter 7

Nationalism and Politics in the Trust Territory of Somalia

In all parts of the Horn, probably the most significant fact about Somali politics is its essentially tribal basis. Politics in the Horn, like the politics of industrial societies, consists of competition among groups for influence in the management of public affairs. The distinction lies in the character of the groups. In developed industrial societies the competing groups are made up of individuals united by common economic or social interests or perhaps a common ideology. Among the Somalis they are determined by common ancestry.

Somali nationalists with modernist tendencies are greatly troubled by the tribal nature of their political system. They are opposed to tribalism because it hinders a rational approach to economic and social problems. Moreover, they view the assertion of tribal interests as diametrically contradictory to the ideal of Somali national unity. Like nationalists in many other African territories, they strive to achieve unity as their most pressing internal political goal.

Yet the eradication of tribalism is not an easy task. It cannot be eliminated by an act of the will. Despite the efforts of modern nationalists, tribalism still pervades all aspects of public life. Political parties are based upon tribes or tribal alliances. Allocations of political spoils or civil service posts are carefully calculated to fit a tribal balance. Recruitment to the police force and the army is also conditioned by the need to preserve a tribal balance—in this case to have all tribes represented. The maintenance of this balance in the lower ranks of the civil service and the police and army is not always easy. In the Southern Region of the Somali Republic—formerly Somalia and before that Italian Somaliland—the Darod, who live in poorer areas, are more readily disposed to join government service than are the slightly better-situated Hawiya; and among the agricultural Dighil and Rahanwein the proportion of those interested in joining government service is the lowest of all.[1]

The eagerness and determination of nationalists to eliminate tribalism lead them sometimes, in conversations with foreigners, to deny that tribes play a role in politics. They apparently believe that the less said about tribalism, the better; and the easier it will be to eliminate it. Yet even the most Westernized Somalis, the most modern ardent nationalists who violently oppose tribalism, are not oblivious of their tribal connections. They cannot be, since their political careers depend essentially on the hard core of support they can generate "at home"—among their own tribe. To understand Somali politics, one must recognize the ambivalence of politicians toward tribalism—their concessions to it as well as their struggle to eliminate it.

The Political Parties of Somalia

The first Somali political organization to emerge in the territory that is now the Southern Region was the Somali Youth Club, which was established at Mogadishu in May 1943, apparently with the encouragement of the British Military Administration. Details on the Administration's role in this development are difficult to ascertain. There is good reason to believe that it was not merely a benevolent onlooker, but provided during the early 1940's guidance and help to the inexperienced Somali politicians.[2]

In 1947, preparing for the arrival of the Four Power Commission of Investigation, the Somali Youth Club reorganized itself as a political party assuming the new name of Somali Youth League

(S.Y.L.). In addition, an association of the Sab, the Hizbia Dighil e Mirifle, also changed from a nonpolitical association into a political party on the eve of the Commission's visit. Still other organizations, more short-lived, were formed in order to facilitate the presentation before the Commission of specific points of view.[3]

Between 1948 and 1950 the question of the political future of what had been Italian Somaliland engendered considerable excitement. But after the Italian trusteeship administration established itself in 1950 the atmosphere gradually calmed down. The Italians were skillful in winning the confidence of some of those who opposed their return; and even the S.Y.L., which had violently opposed the placing of the trust territory under Italian administration, was won over to cooperate.

The new status of Somalia as a U.N. trust territory with a target date for independence, and the political institutions introduced by the administration, provided the framework within which the political parties operated. As independence was assured, the remaining goal of national unification received increased attention. But the political parties and the various tribal groups were mainly occupied with capturing the positions which the Italian trusteeship administration was gradually transferring to the Somalis.

The initial step in Somalia's evolution toward self-government and independence was the establishment of a Territorial Council in 1950. This council was an appointed body with advisory functions. The majority of the Somali representatives on it were tribal leaders; the political parties received only seven out of thirty-five seats. The first elections were held in the territory in 1954, on the municipal level. In 1956, the first territory-wide elections took place, and the appointed Territorial Council was replaced by an elected Legislative Assembly. Also, a government responsible to the Legislative Assembly was formed. After that, two more elections were held: municipal elections in 1958 and general elections to the Legislative Assembly in 1959. The 1954 and 1956 elections were held under universal adult male suffrage; in the 1958 and 1959 elections women too were given the right to vote. The administration of the

TABLE 3 Election Results in Somalia, 1954–1959

Party	Municipal elections				General elections			
	1954		1958		1956		1959	
	Votes	Seats	Votes	Seats	Votes	Seats	Votes	Seats
Somali Youth League (S.Y.L.)	17,982	141	39,178	416	333,820	43	237,134	83
Hizbia Dastur Mustaqil Somali (H.D.M.S.)	8,198	57	38,214	175	159,967	13	40,857	5
Somali National Union (S.N.U.), formerly U.G.B.	2,273	5	6,322	6	21,630	0	0	0
Greater Somalia League (G.S.L.)	0	0	10,125	36	0	0	0	0
Liberal Somali Youth Party (P.L.G.S.)	0	0	11,004	27	0	0	35,769	2
Somali Fiqarini Youth (G.F.S.)	0	0	341	3	0	0	0	0
Somali Democratic Party (S.D.P.)	0	0	0	0	80,866	3	0	0
Marehan Union	0	0	0	0	11,358	1	0	0
Somali African Union (U.A.S.)	2,584	28	0	0	0	0	0	0
Other parties	6,660	50	0	0	7,268	0	0	0
Totals	37,697	281	105,184	663	614,909	60	313,760	90

NOTES: Zeros in this table do not mean that a party tried and failed to obtain a vote; rather the party either did not exist at the time or it boycotted the election.

The Assembly elected in 1956 contained, in addition to the 60 Somali members, 10 representatives of the immigrant communities: 4 Italians, 4 Arabs, 1 Indian, and 1 Pakistani. In 1958 there were contests in only 27 municipalities. In 18 other municipalities only a single list (S.Y.L.) was presented, and 226 council seats in those municipalities went to the S.Y.L. without contest. The 1959 elections were boycotted by the principal opposition parties, H.D.M.S., G.S.L., and S.N.U.; a splinter of the H.D.M.S. participated, and was thereupon expelled from the party. Only 29 Assembly seats were contested; the other 61 seats were assigned to the S.Y.L. without contest.

Sources: Based on A. A. Castagno, "Somalia," *International Conciliation,* March 1959, p. 358; and *Report of the United Nations Advisory Council for the Trust Territory of Somaliland under Italian Administration, from 1 April 1958 to 31 March 1959* (U.N. Doc. T/1444) pars. 103-142 and annex V.

elections among the nomadic population was of course difficult, and left much room for improvement. In all four elections, the S.Y.L. emerged victorious, as shown in Table 3. Since the transfer of executive authority to the Somalis in 1956, the S.Y.L. has been the dominant force in the government as well as in the Assembly.[4]

Fifteen parties participated in the earliest election in 1954—a reflection of the tendency of tribal groupings to establish political parties of their own. But only six parties remained on the Somalia scene in 1958. The disappearance of a large number of local and clan parties can be attributed in part to the growing influence of the major parties and also to the gradually increasing political sophistication of the electorate. Electoral laws, prohibiting parties from employing tribal names, probably contributed to this trend.[5] Furthermore, most of the clan or local parties were not political parties in the normal sense of the term. They were temporary political groupings formed for the purpose of putting up candidates for the elections.

Among the political groupings active in 1960, there were five which maintained permanent organizations and could be regarded as political parties.

The Somali Youth League (S.Y.L.), the party holding a majority of the Legislative Assembly seats and government positions, derived the bulk of its support from the Darod and Hawiya tribes. It was a coalition of a large number of clans and lineage groups, engaged in continuous rivalry and competition. For a number of years the Hawiya predominated in the party and received a greater share of the government posts. Dissatisfaction among the Darod came to a head on a number of occasions. It contributed to a split within the party in 1958 when Haji Mohamed Hussein, one of the party's top leaders, was expelled and formed the rival Greater Somalia League (G.S.L.). Haji Mohamed himself is of the Rer Hamar (the natives of Mogadishu, who are outside the framework of the Somali lineage system). But a sizable number of Mijertain (Darod) followed him out of the party.

Another crisis occurred when Haji Mussa Boqor, a prominent member of the Osman Mahamoud (Darod, Mijertain), quarreled with the then Prime Minister, Abdullahi Issa (Hawiya). Haji Mussa, in what he considered a tactical move, resigned from his post as Minister of the Interior; but, to his surprise, the resignation was accepted.

The internal struggle revolving around personalities, and questions as to the relative share of various clans and tribes in top government posts, were later responsible for a more prolonged crisis, which delayed the formation of a new government after the 1959 elections. Those elections were held in the first half of March, but a government was formed only at the end of June. The composition of the cabinet reflected a victory for the faction of the then Prime Minister Abdullahi Issa. However, a powerful group of Darod leaders, headed by Dr. Abdirashid Ali Shermarke and Abdirazaq Haji Hussein (both of the Mijertain), continued to campaign for a change in leadership and against what they considered excessive attention to tribal interests.[6] The group was expelled from the S.Y.L. but was soon readmitted, and it won a partial victory in early 1960 when the government was expanded and reorganized. Its views finally prevailed after the attainment of independence and the unification with British Somaliland, during the negotiations on the formation of the first government of the Somali Republic. Dr. Abdirashid Ali Shermarke, the leader of the party rebels, became Prime Minister, and his associate, Abdirazaq Haji Hussein, became Minister of Interior. The former Premier, Abdullahi Issa, was named Foreign Minister in the new government.

Although the S.Y.L. represented the majority of Samaale tribesmen in Somalia, it was not the sole representative of the Darod and the Hawiya. Competing with the S.Y.L. for Darod support was the Greater Somalia League (G.S.L.). As mentioned above, the League was established by Haji Mohamed Hussein after a split in S.Y.L. ranks in 1958. Haji Mohamed had been president of the

S.Y.L. The split occurred after his return from a prolonged stay in Egypt. Upon his return he was reelected S.Y.L. president, but differences developed between him and other party leaders including Abdullahi Issa, the Prime Minister, and Aden Abdullah, Chairman of the Legislative Assembly. Probably the differences were, at bottom, of a personal nature. They soon evolved into a dispute over the party's policy. Haji Mohamed insisted upon a more militant Pan-Somali policy, demanded a strong stand against the Italian administration, and advocated that the party orient itself toward Egypt.

After his expulsion from the party and his formation of the Greater Somalia League, the new party criticized the S.Y.L. government for being too closely identified with the Italian trusteeship administration, and for permitting "economic exploitation" by certain Italian companies. The G.S.L. adopted a pro-Egyptian policy, as manifested in its identification with Egypt on international problems, in its campaign for the adoption of Arabic script for the Somali language, and in its promotion of Arabic culture.

The Greater Somalia League seemed to possess a vigorous organization and a considerable following, especially in Mogadishu and among the Darod of the Mijertain and lower Juba provinces. It was weakened, however, by internal differences. In 1959, Haji Mohamed established connections with the Soviet Union and China and has consequently been regarded as having Communist leanings. A conservative and religious-oriented group within the party challenged Haji Mohamed's leadership, accusing him of misappropriations of party funds. These divisions notwithstanding, the party's relative success in organizing a following indicated that among the Darod-Hawiya groupings there was dissatisfaction with the S.Y.L. which could be taken advantage of through skillful manipulation by a rival party, and could indeed lead to a tribal and political realignment.

The Hawiya, like the Darod, are not united in their support of the S.Y.L. The Liberal Somali Youth Party (Partito Liberale Giovani Somali, or P.L.G.S.), which was formed as a result of a union between the Somali Democratic Party and smaller tribal groups, acquired a following among the Abgal branch of the Hawiya. The Liberals' second important source of support was the Bimal (Dir), who inhabit an area south of Mogadishu. The party, however, was weak in its organization, and its stability was therefore doubtful.

The Sab appear to be more united politically than the Samaale. They have been represented mainly by the Hizbia Dastur Mustaqil Somali (H.D.M.S.), which can be translated Somali Independent Constitutional Party. The H.D.M.S., like the S.Y.L., was founded in 1947 in preparation for the arrival of the Four Power Commission of Investigation. The party was originally known by its tribal name Hizbia Dighil e Mirifle (the Party of the Dighil and Mirifle), but changed to its new name in 1958 in preparation for the general elections of 1959, and in conformity with the law prohibiting the use of tribal designations by parties participating in the elections.

The 1959 elections caused a split in the H.D.M.S. The party officially decided to boycott the elections because of alleged intimidations by S.Y.L. supporters. However, a few prominent members, including a former president of the party, a former vice-president, and a former secretary-general, succumbed to what appears to have been a combination of extreme pressure and political inducements, and stood for election.

The complexity of tribal and political loyalties is glaringly illustrated here. Only four of the Rahanwein deputies of Upper Juba were elected on an H.D.M.S. ticket—officially repudiated by the party. The remaining eighteen Rahanwein deputies were elected on the S.Y.L. ticket. Their loyalty to the S.Y.L. seemed uncertain; so the S.Y.L. leadership resorted to the expedient of naming to the government the prominent Rahanwein personalities, and former H.D.M.S. leaders, who were elected to the legislature on the H.D.M.S. ticket, in order to keep the S.Y.L. Rahanwein deputies in line. Thus a former vice-president of the H.D.M.S., Abdinur Mohamed Hussein, became Minister of General Affairs in the 1959 government, and in 1960 became Minister of Public Works and

Communications. The former secretary-general of the party, Abdulqadir Mohamed Aden, became Minister of Finance.

Another party representing a tribal grouping was the Somali National Union (S.N.U.). The mainstay of its support is the Rer Hamar, the natives of Mogadishu. The party was previously known as the Union of Benadir Youth (Unione Giovani Benadir, or U.G.B.), but took its new name in 1958 when preparing for the 1959 general elections.

Of the parties so far mentioned, only the S.Y.L. and (to a more limited extent) the Greater Somalia League could claim to possess a nationwide following. Both of these parties were based upon the Darod and Hawiya, spread throughout Somalia. However, the S.Y.L. also enjoyed some support among the Sab and other minorities, as indicated by the returns in the 1958 municipal elections (the best test available, since the 1959 general elections were boycotted by most opposition parties). Table 4 shows how the parties fared in the provinces of Benadir, Upper Juba, and Lower Juba, the ones that contain significant Sab populations. The Greater Somalia League, too, apparently found some support outside of purely Darod areas. On the other hand, all other parties were strictly limited to a tribal base. The Liberals entered candidates and won a substantial proportion of the votes only in areas having a significant Abgal population. The Benadir Youth Union registered a following only in Mogadishu and Merca. The H.D.M.S. obtained support only in the three provinces covered in the table—those with strong Sab elements.

Parties and Political Issues

The tribal composition of the population provides the key to the understanding of the party structure and of the competition for political influence, but it would be wrong to assume that Somalia's parties have differed only in the genealogies of their followers. Ideological divisions have also begun to appear.

Regarding the fundamental nationalist goals of independence and unification, there were no differences of opinion among the

TABLE 4 Results of 1958 Municipal Elections in Benadir, Upper Juba, and Lower Juba Provinces

(percentage of votes obtained by each list)

Municipality	S.Y.L.	H.D.M.S.	Greater Somalia League	Liberal Somali Youth Party	Benadir Youth Union
Mogadishu	30.4	19.6	14.4	20.3	15.2
Merca	31.4	34.2	14.4	9.9	10.0
Afghoi	32.8	58.8	0.0	8.4	0.0
Audegle	20.3	79.7	0.0	0.0	0.0
Villabruzzi	60.2	12.0	0.0	27.7	0.0
Mahaddei	86.4	0.0	0.0	13.5	0.0
Hauadlei	45.0	0.0	17.6	37.3	0.0
Brava	25.0	73.4	1.5	0.0	0.0
Balad	64.8	0.0	0.0	35.2	0.0
Wanle Wen	26.4	70.0	0.0	3.5	0.0
Baidoa	45.5	54.5	0.0	0.0	0.0
Bardera	27.9	72.1	0.0	0.0	0.0
Dugiuma	35.3	64.7	0.0	0.0	0.0
Saco	44.8	55.2	0.0	0.0	0.0
Lugh Ferrandi	43.0	57.0	0.0	0.0	0.0
Dolo	58.0	42.0	0.0	0.0	0.0
Oddur	46.3	53.7	0.0	0.0	0.0
Wegit	50.0	50.0	0.0	0.0	0.0
Tijeglo	24.7	75.3	0.0	0.0	0.0
Bur Acaba	19.0	81.0	0.0	0.0	0.0
Dinsor	33.4	66.6	0.0	0.0	0.0
Kismayu	37.8	15.7	34.0	0.0	0.0
Margherita	44.0	44.8	11.1	0.0	0.0
Gelib	55.1	44.9	0.0	0.0	0.0
Afmedo	61.8	0.0	38.2	0.0	0.0

NOTES: Zeros mean the party refrained from contesting in that municipality.

Results in the other three Somalia provinces, Mijertain, Mudugh, and Hiran, which are populated exclusively by the Darod and the Hawiya, are not given, because, except in two municipalities, the elections were not contested there. All seats in the uncontested municipalities were captured by the S.Y.L. The Somali Fiqarini Youth (not shown above), a local group in the Kismayu area, obtained 12.4 percent of the votes in Kismayu. In all the above lines except the one for Kismayu, the percentages when added horizontally equal 100, though not always exactly, because of rounding.

Source: Based on election returns in *Report of the United Nations Advisory Council for the Trust Territory of Somaliland under Italian Administration, from 1 April 1958 to 31 March 1959* (U.N. Doc. T/1444), annex I.

parties in 1960. This was not the case during the early stage of Somali political activity. During the 1940's, the S.Y.L. had been the only party with a Pan-Somali ideology. During the 1950's other parties integrated their special tribal or regional interests into a nationalist framework. By the time the Somali Republic was created, all parties in Somalia were nationalist—in the sense that they supported Somali independence and advocated a Greater Somali state.

The S.Y.L.'s program demanding the unification of the Somalilands was voiced by the then president of the party, Haji Mohamed Hussein, in his testimony before the Four Power Commission of Investigation in 1948. The S.Y.L. also submitted a memorandum to the Commission saying:

> We wish our country to be amalgamated with the other Somalilands and to form one political, administrative and economic unit with them. We Somalis are one in every way. We are the same racially and geographically, we have the same culture, we have the same language and the same religion. There is no future for us except as part of a Greater Somalia.
>
> The present international frontiers are artificial and the divisions are placing an unfair strain on the political, administrative and economic welfare of the country. The existence of several foreign official languages within the several territories, is enough, in itself, to make aliens out of brothers of the same race, religion and country, and, put back our national advancement indefinitely . . . We want it [unity] and the Somalis of the other territories also want it. By this union only can we have the opportunity to give full expression to our national spirit and work out our destiny as a nation of normal human beings.
>
> Union with the other Somalilands is our greatest demand which must take priority over all other considerations.[7]

The S.Y.L.'s position on Somali unity has not changed since this statement in 1948. In order to further its Pan-Somali objectives the party has maintained branches in British Somaliland. It also had branches in Jibuti and in Kenya, but these were proscribed by the authorities.

The Sab-oriented H.D.M.S., in the early stage of its evolution, had a narrow tribal outlook upon political problems, although even then the party supported certain broad nationalist objectives. In 1947, in preparation for the Four Power Commission, the H.D.M.S. (then called by its tribal name Hizbia Dighil e Mirifle) joined in forming the "Somalia Conference"—a convention of associations demanding that the territory be placed under Italian trusteeship—a step violently opposed by the S.Y.L. The first point of the manifesto of the conference stated that "the Somali people aspires to its full political independence and to its admission—as between equals—into the peoples' international community." The declaration went on to ask that Italy be given trusteeship over the territory under the auspices of the United Nations, in order to prepare the country for independence.[8]

This, however, was the limit of the H.D.M.S.'s nationalism. Its narrow tribal outlook on political problems was reflected in the testimony of its representatives before the Commission. Sheikh Abdullah, then the party president, when asked by the Soviet member whether "he is not interested in the political activities of the country," replied: "I have only interest in the Dighil Mirifle." In answer to another query, he stated: "When we asked for the trusteeship, we only meant for the country where the Dighil Mirifle live, not the rest of the country. We do not mean the rest of Somalia."[9]

The H.D.M.S. later adapted itself to the nationalist spirit of the times and has joined in espousing the goal of a Greater Somalia. On the question of the constitutional form of the proposed union, however, the H.D.M.S. retained a distinct point of view, advocating a federal constitution for the future Somali state. A federal arrangement whereby the component units would enjoy considerable autonomy was viewed as the best safeguard for the special interests of the agricultural population, in an otherwise nomadic society. This position was reiterated in 1958 when Jelani Sheikh bin Sheikh, at that time the party president, said in a speech to the party convention that "the party has become convinced that the only method of unifying the Somalis . . . is through a federal constitution which accords full regional autonomy."[10]

On the other hand, the S.Y.L. favored a unitary centralized state. The view was restated by Prime Minister Abdullahi Issa when he outlined his government's program to the new Legislative Assembly on July 26, 1959. He declared: "In the interest of union among the Somali and in the interest of the very safeguarding of the Nation, the Government herewith declares that it does not pursue any regionalist or federalist goal, because unity alone can ensure the durable existence of a Somali national life."[11]

This position stemmed in part from a recognition of the economic needs of the territory. The Rahanwein and Dighil areas (roughly corresponding to the Upper Juba and Lower Juba provinces) offer the greatest potential for agricultural development in Somalia, which of course is now the Southern Region of the Somali Republic. All plans for future economic development hinge upon large-scale development of the water resources, the extension of agriculture, and the settlement of hundreds of thousands of nomads in the two provinces. But, perhaps even more important in determining the S.Y.L. position was the leaders' commitment to nationalist centralist principles, very much in the spirit of the general trend of nationalist movements in Africa. This commitment is the more remarkable because it implies the voluntary acceptance of a significant diminution of Hawiya political influence, which was bound to occur if a centralized government were established in the unified Somali state.

Despite the general agreement among all parties about the nationalist goals, nuances in emphasis have marked a distinction between the Greater Somalia League and the other parties. The S.Y.L. leaders, entrusted with governmental responsibility, have tended to be more moderate in their pronouncements regarding the Somalis of Ethiopia, Kenya, and French Somaliland than have the leaders of the Greater Somalia League. Unification was part of the government's official program. But, while declaring themselves dedicated to the goal of unification, government leaders have always been careful to emphasize that it should be accomplished peacefully. The government's official position on unification was stated by the Prime Minister in his address to the Legislative Assembly in July 1959, when he declared that

> all means must be employed—within the framework of legality and the pursuit of peace—in order to obtain the union of all Somali territories, and their reunification under the same flag. This constitutes for us not only a right, but a duty which one cannot neglect, because it is impossible to want to distinguish between Somali and Somali.[12]

The Greater Somalia League did not advocate war as a means to unification; but its leaders have enjoyed the political advantage of being able to be more extreme than the government in their attacks on Ethiopia and on "imperialism" which is obstructing unity, and to omit any assurance regarding the method of achieving unification. Their ambiguity regarding methods has been explained by the romantic, yet perhaps not invalid, proposition that independence and national unification have seldom been granted to nations for the asking; rather, they had to be won by fighting.

A question that had aroused considerable controversy in Somalia by 1960 was the selection of a script for the Somali language. The matter had not become a clear-cut party issue, but, as mentioned above, the Greater Somalia League had become identified with those urging the adoption of Arabic.* In this it received support from Egyptian representatives and teachers in the country as well as from Moslem religious authorities. The thesis is that because the Somalis are a Moslem people, it is only natural that their culture should have an Arab orientation.

Those who were opposing the adoption of Arabic were not particularly identified with any political party. They were mainly

* The author, during his visit to the Greater Somalia League headquarters in Mogadishu at the end of 1960, was struck by the fact that the language spoken among the members was Arabic, rather than Somali.

young intellectuals, who advocated the development of a Somali culture and a distinct "Somali personality," and feared that the adoption of Arabic would result in cultural assimilation and in the loss of Somali cultural identity. There were differences of opinion among them. Some favored the adoption of the Osmaniya alphabet, specially devised for the Somali language in the 1920's by an early Somali nationalist, Yusuf Kenadid Osman. The advocates of Osmaniya, however, lost ground after a conference of educators and linguists from Somalia and British Somaliland recommended its abandonment in 1955, because its adoption, they argued, would impose upon school children the burden of learning three alphabets: Osmaniya would be taught as the national language, Arabic would be taught for religious purposes, and the Latin alphabet would be taught with European foreign languages.[13]

A larger section of the young secular intellectuals favored the adaptation of the Latin alphabet to the Somali language. They argued that the adoption of Osmaniya would encourage cultural isolation. The adoption of the Latin alphabet, on the other hand, would make the contact between the Somali and Western cultures easier. These intellectuals were not concerned primarily with Western humanistic traditions, but rather with the scientific achievements of Europe and America, the adaptation of which they regarded as essential for the development and prosperity of their country.

At the time of writing, the controversy regarding a Somali script has not been resolved. The matter is still in the hands of committees studying the problem.[14]

On foreign affairs there was a distinct divergence of views among the parties. All parties advocated "neutralism," a principle which has been gaining favor among African nationalists. However, while the S.Y.L., the H.D.M.S., and the Liberals could be described as "neutral with a pro-Western bias," the Greater Somalia League and the Somali National Union appeared to be "neutral in favor of the Communist powers." Both Haji Mohamed Hussein and

Abubakr Hamud Socorro, presidents of the Greater Somalia League and the Somali National Union respectively, had paid visits to Moscow, Peiping, and other Communist capitals. They were generally believed to have received considerable financial support from China, and their followers had been granted scholarships for study in Communist countries.

These issues of internal and external policy have been gradually gaining public interest. The increasing attention being paid to such issues marked a new trend in political life, whereby political controversies were gradually ceasing to revolve exclusively around personal and tribal interests. As the population of what used to be Italian Somaliland becomes more sophisticated politically, and as economic and social development takes place, new interests are beginning to assert themselves, and issues of principle and ideology are gaining in prominence.

Chapter 8

Nationalism and Politics in British Somaliland

THE nationalist movement developed more slowly in British Somaliland than in the trust territory of Somalia. The reasons were that British Somaliland was behind Somalia in economic and social change and was less subject to external influences. Incipient nationalist organizations had existed in the Protectorate since the early 1940's, but no mass-supported nationalist movement emerged there until the late 1950's.

The slow rate of economic and social progress in British Somaliland during sixty years of British administration is to be attributed in large measure to the territory's poverty in natural resources. Opportunities for developing agriculture or industry are not favorable, and the territory barely provides subsistence for a population of 650,000, nine tenths of whom are nomads. British Somaliland was believed to be poorer than the neighboring Italian Somaliland. The Italians viewed their Somali colony as a territory to be settled by immigrants from Italy, and to be developed by them; and, as a result of public works projects and private enterprises there, the local Somalis were more exposed to Western ways than the inhabitants of British Somaliland. The British never attempted to settle in their Somali territory, for their interest in it was purely strategic. Since the territory could serve strategic purposes regardless of its state of development, the British government had no incentives to initiate economic or social undertakings. The territory's protectorate status provided a convenient justification for the absence of such initiative.[1] Development projects were started in the Protectorate only in the 1950's, and they appear to have been prompted by the belated political awakening in the territory.

As already mentioned, the sluggishness of education had retarded the awakening of political consciousness. The literate middle class is still very small, and consequently the number of people capable of organizing and sustaining a modern political movement is limited.

Tribal feuds, which appeared to be more widespread in British Somaliland than in Somalia, powerfully inhibited the development of Protectorate-wide political movements. British Somaliland, poorer in water and grazing resources than Somalia, saw more conflicts between tribes competing for the scarce resources, upon which their existence depends. Antagonisms are still intense. Moreover, the population is remarkably attached to traditional tribal customs. All these tendencies inhibit the development of cohesive forces and modernist secular-nationalist organizations.[2]

The emergence of a nationalist movement in the face of such difficulties was largely due to external influences (as in the rest of the Horn), though these were not as intense as in Somalia. The placing of all Somali territories under the British Military Administration after the war, resulting in the intensification of interterritorial contacts—official, commercial, and personal, had made a strong impression on the population of the Protectorate. British Somaliland, unlike its Italian counterpart, faced no question about the territory's government after the war. No outside commissions of investigation came inquiring about the wishes of the population. Nevertheless, people in the Protectorate were interested in the negotiations on the future of Somalia, and especially in the British proposal for the unification of Somalia, British Somaliland, and the Ogaden under British trusteeship. Subsequently, the assertion of nationalist feelings in Asia and the Middle East, and especially in Moslem countries, made a great impression; the Protectorate's close contacts with Aden and the Arab world facilitated the spread of information about such developments.[3]

But the most important spur to political interest in British Somaliland was the return of the Haud to Ethiopian administration in 1955. The story of those controversial territories will be told more fully in our chapter on border disputes. Only a few facts are needed here. The Haud territories are the rich grazing grounds on the Ethiopian side of the border. Half the population of the Protectorate depend on them for livelihood. After being under the jurisdiction of the British Military Administration during the war as part of the "Reserved Area" in Ethiopia, the territories were retained by the British until after a new Anglo-Ethiopian agreement was concluded in November 1954. Their transfer to Ethiopia aroused excitement throughout the Protectorate. Until then, interest in politics had been confined to the small urban population and educated elite; now it spread to the nomadic tribes of the interior. In February 1956, Michael Mariano, one of the foremost nationalist leaders at the time, said in a broadcast over the Hargeisa radio that what the Somalis of the Protectorate had regarded as a "great calamity" might in the long run, because of the great political awakening it had caused, be their "greatest blessing."[4]

The first political organizations set up in the Protectorate after the military campaigns of the Second World War were branches of the Somali Youth League (S.Y.L.) from Italian Somaliland. These were followed in 1945 by the establishment, through local initiative, of the Somali National Society. During the next few years the Society merged with some of the political clubs which had been active in the Protectorate since 1935, and gradually evolved into a new organization, which in 1951 took the name Somali National League (S.N.L.).

The political programs of the two parties, S.Y.L. and S.N.L., were fairly similar. The S.Y.L. program was essentially the same as that of the Somalia S.Y.L., that is, the independence and unification of the Somali people, the cessation of tribal feuding, and the encouragement of economic, social, and political development. The S.N.L. program emphasized the same goals.[5] The main difference between the parties was in their tribal bases. The S.Y.L. derived its principal support from Darod tribes (Dolbahanta and Warsangeli) and the S.N.L. drew its main support from the Ishaq tribes. To the extent that there was competition for political support between the parties, the S.Y.L. was at a considerable disadvantage because of its links with Mogadishu, whereas the S.N.L. was viewed as a truly indigenous organization. Both parties were limited to the principal towns and administrative centers; neither had much support among the population in the bush.

The Haud question prompted the existing political parties, which hitherto had exerted little influence, to combine and jointly press for the reversal of the Anglo-Ethiopian agreement restoring the Haud to Ethiopia. A new organization, the National United Front (N.U.F.) was formed for that purpose in 1955. The Front was at first a convention of associations, and provided a framework for cooperation among political parties and other organizations, such as the Somali Officials' Union, which represented the civil servants. However, the parties' cooperation was short-lived, and they soon reverted to independent action. This reversion has been attributed to the Front's failure to attain its avowed aim of returning the Haud to the Protectorate. Probably a more important reason for the parties' withdrawal from the Front was the age-old problem of tribal rivalries.

As the S.N.L. and S.Y.L. withdrew, the National United Front gradually evolved into a political party in its own right, deriving its principal support from the Habr Toljala, a branch of the Ishaq. But it never succeeded in broadening its basis. Its inability to turn into a mass party was due in large measure to the fact that its most prominent leader, Michael Mariano, is a Christian. This appears to be a great liability in a country in which the nationalist movement is so closely linked with Islam. Mariano's great service to Somali nationalism is acknowledged. He was one of the founders of modern Somali nationalism in the 1940's. In the late 1950's, however, in comparison with the militancy of the S.N.L. leaders, Mariano appeared to many Somalis as excessively moderate.

A fourth party appeared on the British Somaliland scene early in 1960. Its founding was prompted by the forthcoming February elections to the Legislative Council. The new organization, the United Somali Party (U.S.P.), was a coalition of the minority tribes: the Dolbahanta and Warsangeli (Darod) in the eastern part of the Protectorate, and the Issa and Gadabursi at the western end.

The results of these general elections seem to indicate that the votes were not divided along the clear lines of principal tribal divisions. (See Table 5.) It appears that the political loyalties of certain sections and clans are not always the same as those of the majority of the tribe. In these elections the support of the Habr Toljala was divided between the National United Front and the S.N.L. Also, sections of the Dolbahanta and Warsangeli voted for the S.Y.L., though the majority of these tribesmen supported the United Somali Party. The discrepancy between the number of seats a party won and the number of votes it received stems from the division of the territory into constituencies which resulted in the wastage of a large proportion of the votes cast for the National United Front and the S.Y.L. The only Front candidate to win a seat was Michael Mariano. The S.Y.L., which for this election allied itself with the Front, failed to return a single candidate.

The political competition of the parties and the tribes did not prevent the nationalist leaders from cooperating for their commonly shared objectives; for the political parties still had similar programs. They all agreed on the fundamental nationalist goals of independence and unification.

The Pan-Somali goals of the Protectorate parties were essentially the same as those of the Somalia parties, except for a slight, but nevertheless significant, difference in emphasis. The Somalia parties'

TABLE 5 Results of February 1960 General Elections in British Somaliland

Party	Number of seats won[a]	Percentage of elected seats	Percentage of votes received[b]	Principal tribal basis	Approximate strength of those tribes as percentage of total population[c]
Somali National League (S.N.L.)	20	60.6	68.75 (S.N.L. and U.S.P.)	Ishaq tribes with exception of Habr Toljala, the majority of whom supported N.U.F.	50.0
United Somali Party (U.S.P.)	12	36.4		Dolbahanta, Warsangeli, Gadabursi, Issa	34.4[d]
National United Front (N.U.F.)	1	3.0	31.25 (N.U.F. and S.Y.L.)	Habr Toljala, except for a segment which supported the S.N.L.	15.6
Somali Youth League (S.Y.L.)	0	0.0		Sections of the Dolbahanta and Warsangeli	n.a.
Totals	33	100.0	100.00		100.0

[a] As reported by *Commonwealth Survey,* vol. 6, no. 6 (March 15, 1960), p. 271.
[b] Based on Sir Douglas Hall, "Somaliland's Last Year as a Protectorate," *African Affairs,* January 1961.
[c] Based on estimates in the *Report of the Commission of Inquiry into Unofficial Representation on the Legislative Council,* Hargeisa, June 1958 (mimeo.).
[d] Includes all Dolbahanta and Warsangeli, even those sections which voted for the S.Y.L.

Pan-Somali aspirations were directed primarily toward the Ogaden, largely because of the division of the Marehan and Mijertain tribes, important sections of which live in Ethiopia. The aspirations of the Protectorate parties were directed first toward some form of unification with Somalia. Demands for the Haud were and remain annexationist rather than Pan-Somali in character. They were prompted by immediate and vital interests in the grazing areas on which half the population depends, rather than by nationalist ideals. The rest of the Ogaden was not particularly coveted by the Somalis of the Protectorate and was regarded only in the context of a distant ideal of a "Greater Somalia." Their absence of fervor in claiming the Ogaden was probably the result of the frequent clashes between the Ogaden tribes and the British-protected tribes in the common grazing areas of the Haud. These clashes have apparently produced strained relations and an awareness of a conflict of interest between them over the grazing areas.

The political awakening that followed the return of the Haud to Ethiopian administration in 1955 accelerated the progress toward self-government in the Protectorate. Some of the early measures for self-government had been taken on the initiative of the British authorities before the development of nationalist demands. An Advisory Council was appointed on a tribal basis in 1947, its main purpose being "to stimulate the interest of the people themselves in the administration of the country and in the collection and expenditure of public funds." [6] In 1951, the government established the first district advisory councils. Town councils, responsible for the collection of local revenue and for the administration of services, were introduced in 1953, but met with some opposition, apparently because of the unpopularity of taxes. The first Legislative Council, with six unofficial members, all appointed, came into being in 1957.

The growing political agitation in the territory prompted the British government to introduce a new constitution in 1958. Constitutional reform was not an easy task to accomplish. In the towns, political consciousness was widespread and the parties were the most influential political factor. In the bush the new political organizations had often to compete for influence with the tribal elders. The absence of a sufficient number of educated people qualified to assume executive responsibility was another obstacle. The Commission of Inquiry into Unofficial Representation on the Legislative Council estimated that there were only eight persons outside the civil service whose ability to use English was up to secondary school level; there were about thirty whose ability was up to seventh-form level. The 1958 constitution provided for an increase in the unofficial representation on the Legislative Council; and, for the first time, these unofficial members were to be elected. But, because the new constitution failed to provide for a Somali majority in the Legislative Council, the S.N.L. boycotted the 1959 election. Nevertheless, nationalist politicians did get a taste of the system; for a number of prominent National United Front and S.Y.L. members were elected.[7]

Pressures for more rapid progress toward self-government now were mounting. In the course of 1959, the Protectorate government introduced a new constitution providing for an elected majority of unofficial members in the Legislative Council, and a majority of elected Ministers. The general elections already mentioned were held on a basis of universal adult male suffrage on February 17, 1960. Not only were thirty-three Somalis elected to the Legislative Council, but four Somali members received ministerial posts for the first time.

On April 6, the new Legislative Council adopted a motion calling for independence and union with the trust territory of Somalia as soon as Somalia became independent on July 1, 1960. A constitutional conference, hastily convened in May, agreed on a date for independence and upon the arrangements to accompany it. The Protectorate came to an end on June 26, 1960.[8] Thus, approximately four months after the assumption of ministerial responsibility by Somali political leaders, British Somaliland became an independent state. As planned, it united on July 1 with the trust territory of Somalia to form the Somali Republic.

Chapter 9

The Problems and Politics of Unification

THE unification of British Somaliland and the trust territory of Somalia created problems—economic, political, and administrative. These problems arose despite the underlying conditions in the two territories favoring unification, that is, the common language, culture, and religion, and the almost unanimous support for unification among the articulate persons of the two territories.

Seventy years of British and Italian rule had imparted to each territory a distinct character, and accentuated whatever regional differences might have existed before. The nomadic tribes had been influenced by the British or Italians only to a very limited extent, and the nomadic population had remained culturally homogeneous; but a cultural gap had developed between the new urban elites in the two territories. Besides, different economic, political, and administrative patterns had developed. A successful and lasting union required that the two territories become more closely integrated in those respects.

The problems facing the new unified state do not detract from the advantages and desirability of the union. The prospect at this writing is that in the course of time the constitutional act of unification will be consummated by actual integration; and on that assumption it can be said that there are considerable political and economic benefits to be derived from the union. For one thing, it seems to be a modest step toward diminishing the danger of the balkanization of Africa and its attendant political instability. Furthermore, considerable economies can be derived from merging the apparatus of government; these are particularly significant in view of the relative poverty of the region in natural resources. Unification also greatly facilitates the planning and execution of development projects, which are essential for the ultimate prosperity of the region. Most programs for the alleviation of the harsh living conditions of the nomadic population of the north envisage the resettlement of a portion of these nomads in the agriculturally more promising southern regions.

For the very reason that union seems to offer important benefits, the problems it faces require careful examination.

The Precipitate Union

The possibility of territorial unions in the Horn of Africa has been widely discussed since the inception of Somali nationalism in the 1940's. It may seem strange, therefore, that the unification of Somalia and British Somaliland was carried out without adequate preparation. It seems that the British, the Italians, and the United Nations (under whose auspices the trusteeship over Somalia was exercised) viewed it as an eventuality for which they would prefer not to share responsibility. To be sure, the British government declared in February 1959:

> Her Majesty's Government is aware of the desire expressed by many Somalis of the Protectorate that there should be a closer association between this territory and Somalia. If, therefore, when Somalia has become independent, the Legislative Council of the Protectorate formally resolves that negotiations with the Government of Somalia be instituted to determine the terms and conditions on which a closer association of the two territories might be achieved, Her Majesty's Government in the United Kingdom would be ready to transmit this resolution to the Government of Somalia and enquire whether that Government would be willing to enter into negotiation. If so, Her Majesty's Government would arrange for negotiations of a suitable nature to take place.[1]

It is unlikely, however, that the British government desired to become involved in these negotiations. Britain, Italy, and the United

Nations all appear to have considered their responsibility limited to preparing their territories for self-government.

Be that as it may, unification caught all concerned by surprise, and very little time was available for any preparations. This undoubtedly handicapped the smooth functioning of the administration, and may have produced an element of political strain in the early months of independence. Yet it might be argued that, had preparatory negotiations been held, they would have led to the crystalization of diverse interests and thus inhibited unification.

Union suddenly became imminent in the spring of 1960. In British Somaliland the Somali nationalists who now found themselves a majority in the Legislative Council had repeatedly declared their dedication to the early independence of the Protectorate and its unification with Somalia. They felt themselves under political pressures because of their promises. But this was not the only reason for the big rush. The feeling of urgency stemmed in part from apprehension that if the Protectorate's independence were delayed much after that of Somalia, the Protectorate Somalis would be regarded as "younger brothers" by their brethren to the south. Consequently, they would have been at some disadvantage in applying for unification later on. Thus the political leaders, in their resolution of April 6 in the Legislative Council, declared

> That it is the opinion of this House that practical steps should be taken forthwith for the immediate unification of the Protectorate and Somalia; that prompt action is essential to achieve this most cherished aim, and can be fully justified by the special importance which popular feeling in this country attaches to its early achievement; that bold and definite action be taken and that the date of our independence and unification with Somalia must be 1st July, 1960, the date when Somalia will attain its full freedom.[2]

The British government was most accommodating to the Somali views. It had apparently reached the conclusion that the primary British interest of safeguarding sea communications through the Red Sea and Indian Ocean would be served better by preserving

Somali friendship and good will than by retaining possession of the territory in the face of Somali opposition. To postpone the date of independence by one or two years did not seem to make any basic difference with respect to the territory's readiness for it. On the other hand, any attempt to delay independence after the Somalis had asked for it would have only generated bitterness and misunderstanding.

Having received the British government's agreement in principle for the independence of British Somaliland on or about July 1, 1960, the Somali leaders were confronted with the task of negotiating the details of unification with their counterparts in the trust territory of Somalia. A conference was held in Mogadishu in the middle of April. The conference agreed that after the two territories attained independence they would be united "under one flag, one president, one parliament, and one government." It also agreed that the central governmental institutions of the new republic would be a presidency, a council of ministers, and a legislative assembly; that the constitution of Somalia would serve as the basis for the constitution of the new republic; and that the administrative, judicial, and economic systems of the two territories would function separately until provision was made for their integration. It was envisaged that each territory, upon becoming independent and prior to the unification, would conclude a separate agreement with the respective administering power regarding the transfer of authority, and regarding economic aid and other arrangements.[3]

On July 1, the legislatures of the two newly independent states met at Mogadishu in joint session, and proclaimed the establishment of the Somali Republic. The republic was declared a unitary state, consisting of two regions, the Northern and the Southern, corresponding to the former British Somaliland and the former trust territory of Somalia, respectively. The two legislatures merged into one and became the National Assembly of the Somali Republic. On the same day, the Assembly elected Aden Abdulla Osman, a prominent leader of the S.Y.L. and former president of the Legislative Assembly of Somalia, as president of the republic. The Assembly also resolved that a referendum would be held within one year to ratify the new constitution.[4]

The election of the president seems to have been agreed upon in advance, and it proceeded smoothly. But the formation of a government, and elections to certain other offices, apparently encountered political difficulties and required time. Thus, the president of the National Assembly was elected on July 7. The post was filled by Jama Abdullahi Galib, a member of the S.N.L. (Somali National League) from the Northern Region. The formation of the government required prolonged negotiations. Two issues had to be resolved. First, the relative share of each region in the executive offices had to be agreed upon. Second, the political plums had to be distributed among various sections within each region. A complicated political struggle ensued within the S.Y.L., as a result of which Abdirashid Ali Shermarke, the leader of the opposition group within that party in the Southern Region, was nominated Prime Minister. Another prominent member of the opposition group within the S.Y.L., Abdirazaq Haji Hussein, became Minister of the Interior. The former Prime Minister of Somalia, Abdullahi Issa, became Minister for Foreign Affairs. The Northern Region received four ministerial posts out of fourteen. Among them were the posts of Deputy Prime Minister, assumed by Abdi Hassan Boni of the United Somali Party, and Minister of Defense, filled by Mohamed Haji Ibrahim Egal, the leader of the S.N.L.

The newly formed government was charged with the central direction of the affairs of the republic. However, at this initial stage, unification did not proceed much further. As planned beforehand, the separate administrative, judicial, and economic systems of the two regions remained intact. A special committee, aided by experts provided by the United Nations, was charged with proposing measures for accomplishing the integration of the two systems.

The Problems

Amalgamating different administrative, judicial, and economic systems is difficult at best; and in this case it is complicated by the size of the territory and the inadequacy of communications. It is not only that the distance between Mogadishu, the capital of the republic, and Hargeisa, the administrative center of the Northern Region, is about 530 miles. For many months after unification there was no direct telephone link between the two towns and there were only two flights weekly between them. The roundabout trip by automobile—staying in Somali Republic territory and bypassing Ethiopia which sits athwart the direct land route—required about three days, except during the two rainy seasons each year, when the roads were frequently impassable.

Another complication is a linguistic one. As already noted, Somali is only a spoken language. Each region had been using a different written language: English in the Northern and Italian in the Southern. Some of the ministers from the Southern Region had learned English at the time of the British Military Administration, but only a few of the civil servants were bilingual. As a result, most civil servants in one region could not communicate in writing with those in the other. Letters, memoranda, and other documents were not understood from region to region. Competent interpreters were scarce; therefore these hurdles have been difficult to overcome, pending the adaptation of the Somali language to administrative purposes.

If the written languages used by the two civil services differed, so did their standards and terms of employment. Civil servants in the Northern Region, because of the slower rate of Somalization there, had had less experience in senior posts; yet they appeared, on the whole, to be better trained than those in the Southern Region, and indeed were a highly professional, nonpolitical corps. The civil service in the Southern Region was deeply involved in politics, and there have been reports of corruption. In many cases the civil servants of the Northern Region received higher salaries than their counterparts in the Southern. Any attempt to unify the services would presumably have to be achieved within the framework of the unification agreement whereby government employees in each region were to continue in the service of the government of the Somali

Republic "under conditions no less favorable" than those they had enjoyed prior to unification. The legal situation in this respect was unclear, since the agreement received formal legislative approval prior to unification in the Northern Region, but not in the Southern Region.

A different set of problems arose in connection with the judiciary. The legal system in the Northern Region was based on the English common and statute law, upon the Indian Penal Code, and upon Somali custom. Matters of family concern were administered in accordance with Islamic law. In the Southern Region a different system based on customary law and on Islamic law had been established. Unification did not impose any great difficulties upon the administration of justice at the lower level, but it raised questions with regard to the operation of the higher courts. Before unification, appeals against decisions of the High Court of the Somaliland Protectorate were referred to the Court of Appeals for Eastern Africa in Nairobi. The trust territory of Somalia had its own appellate arrangements.[5] Pending the introduction of a uniform legal system, it was necessary to establish separate sections of the supreme court of the Somali Republic to deal with cases from the two regions.

There were also problems in connection with merging the police forces and military establishments. Those in the Northern Region were British-trained and used British equipment. Those in the Southern Region were Italian-trained and used Italian equipment. The Somaliland Scouts, the military force in the Northern Region, retained British officers in command positions for the first six months after independence,[6] while in the Southern Region the Somali National Army was commanded by local Somali officers. Both establishments retained foreign advisers in a technical capacity. With the formation of a central government, both of the police forces had come under the authority of the Minister of the Interior, and both of the military establishments had come under the Minister of Defense. But no unified police command nor unified military command was immediately established. Unified commands were planned, but, because of the variety of equipment and traditions, actual amalgamation of the forces would take a while to accomplish.

In the economic sphere, unification raised questions with respect to trade patterns, customs, tariffs, and currency.

The economies of the two territories were competitive rather than complementary. Their principal resources were the same: camels, cattle, hides and skins, and other animal products. The Southern Region exported bananas—to Italy, where they were needed, not to the Northern Region. The Southern Region also produced some grain and sugar cane, which could be used in the North, but these did not suffice for internal consumption and were not normally exported. At the end of the 1950's less than one percent of the value of Somalia's and British Somaliland's foreign trade was with each other, thus:

Of Somalia's exports, 0.8 percent went to British Somaliland.
Of Somalia's imports, 0.8 percent came from British Somaliland.

Of British Somaliland's exports, 0.1 percent went to Somalia.
Of British Somaliland's imports, 0.2 percent came from Somalia.

Most of Somalia's foreign trade—77.1 percent of its exports and 51.1 of its imports—was with Italy. Similarly, more than half of British Somaliland's foreign trade—55.1 percent of its exports and 54.9 percent of its imports—was with its sister countries in the British Commonwealth.[7]

Unification is not likely to have a major early effect on trade patterns. For example, bananas accounted for an average of 60 percent of the annual value of Somalia's exports between 1953 and 1959; almost all of these bananas were sold to Italy through the Italian state banana monopoly, and this arrangement was continued after unification as part of Italy's contribution of economic aid.[8] British Somaliland, as the Northern Region of the new republic, is no longer in the British Commonwealth, but the United Kingdom and India could be expected to remain major suppliers. Moreover, British

Somaliland's chief customer, buying approximately half of its export goods, was Aden; and this export flow, consisting mainly of camels, cattle, sheep, and goats, was not likely to be greatly affected by the termination of Commonwealth membership.[9]

In the long run more internal trade will probably develop between the Southern and Northern Regions. When the development projects planned for the area between the Juba and the Webi Shebeli are completed, it is possible that the Southern Region will become able to supply grains and sugar to the North. For the next decade, however, if not longer, trade between the two regions is likely to remain small. The only short-range commercial benefit of the merger was that it facilitated transit trade, which is particularly important for the Mijertain. A considerable proportion of the imports to this province, and also some of its exports, have traditionally moved through the ports of British Somaliland.

Differences in tariff levels also caused difficulties. To reach uniformity it appeared desirable to raise the lower rates of British Somaliland to the level of the tariffs in Somalia. The alternative of reducing the Somalia tariffs would have deprived the government of an appreciable portion of its revenue. Yet, increasing the tariffs of British Somaliland would have brought about considerable increases in the prices of foods, gasoline, and fuel oil, which could have caused political repercussions. While a solution was being sought, different tariffs remained in force, and the movement of goods between the regions was still subject to payment of duties a year after unification.

The unification of currencies also required time. The currency in circulation in the Northern Region was the East African shilling, linked to the pound sterling. In the Southern Region it was the somalo, linked to the Italian lira. At the time of independence a central bank, empowered to function also as an issuing bank, was established. However, until a uniform currency could be worked out, restrictions on the movement of monies between the two regions remained in force. Thus, many months after formal unification had taken place, the free movement of goods and services between the two regions remained inhibited.

The Politics

Finally, the unification of the two territories raised a number of intriguing questions regarding future political evolution in the new state. The political groups which had enjoyed a leading position in their respective territories agreed on unification under terms which necessarily led to a diminution of their own influence. For example, it was undoubtedly obvious both to the Ishaq in the North and to the Hawiya in the South that their relative weight and political influence were bound to decline if the two territories were merged into a unitary state. Table 6 tells that story at a glance. Assessed in the light of normal considerations of political interest—namely, that groups normally strive to preserve or increase their influence—the decision to form a unitary state therefore seems surprising.

The decision is explainable by the political leaders' commitment to nationalist ideals. Nationalism is an ideology inspiring people to

Table 6 Tribal Composition of Somalia, British Somaliland, and the Somali Republic

(in percentages of total population)

Tribe	Somalia [a]	British Somaliland [b]	Somali Republic
Darod	22	19	21
Hawiya	36	0	24
Ishaq	0	66	22
Dighil and Rahanwein	25	0	17
Dir	8	15	10
Other	9	0	6
Total	100	100	100

[a] Based on Lewis, "Political Movements," p. 355*n*3; and *Rapport sur la Somalie 1959*, p. 211. For full citations see list at beginning of the notes in the back of this book.

[b] Based on figures from *Report of the Commission of Inquiry into Unofficial Representation on the Legislative Council*, Hargeisa, June 1958 (mimeo.).

identify themselves with a nation "most intensely and most unconditionally . . . even to the extent of being prepared to lay down their lives for it . . ."[10] The fervor of nationalist zeal fluctuates. At times, its intensity is such that other interests which normally determine political behavior are overridden. It seems that such a situation existed at the time that the terms of unification were agreed. One would be incorrect in concluding from this that the ordinary standards of politics are no longer important in the Horn, or that tribalism and personal ambitions no longer flourish. The political struggle over the relative share to be held by different groups in the first government of the unified Somali state indicates that these factors continued to play a role in Somali politics.

When the formation of a unitary state disturbed the political balance that had existed in each of the two territories, changing the relative weight and influence of different tribal groupings, a realignment of political forces seemed likely. Tentative moves were made in two directions: one, toward consolidation of the political parties of a single region, and the other, toward a regroupment cutting across regional lines.

There were grumblings of discontent in the Northern Region in the months following unification. Their main cause seems to have been the economic decline experienced in the region as a result of the exodus of British and other expatriate staff members and the transfer of political and governmental activity to Mogadishu. Although the number of people involved in both movements was not large, their effect upon the North seems to have been considerable. The economic decline brought suggestions for a merger of the political parties of the region in order to form a strong common front capable of defending the region's interests.

A first step in that direction was taken in September 1960 with the merger of the Somali National League and the United Somali Party—the S.N.L. and U.S.P. Very like two New York banks which merge but hang on to both their names, the amalgamated party assumed the name Somali National League United Somali

Party (S.N.L.U.S.P.).[11] The merger was followed by negotiations for a possible inclusion of the National United Front in the new grouping, which was thus supposed to assume a truly regional character. This alignment did not fully crystallize. Other possibilities were considered as well. A number of political leaders were opposed to the formation of a regional party because they viewed it as inhibiting the integration of the two regions, and as detrimental to national unity. They preferred a regrouping cutting across regional lines.

One basis for such a regrouping could be tribal affinity, namely bonds of kinship between Northern and Southern tribes. At one time, prior to the S.N.L.–U.S.P. merger, the possibility of forming a joint party of the Ishaq (S.N.L.) and the Hawiya was contemplated. This would have presumably involved a split within the Somali Youth League (S.Y.L.). The plans were abandoned because such a merger would have laid itself open to charges of tribalism, which had been pressed in the past against the Hawiya S.Y.L. leaders by the Darod wing of that party.

A North-South grouping on the basis of affinity in political outlook was also considered. As already indicated, differences in political outlook have recently begun to develop among parties. Thus, the tendency toward extremism which has at times been displayed by sections of the S.N.L. suggested certain similarities in outlook with the Greater Somalia League (G.S.L.). The pro-Western attitudes of the National United Front (N.U.F.) were close to the points of view of both the S.Y.L. and the Somali Independent Constitutional Party (H.D.M.S.).

The state of flux of Somali politics in the period following unification was reflected in the referendum on the constitution and the subsequent election of the president of the republic.

The referendum, held on June 20, 1961, turned into a vote of confidence in the government. In the republic as a whole, 1,760,540 votes were recorded in favor of the constitution, and only 182,911 against. Among the parties which expressed their lack of confidence in the government by campaigning against the constitution were the principal opposition parties in the Southern Region, the Greater Somalia League and the H.D.M.S.; meanwhile in the Northern Region the main opposition came from the S.N.L.U.S.P., which had been formed by merger the preceding September, and whose leaders were members of the government.

In the Southern Region the "no" vote was reported as 128,627, and the "yes" vote was reported to be a resounding 1,711,013, considerably higher than the estimated total population of the Region.*

In the Northern Region, participation in the referendum was relatively small. But, of those who participated, a majority voted against the constitution. The vote was reported as 54,284 against and 49,527 for. This result reflected the widespread discontent in the Northern Region over the economic decline there, and over the growing political influence of Mogadishu. It also reflected the gap which had developed between the party organizations and the region's representatives in the National Assembly and government. This gap was in part the consequence of the rules adopted by the parties in the Northern Region barring members of the National Assembly from holding office in the party executive.

Discontent in the Northern Region continued to manifest itself in the months that followed. On December 9, 1961, a group of junior officers tried to seize power in Hargeisa with the object of effecting the secession of the Northern Region from the Somali Republic. Their attempt was poorly organized, and apparently did not enjoy popular support, as it was quickly suppressed. In October 1962 another crisis ensued, resulting in the resignation of the Northern Region ministers from the government. A few days later, the Northern Region deputies walked out from a session of the National Assembly and threatened to boycott the legislature. These periodic crises did not assume the character of a clear-cut North-South con-

* The source of these figures, and of those for the Northern Region, is Agence France Presse, June 28, 1961. The 1,711,013 figure can perhaps be explained by the difficulties involved in counting votes in tribal areas where the voting was by acclamation, and by the tendency of tribes, in reporting the vote, to exaggerate their numerical strength.

frontation, as factions of the southern Somali Youth League, Greater Somalia League, and other opposition groups occasionally sided with the northern politicians. The divisions within the S.Y.L. remained strong. Thus, the party had been deeply split in the presidential election taking place after the referendum of June 1961. President Aden Abdulla Osman was reelected by the National Assembly, but only on the third ballot, and by a narrow margin, over Sheikh Ali Giumale, one of the leaders of an opposition faction within the party. Despite the heated election dispute, Sheikh Ali Giumale was at first retained in the government as Minister of Health and Labor; but he was forced to resign in December 1961.

Clues that might help us predict the future course of Somali politics are scarce. It appears that tribal divisions and differences between the North and the South will continue to play an important role for many years. But perhaps even more important is the aspiration for the broadening of the union to include the Somali populations of French Somaliland, Ethiopia, and Kenya.

Chapter 10

The Politics of French Somaliland

FRENCH Somaliland, unlike the Somali Republic, has an ethnically mixed population. Its lack of homogeneity has greatly influenced the trend of local politics; and so has the distinct character of Jibuti's economic life.

The name Somaliland is misleading for this little territory of 67,000 population. Although the Somalis are the largest single group, they are a minority of the inhabitants. They number approximately 29,000—of whom some 25,000 are indigenous and 4,000 are immigrants from neighboring territories—and they constitute 43 percent of the total population. The Danakils number approximately 27,000 and comprise 40 percent of the total. The rest of the people, about 11,000, or 17 percent, consist of immigrant communities of Arabs, Indians, and Europeans.[1]

Somalis and Danakils are similar in some ways. Both lead a pastoral life, adhere to Islam, and are believed to be descended from the same Hamitic stock. But they also differ. They are geographically separated, the Somalis inhabiting the southern third of the territory and the Danakils the northern parts. There is very little intermingling. They speak different (though related) languages. Most important of all, each group considers itself a separate community and is conscious of its own special identity.

Next to ethnic composition, the strongest factor in the trend of local politics is the economics of the territory. Much of the population is nomadic, but nearly half is concentrated in Jibuti, a busy port whose economy is wholly geared to international commerce. Jibuti is connected by a railroad with Addis Ababa, and provides Ethiopia's principal outlet to the sea. Although the Eritrean ports of Massawa and Assab, now parts of Ethiopian territory, handle an increasing proportion of Ethiopian foreign commerce, Jibuti, because of its rail link with the interior and its modern installations, still handles over 50 percent of it. Ethiopian transit trade makes up between 70 and 75 percent (by value) of the traffic through the port of Jibuti.[2] The urban population is fully aware of the importance of international trade for its prosperity, and of its economic interest in continued good relations with Ethiopia. Moreover, Ethiopian dislike for the "Greater Somalia" ambitions of the Somali nationalists is well known. Jibuti's dependence upon Ethiopian trade makes it highly vulnerable to pressure, which could be exerted through the diversion of trade to Assab and Massawa. Already, the competition of the newly constructed Ethiopian port of Assab is keenly felt.

The commonly accepted generalization that the growth of nationalist movements is directly related to economic development and the accompanying social change, did not hold true in French Somaliland (as it did not in the Somali Republic either). Despite the relatively high level of urbanization, political pressures began to build up in the territory only in the 1950's, mainly as a result of external influences rather than internal developments.

The territory's constitutional progress was initiated by the French government after the Second World War. A Representative Council was established in the territory in 1946. Its functions involved voting on the budget and approving public works projects, administrative measures, and the like. The Council was composed of two sections of ten members each, one representing the French community, the other the indigenous population. Six of the representatives of the indigenous population—two Somalis, two Danakils, and two Arabs—were elected through separate electoral colleges, by restricted electorates. The four remaining indigenous members were chosen by the governor from lists presented by the Chamber of Commerce, professional groups, and trade unions. The territory sent a deputy elected in popular elections to the National Assembly in Paris, and sent delegates chosen by the Representative Council to the Council of the Republic and the Assembly of the French Union.[3]

The constitutional reforms introduced in French Overseas Territories by the *loi cadre* of 1956 brought about changes in French Somaliland. A new constitution promulgated in 1957 provided for the establishment of a Territorial Assembly elected by a common roll of voters, and the extension of suffrage to all adult males. In addition, it established a Council of Ministers, to be presided over by the governor (a Frenchman), with the leader of the majority group in the Territorial Assembly serving as vice-president. The election to the new Territorial Assembly was won by the Union Républicaine, led by Mahmoud Harbi, an Issa Somali. The party received support from all communities, and for a while skillfully managed to balance the diverse interests of its supporters. The Council of Ministers was composed of four Somalis, two Danakils, one Arab, and one European. Mahmoud Harbi duly became vice-president of the Council and also served as deputy in the French National Assembly. Another Somali, Hassan Gouled, was chosen to represent the territory in the Council of the Republic. The representative in the Assembly of the French Union was a Danakil. The fact that the Somalis' share in the government and among the representatives sent to Paris was larger than their share of the population reflected their greater political sophistication as compared to the Danakils.[4]

Although the territory experienced some political unrest, caused by the growing force of Somali nationalism in Somalia and British Somaliland and by nationalist propaganda from the Cairo radio, the situation remained relatively calm until 1958. The calm was broken by the referendum on the proposed constitution of the French Fifth Republic held in September of that year. The referendum was the occasion for the introduction of Somali nationalism into local politics. The choice in the referendum was presented as between continued association with France ("yes"), and independence with the object of joining a "Greater Somalia" ("no"). The campaign aroused great controversy among the Somalis, and also stimulated political interest among the Danakils, up to then not politically minded. Mahmoud Harbi campaigned against the constitution on a Somali nationalist platform, arguing that continued association with France would hinder the territory's joining a Greater Somalia. Hassan Gouled campaigned for a "yes" vote.

The "yes" forces won handily; 75 percent of the votes cast were in favor of the new French constitution and of the continued association with France.[5] These "yes" voters amounted to 55 percent of the total registered electorate; 18 percent of those registered voted "no," and 27 percent of them did not vote. Here are the results:

Total registered voters	15,833
Total votes cast	11,579
Valid votes cast	11,512
Yes	8,661
No	2,851

As for the distribution of the vote, it appears that a very high proportion of those registered who did not cast their ballots were Somalis. Of those Somalis who voted, the majority voted "no." The Danakils and Europeans voted almost unanimously "yes." Thus, the over-all majority which voted for the constitution was made up of the Danakils, the Europeans and other communities, and a minority of the Somalis.

Mahmoud Harbi, despite the defeat of his views in the referendum campaign, was confirmed in office as vice-president of the Council of Ministers by the Territorial Assembly, but was suspended on October 2 by the governor. This brought on a political controversy in which the Union Républicaine disintegrated. New elections then had to be held, and a number of new parties sprang up; indeed, seven parties won seats in the new Assembly.

The elections, held in November 1958, were the occasion for leadership contests within both the Somali and the Danakil communities. Among the Somalis, Hassan Gouled was competing with Mahmoud Harbi. Among the Danakils the contestants were Mohamed Kamil and Abu Bekr. The voters divided in accordance with their tribal (lineage group) allegiances. The contests resulted in the formation of two competing Somali-Danakil coalitions: Hassan Gouled allied himself with Mohamed Kamil, and Mahmoud Harbi with Abu Bekr. The Hassan Gouled–Mohamed Kamil coalition won the elections, mainly, it seems, because of Danakil and European support. The majority of the Somalis seem to have supported the Mahmoud Harbi–Abu Bekr bloc.

Hassan Gouled now became vice-president of the Council, while Mahmoud Harbi went into voluntary exile to Cairo and later established headquarters in Mogadishu. Mahmoud Harbi was killed in an air accident in October 1960 when returning from a visit to Eastern Europe and China.

In April 1959, Hassan Gouled was elected deputy to the French National Assembly, whereupon he resigned his post as vice-president of the Council.* A Danakil, Ahmed Dini, took his place, and retained the position until June 1960, when he was ousted as a result of a political revolt among the members of the Territorial Assembly led by a young Danakil by the name of Ali Aref Bourhan.

But this 1960 contest was fought mainly on a personal, not a nationalist, basis. Indeed, with the passing of the excitement caused by the events of 1958, political life in the territory had resumed its former character of small-town, parochial rivalries. During the 1958 campaigns on the referendum and the membership of the Territorial Assembly, the Somali nationalist issue had become superimposed on the traditional pattern of personal and clan rivalries. However, the

* He was elected on the Gaullist list of the Union pour la Nouvelle République.

nationalist agitation gradually subsided, and the political parties that had been formed to contest the 1958 elections soon fell apart. Personal and clan jealousies regained their pre-eminence as political issues.

Why did the politics of French Somaliland resume their essentially parochial character instead of erupting into a violent conflict with Somali nationalist claims as the dividing issue? Common sense suggests that the small size of the population, 67,000, is partly responsible. Political contests normally take place within the ethnic communities, 29,000 Somalis and 27,000 Danakils. Jibuti, the political and economic center, has a population of 31,000. Individual rivalries which develop within such limited circles, where a large proportion of the population is personally acquainted with the contestants, are not easily presented as great ideological or constitutional issues, as they might be before bigger and more diffuse political audiences. Clans rally around their leaders, and take positions on the basis of traditional relationships with other clans, or on the basis of the personal appeal of the political aspirants.

Perhaps one of the causes of Mahmoud Harbi's failure was his personality. He was regarded as clever, but not wise, possessing a dictatorial manner which alienated many supporters. His political past was an unstable one. While a member of the French National Assembly he shifted political allegiances a number of times, thus acquiring an opportunistic image which hindered him in his attempt to appear as a dedicated fighter for nationalism. He gathered considerable support, but his personality prevented him from becoming the generally acknowledged nationalist leader he aspired to be.

The development of a modern nationalist movement in the territory has also been hindered by the special characteristics of the Somalis there. The indigenous Somali population belongs to the Issa tribe, which is renowned for its separatism.[6] To be sure, the Issa are divided between French Somaliland (about 25,000), Ethiopia (between 50,000 and 100,000), and the Northern Region of the Somali Republic (about 55,000), and they would like to be rid of the alien governments and the interposing boundaries. But their primary concern is the unification of the Issa; the unification of the rest of the Somalis is of only secondary interest.

Issa separatist sentiments have led to an attempt to form a political movement. In September 1960, Issa tribal leaders and politicians met near Zeila and issued a call for the establishment of an Issa state. Presumably, they intended this state to be associated with the Somali Republic; however, the form of this association was left ambiguous. The conference resolved to convene regularly in the future and to establish a fund for the purpose of furthering Issa political aspirations. It is unlikely that Issa separatism will develop into an influential political force. Pan-Somali nationalists, the French authorities, and Ethiopia—all oppose it. But whatever the outcome of this attempt to form a political movement, Issa separatist tendencies will continue to exist and may hinder the spread of Pan-Somali organizations.

These inhibiting factors notwithstanding, the potential impact of Somali nationalism upon the territory is evident in all spheres of public life. Somali nationalism, though not a burning issue in the early 1960's, could become so at any time, and was therefore very much on the minds of people in the territory—the politicians, the business community, and the French officials. Even Issa separatism could be considered as essentially an expression of Somali nationalism, and its assertion was an indication of the political unrest among the Somali population. This unrest is kept alive by events in the neighboring territories, by agitation from the outside, and also by local grievances. There is a strong desire for greater educational opportunities and for more rapid economic development, and the French administration is criticized for lack of initiative in these spheres.

When Somali nationalism became an important political factor in the territory, one of its main effects was upon the Danakils, who have become sensitive about the Somali primacy, and have begun to claim what they regard as their rightful place in the government and in economic life. The French authorities seem to have recognized the validity of Danakil grievances, and have been attempting to maintain a balance between the two groups. The local trade unions have begun insisting upon strict parity between Somali and Danakil employees. The Somalis protest that Danakil claims have been inspired by the French authorities because the French would like to see the Danakils become a counterforce to Somali nationalism in the territory. Be it as it may, the Danakils are becoming increasingly consciously politically and are opposed to the Somali nationalists' attempts to shape the political future of the territory. The rivalry between the two groups is growing, and will in the long run greatly complicate the political situation in the territory.

What is the political future of French Somaliland—a barren and arid territory a little larger than Massachusetts, constituting a vital outlet to the sea for Ethiopia, furnishing a valuable base for the control of sea communications between Europe and the Indian Ocean, and inhabited by two rival ethnic groups of approximately equal size?

For the foreseeable future it will probably remain associated with France in one form or another. To be sure, the nature of French interest in the Horn of Africa has changed since the nineteenth century. As we have seen, the establishment of the French colony was motivated primarily by the need for a naval supply station on the route to Indochina, and in the 1890's the colony played a significant part in the rivalry with Britain over influence in Ethiopia and the control over the sources of the Nile. The French are no longer in Indochina. Even so, the strategic value of French Somaliland as a sentry at the entrance into the Red Sea and as the terminal for the Ethiopian rail link remains considerable. The determination of the French to safeguard their position in the territory was emphatically stated by General de Gaulle during his short visit to Jibuti in July 1959. In an address before a gathering of local notables the General said:

The present, and even more the future, make Jibuti and the entire Coast exceptionally important. You understand the reasons, which are political—and I do not shy from the word—but which are also economic and humanitarian. A number of things depend on what will happen here in this territory, among them the influence of France. I am, as is France, particularly aware of what happens here. With you, we have made, and we shall make progress.*

General de Gaulle further declared that "whatever may happen to others, France will not relinquish its humanitarian task" in the territory. Empires, however, are not eternal. Sooner or later, circumstances are likely to arise under which France may consider it advantageous to divest itself of its direct responsibility for the territory.

If and when this occurs, French Somaliland is unlikely to become an independent state. Even assuming that the economic difficulties could be overcome, the political obstacles to such a solution seem decisive. Cooperation between Somalis and Danakils, which would be a prerequisite, would be unlikely. Moreover, the territory's importance for Ethiopia and its strategic location render its ability to sustain its independence highly questionable.

A more realistic expectation regarding the territory's future is that it will be annexed to Ethiopia, or conceivably, partitioned between Ethiopia and the Somali Republic. It would seem idle to speculate about how this might happen. Much would depend upon the circumstances of French departure, upon the internal situation in Ethiopia, and upon the involvement of other international factors. However, one must bear in mind Ethiopia's historic drive toward the sea, its aversion to foreign influence along its borders, and most of all Jibuti's supreme importance for Ethiopian trade.

* The expressive French text, as it appeared in *Le Monde* (Paris), July 5–6, 1959, follows: "Il y a le présent et il y a surtout l'avenir, qui donne à Djibouti et à l'ensemble de la Côte un intérêt exceptionnel. Vous en comprenez les raisons, qui sont politiques—et je tranche le mot,—mais qui sont aussi économiques et humaines. De ce qui se passera ici, sur ce territoire, dépend une quantité de choses, dont le rayonnement de la France. Je suis, et la France est, particulièrement conscient de ce qui se passe ici. Avec vous nous avons fait et nous ferons davantage."

Chapter 11

The Problem of the Ethiopian Somalis

SOMALI nationalism confronts Ethiopia with a grave challenge. It claims the right for the Somali-populated region to secede and join a Greater Somali state. This claim concerns one fifth of Ethiopian territory. But far more threatening than the loss of territory and population is the effect of the Somali challenge upon the political stability of this polyethnic state.

THE INHABITANTS

The Somalis inhabit the entire southeastern portion of Ethiopia, an area of about 80,000 square miles. The map presented earlier in this book shows the region in question. Administratively, it falls within Harar and Sidamo provinces. The exact number of the Somali population is not known, but on the basis of available information and our local inquiries it seems reasonable to estimate that the figure is between 850,000 and 1,000,000. The area is populated almost exclusively by Somalis, except at its fringes where the population is intermixed and ethnic divisions are sometimes blurred. This is the case especially in the Diredawa-Harar-Jigjiga area where a number of agricultural tribes are of mixed Somali and Galla origin and do not readily identify themselves with either ethnic group. Moreover, the Somalis are a minority in the three towns, which have large Amhara and Galla populations. Elsewhere in the region the non-Somali population consists of a few hundred Amhara administrators and police with their families, and scattered individual Arab and Galla traders. Thus it is not far wrong to consider the entire 80,000 square miles—except for the three above-mentioned towns—as being ethnically homogeneous, inhabited by the Somalis.

The Somali population belongs to a variety of tribes. It can conveniently be divided into five main groups.

In the northern portion of the Somali-populated region, between Harar and French Somaliland, live the Issa. They are all nomads, and number between 50,000 and 100,000.

To the south of them, in the vicinity of Jigjiga, there is a concentration of settled agricultural Somalis. Some of them belong to the Gadabursi tribe, which is divided between Ethiopia and the Northern Region of the Somali Republic. Others are sections of the Darod referred to as Absame and Jidwak. The agricultural Somalis in this area number close to 250,000.

A third group are the Ogaden who occupy the central portions of the Somali-inhabited region. The Ogaden are Darod and number between 350,000 and 400,000. They are nomads, and graze their stock exclusively within Ethiopian territory all year round.

A fourth group are nomadic tribes whose main center is in the Somali Republic—the Ishaq, Dolbahanta, Mijertain, and Marehan. Most of these tribes used to cross into Ethiopia only for seasonal grazing. However, during the last forty years, some sections have ceased to return to British Somaliland and Somalia, and now stay in Ethiopia throughout the year. This change was brought about partly by a deliberate Italian policy encouraging them to do so. But, to some extent, their penetration into Ethiopia is a manifestation of the traditional Somali pattern of southward migration.[1] The process resulted in a partial displacement of the Ogaden tribe from the rich grazing area of the Haud, and from a series of wells running parallel to the border of the Southern Region of the Somali Republic. The Ethiopian portions of the Ishaq, Dolbahanta, Mijertain, and Marehan are estimated at approximately 150,000 (Ishaq 50,000, Dolbahanta

30,000, and Mijertain and Marehan 70,000). One difficulty in estimating these tribes is that some of them are included in the population estimates of the Somali Republic, and are thus counted twice.

A fifth group are tribes of the extreme south of Ethiopia, some of which are divided between Ethiopia and the neighboring areas of Kenya and the Somali Republic. These are sections of the Marehan (Darod) and Digodia, Gurreh, and Ajouran (Hawiya). They number between 50,000 and 100,000.

The degree of political consciousness among the Somali population is difficult to assess. In the early 1960's no political parties had yet made their appearance in Ethiopia, and there were no political organizations of any kind among the Somalis. During the period when portions of Ethiopia were under British Military Administration, the Somali Youth League (S.Y.L.) from Somalia established a number of branches in Ethiopian territory. These were disbanded when Ethiopian authority was restored in the region. There is no doubt, however, that the Somalis have kept themselves informed about political developments around them. They are aware of the progress made by Somali nationalism, including the unification of British Somaliland with the Italian-administered trust territory of Somalia. News and nationalist propaganda have reached the Ethiopian Somalis regularly through the continuing seasonal migrations back and forth across the border, and also by means of radio, though the effect of this medium was limited for the time being by the scarcity of receivers.

General sympathy for Somali nationalism is apparently found among all sections of the Somali population of Ethiopia. They differ, however, in the intensity of nationalist feeling and the degree of identification with nationalist causes.

It seems that the most fervently nationalist are the Ishaq, Dolbahanta, Mijertain, and Marehan, whose main centers are across the border in the Somali Republic. The Ogaden, on the other hand, seem to be less influenced by Somali nationalism. The divergent attitudes of these two groups reflect to a considerable extent their conflicting economic interests. The Ishaq, Dolbahanta, Mijertain, and Marehan all seek to fortify and extend their rights with respect to rich grazing lands and wells inside Ethiopian territory. On the other hand, the Ogaden, some of whom have been displaced from areas they previously occupied by the tribes from across the border, would like to have their pre-eminent rights for the shared grazing areas recognized. They suspect that the incorporation of the Ethiopian territories in a "Greater Somalia" would result in their losing their pre-eminence over the areas in question.

The agricultural Somalis around Jigjiga also seem less fervently nationalist than the neighboring nomadic Ishaq. The Issa appear to be strongly anti-Ethiopian, as the frequent clashes between them and the authorities indicate. Their antagonism to the Ethiopian authorities renders them at the same time strongly pro-nationalist. There is no information about the attitudes of the fifth group, the Somalis of Sidamo province in the south. The absence of information suggests that their sympathy for Somali nationalism has not reached violent proportions.

Expressions of Somali nationalist sentiments in Ethiopia are few and sporadic, and are quickly suppressed by the authorities. The most overt manifestations of nationalism take the form of Somali defiance of established Ethiopian authority. Usually, however, it is difficult to distinguish between politically motivated incidents and common lawlessness. An incident which was explicitly nationalist in character occurred in Jigjiga in 1948. On the eve of the restoration of the town to Ethiopian administration, the S.Y.L. flag was hoisted on a public building. When the British authorities lowered it, a riot followed, resulting in a number of casualties. From time to time, public displays of disrespect toward the Ethiopian flag during hoisting and lowering ceremonies are known to occur. During such ceremonies, which take place twice daily everywhere in the country, all persons present are supposed to stand at attention. Occasional defiance of this custom by Somalis has reportedly been accompanied by statements that this was not the Somali flag, and that as Somalis they did not owe it respect.

Armed clashes between tribesmen and Ethiopian security forces also occur, but are more difficult to assess. A serious incident in 1956, involving the Issa, apparently had nationalist undertones. An even more serious incident, the Issa attack on the railroad between Addis Ababa and Jibuti in August 1960, apparently had mixed motives: it was a raid for looting purposes as well as a politically inspired challenge to Ethiopian authority. In the following months the frequency of incidents seemed to be increasing. Between January and April 1961 there were three major ones: at Damot in the Haud, at Aisha on the railway line, and at Dagahbur in the Ogaden. The episodes at Aisha and Dagahbur appear to have been purely political in character. They are disquieting reminders to the Ethiopian government that the dormant Somali nationalism may erupt any time into a major conflagration.

The Challenge

The territory coveted by the Somalis is mainly a semi-arid plateau. At present it is a poor and desolate country, but it has potentialities for agricultural and mineral development. Water resources in the Ogaden have not been extensively explored. It seems probable that with modern well-drilling techniques, the damming of river beds, and perhaps irrigation schemes involving waters from the Webi Shebeli, parts of the Ogaden could become fit for cultivation. As for mineral resources, they too have not been fully explored. From the sketchy surveys undertaken, it appears that in the Harar area there are iron ore, lead, copper, tin, and clays. Farther east, near Jigjiga, mica has been mined for some time, and other mica deposits are reported in the Ogaden. Small veins of asbestos have been found near Diredawa. Oil explorations were conducted in the Ogaden for several years by the Sinclair Oil Company, which apparently considered the prospects unpromising and discontinued their operations in 1957.[2] Recently a German-owned oil company started explorations in the southwest of Harar province. Even the remote possibility of the presence of oil increases Ethiopian determination to hold on to its territory.

Demands upon Ethiopian territory are by themselves sufficient to cause concern to the Ethiopian government. Their example is even more alarming, for the Somali demands might encourage demands by other peoples.

The population of Ethiopia is a conglomeration of ethnic groups and tribes, belonging to different races and divided by language, culture, and religion. There are well over a hundred different groupings, speaking at least fifty different languages.[3] In the context of Ethiopian history and society, the diversity of the population poses for that country extremely grave problems. The history of Ethiopia was a continuous struggle of the Christian polity against Moslem and pagan tribes, either warding off their attacks or striving to expand the Ethiopian domain over them. Although the warfare has subsided, traditional antagonisms are engrained among the people.

The forging of new nations from multiple tribes can be attempted either through a process of amalgamation or through assimilation. In Ethiopia, national integration is achieved through the assimilation of minorities by the ruling Amharas, rather than through a process of cultural, economic, and social amalgamation of different ethnic groups. Assimilation involves the acceptance by the minority of Amhara culture, language, religion, and customs. In the newly independent countries of Africa, nationalism does not usually reflect the cultural heritage of any single particular tribe or ethnic group to the exclusion of others, but Ethiopian nationalism is actually Amhara nationalism.

Assimilation is hindered by the religious divisions: approximately 40 percent of the population are Christian, 40 percent Moslem, and 20 percent pagan. The ruling Amharas are Christian, and the minorities are mainly Moslem and pagan. Racial antagonisms are another complicating factor. The Amharas are Hamitic, whereas many of the western tribes are Negroes who have long been subject people and are sometimes still regarded as such.

The Amharas are concentrated mainly in the center and north of the country. The minorities live along the borders and inhabit almost the entire southern half of the country. Moreover, the minorities are usually related to peoples living across the border in the Sudan, Kenya, and the Somalilands. In view of the cultural and religious divisions, and of the historical antagonisms, it is quite possible that tribalism in Ethiopia may assume the character of secessionist movements.[4]

The Somali claims are unique in some respects, since there is no other ethnic group of the same size and degree of national cohesion, occupying so extensive a territory. Nevertheless, there are groups which potentially pose similar problems.

Eritrea, for example, is often regarded as a potential trouble spot. Prior to its federation with Ethiopia in 1952, there existed a powerful movement demanding independence for the territory, deriving its principal support from sections of the Moslem population.[5] The calm in Eritrea during the attempted *coup d'état* in 1960 suggests that the current strength of separatism there has been overestimated. Yet any concessions to the Somalis might encourage its revival.

Sections of the Galla population may also be encouraged to press for a change in the *status quo*. The Galla migrations into the Ethiopian highlands took place during the sixteenth and seventeenth centuries. These people are spread throughout the country, and in some areas constitute the great majority of the population. Most of the Gallas are Moslem and speak their own language. Among some of them, notably in the southwest, memories of their past political independence, which they lost at the end of the nineteenth century, are still very much alive.[6] Others have been assimilated by the Amharas and have adopted Christianity. Since the eighteenth century the Gallas have been influential in Ethiopian politics and their support has at times decided the outcome of internal political rivalries. During the constitutional crisis which followed Menelik's death, they, along with the Somalis, supported Lij Yasu who reportedly leaned toward Islam. Their record in the Italian-Ethiopian war was mixed. There were numerous cases of Gallas aiding the Italians, while other Galla troops rebelled and became *shiftas* (bandits). Although there is no Galla "nationalism," and the Gallas are less conscious of their separate identity than the Somalis, the possibility of the development of some form of Galla self-assertion cannot be ruled out.[7]

These possibilities probably cause great concern to the Ethiopian government. The Ethiopians' worries are further augmented by the fear that their troubles might be exploited by foreign powers, or, perhaps, are partly the product of foreign intrigues. This fear may be greatly exaggerated. Yet, beliefs, however ill-founded, sometimes become political factors more significant than reality. The Ethiopians have been traditionally suspicious of foreigners, and their suspicions were nurtured by their experiences. Somalia and the Ogaden plateau figured prominently in the Italian scheme for the conquest of Ethiopia in the 1930's. First, the Ogaden was penetrated with the help of Somali irregulars; then the Wal-Wal incident was provoked on the pretext that the area in question actually belonged to Italian Somaliland; and finally, Italian Somaliland served as a base for the invasion. The Somali-inhabited areas were a source of friction between Ethiopia and Britain as well. The retention of British Military Administration over the Ogaden until 1948, and over the Haud near the British Somaliland border until February 1955, ten years after the war had ended, was viewed with considerable suspicion by Ethiopia. The "Bevin Plan" whereby the Ogaden was to be detached from Ethiopia and joined with other Somali territories under British trusteeship aggravated the suspicions.

The encouragement given to Somali nationalism by Cairo is another source of concern for Ethiopia. The Islamic content of Egyptian propaganda may have an influence not only on the Somalis, but upon other Moslem minorities as well.[8]

At stake for Ethiopia is not only one fifth of its territory, but the very foundations of the Ethiopian state. If the principle of secession is conceded to the Somalis, it may stimulate similar demands by other sections of the population and gravely threaten the continued existence of the Ethiopian state in its present form.

The Response

The Ethiopian response to this challenge to its integrity and stability is threefold: the strengthening of Ethiopia's international position; a call on the Somalis throughout the Horn to achieve unity through joining Ethiopia; and increased efforts to win the loyalty of the Ethiopian Somalis and assimilate them.

Until 1958, Ethiopian policy was closely allied to the West on issues in the cold war. Ethiopian forces participated in the Korean War, and Ethiopia provided facilities for the establishment of an American military communications station on its territory. The same policy had manifested itself at the United Nations on numerous occasions. However, as the Somali threat increased, so did Ethiopian doubts about the advisability of trusting in Western support in case the Somali issue ever came to a head. These doubts were induced in part by memories of the 1930's, when Ethiopia was abandoned by the League of Nations. Moreover, British policy since the Second World War, and especially the "Bevin Plan" and the retention of British administration in Ethiopian territory long after the war had ended, instilled a conviction in Ethiopia that Britain favored Somali unification at Ethiopian expense. American support for the British policy statement of February 1959, offering Britain's good offices for arranging negotiations between Somali representatives on the subject of closer association between British Somaliland and Somalia, aroused Ethiopian suspicions toward the United States as well.[9]

As subsequent events have shown, Emperor Haile Selassie concluded that the path of prudence lay not in trusting friends, but in the avoidance of making enemies. The Somalis, even standing alone, could not be taken lightly; but Somali nationalism, if supported by the Soviet Union or China, could become a very grave threat indeed. Ethiopia's desire for a rapprochement with the Soviet Union was motivated in large measure by the fear that the Somalis might be able to obtain such support. In an attempt to forestall this potentially threatening development, the Emperor visited Moscow in 1959, and

Ethiopia accepted a Soviet offer of economic assistance. Ethiopia's apparent desire to mend its relations with China is reflected in its voting on the question of Chinese admission to the United Nations. Until 1958, Ethiopia voted consistently with the United States against the consideration of the proposal to admit China. In 1959, it abstained. In 1960 it voted for the first time in favor of the resolution.

Ethiopia also seeks to strengthen its position within the bloc of independent African states. Ethiopia, showing pride in being the oldest independent state in Africa, has displayed interest in African affairs. Although its aspiration for recognition as a leading member of the African bloc is not a product of its concern about the Somali issue, the consistent Somali appeals to African conferences have heightened Ethiopia's interest in enhancing its African influence.* The more influential Ethiopia's general position in the bloc, the less likely African states will be to support the Somalis. Any moral support the Somalis might get would not be of great practical significance, but it would, nevertheless, make the situation more uncomfortable for Ethiopia.

The Ethiopian call upon the Somalis to join Ethiopia is both a response to the Somali desire for unity and a manifestation of Ethiopia's own nationalist aspirations. On various occasions in recent history, the Ethiopian government laid claim to the entire Horn of Africa. In April 1891, as mentioned earlier, Emperor Menelik sent a circular to the European powers contending that his territories extended to Khartoum and Lake Victoria in the west, and to the sea in the east and southeast. Ethiopian claims to Italian Somaliland were renewed during and after the Second World War. These claims were based on the argument that at some time in history the Somali territories were part of the Ethiopian Empire. Additional arguments were Ethiopia's need for outlets to the sea, and the racial affinities between Ethiopians and Somalis.[10]

* The Somalis won qualified support for their goals at the All African People's Conference in Tunis in January 1960. They were rebuffed, however, in their attempt to raise the question at the Conference of Independent African States held in Addis Ababa in June 1960.

The claim to Italian Somaliland failed to gain support and, Ethiopian protests notwithstanding, the country was placed under United Nations trusteeship with Italy as the administering power. However, Ethiopia has not abandoned its hope to incorporate the Somalilands within its domain. The Ethiopian point of view was expressed by the Emperor in his speech at Gabredare in the Ogaden on August 25, 1956:

> The people of ex-Italian Somaliland are to achieve independence in the near future. We are confident that they will also remember that unity is strength, even as the Eritreans recognized that unity is strength. Not only they, but the whole world will recognize that we are united by race, colour, economics, and that we all drink from the same great river . . . As to the rumours of a greater Somalia, we consider that all the Somali peoples are economically linked with all Ethiopia and, therefore, we do not believe that such a state can be viable standing alone separated from Ethiopia. We will speak of this more fully when the proper time comes.[11]

It is doubtful that the incorporation of the Somali areas would solve more political problems for Ethiopia than it would create. The problem which would find a solution is Somali irredentism; and the step would also relieve some of the anxieties the Ethiopians may have about the establishment along their borders of foreign influence that might be inimical to their interests. But the addition of a sizable Moslem minority to Ethiopia's existing minorities would only complicate the already difficult internal situation, and would undermine the precarious balance between the Christians and the Moslems. Intensified contact between the politically conscious Somalis and other minorities might provide the stimulus to the awakening of political consciousness among other groups, and their presence would tend to hinder Ethiopian efforts to assimilate the minorities. Thus, there may be more danger for Ethiopia in the incorporation of the Somali territories than in their independence.

Ethiopia's efforts to encourage assimilation of the Somalis now within its jurisdiction represent a different approach to the Somali problem. If the Ogaden is to remain part of Ethiopia, the assimilation of its population into Ethiopian society seems imperative. The Ethiopians, as pointed out above, have traditionally encouraged assimilation; the minorities, which are mainly Moslem and pagan, were encouraged to adopt the Amharic language and to convert to Christianity, and often, political bonds were cemented through marriage alliances between the royal house and the minorities' ruling families. The absorption of those of the Gallas who have settled among the Amharas is a process that has been going on for centuries. After the restoration of Ethiopian independence during the Second World War a more deliberate and comprehensive policy of assimilation directed at the minorities was embarked upon. With the beginning of modern economic and political development in Ethiopia the traditional methods of the past no longer suffice. It has become necessary to integrate the minorities within the new social, economic, and political fabric which is being created. This applies in particular to the growing numbers of educated young people in the country.

Efforts to encourage the assimilation of the Somalis are limited for the time being to educational measures and to the appointment of Somalis to administrative positions, mainly in Harar province.

No significant attempt has been made to convert the Somalis to Christianity. Any such attempt would probably backfire because of the passions it would arouse. Economic and social integration has not commenced because of the relative isolation of the Somali regions from the rest of Ethiopia. Nor have attempts at political integration gone far. There were in 1960 six Somali deputies and one senator in the Ethiopian parliament, and there were a few Somalis in high-ranking positions in the central government. The main importance of the recent appointment of Somalis to civil service posts in Harar province lies in the employment and status it provides for some of the educated young men. The Ethiopian authorities also hope that the presence of Somali administrators may help reduce tensions between the government and the tribes and diminish the attraction of the all-Somali administration across the border. Yet the effect of these measures, intended to help win Somali loyalty and good will, is questionable.

The government's policy with respect to the assimilation and integration of the Somalis was outlined in the course of the Emperor's 1956 speech in the Ogaden:

> We have seen the elimination of the spirit of strangeness which you formerly had with one another, and instead, as Ogaden is but one of the integral parts of Ethiopia, our police live happily with you. You are now linked with them in fraternity, in mutual confidence, and in brotherly love. Intermarriage has followed, and has cemented your unity . . . We have, in the first place, given orders for the establishment of schools in the various districts, whereby your children will be educated so as to help their country, themselves and their parents. It is our desire that these schools will not only impart education, but also will foster understanding and co-operation among the military, the police and the civilian population . . . It is imperative for you, the people of the Province of the Ogaden, who form part of the great family of the Empire of Ethiopia, to acquire the necessary education whereby you will be able to take over the various positions and responsibilities that await you in the Central Government Administration. Difference in language often creates misunderstanding, and can seriously affect the responsibilities that are being bestowed on you. Lack of knowledge of the national language will be a barrier for the education we have in mind for you . . .[12]

In pursuance of this policy, the government has paid special attention to the development of educational facilities in Harar province. Elementary schools were established in a number of administrative centers, with the purpose of providing education to children from the Somali tribes. This is complicated by the nomadic way of life of these tribes, and the difficulty of keeping the children in school throughout the school year while their tribes migrate. The authorities have attempted to cope with this problem by provision of boarding facilities. One such boarding school was set up in Gabredare, and others were planned elsewhere. Compared to other provinces, Harar province has also been well provided with secondary education facilities. An academic secondary school for boarding students has been functioning in Harar for a number of years. Select Somali students, usually the children of prominent chiefs, were sent to secondary schools in Addis Ababa.* Moreover, there are Somali students studying at the University College in Addis Ababa.

It would be naive to suppose that educating people makes them loyal citizens, or that teaching young Somalis the Amharic language accomplishes their assimilation. Rather, after having provided them with education the government faces the responsibility of placing the young people in appropriate jobs, because the literate young men are unlikely to find satisfaction in return to a nomadic way of life. Thus far, employment has been found for most Somalis who completed their secondary education, mainly in the Harar provincial administration. No information is available about elementary school graduates, but presumably jobs can be found for them too in the rapidly expanding government service. As the number of educated Somalis increases, however, an acute problem is likely to arise because of the slower rate of increase in employment opportunities. This is a general problem throughout Ethiopia, but seems more acute among the Somalis because of the almost total absence of any economic development in the Ogaden.

The integration of the Somalis in Ethiopia's economic and social life is an important aspect of assimilation. But the continued isolation of the Ogaden region imposes a formidable barrier. The great majority of the Somalis, whether settled or nomadic, are engaged in production of food necessary for their subsistence. With the exception of the settled agricultural Somalis in the Harar-Jigjiga-Diredawa area, the Somali population moves around in places that have inadequate communications with the rest of Ethiopia and no economic intercourse with it. In the early 1960's it took about eighteen hours to travel by car or truck from Harar to Gabredare in the Ogaden, a straight-line distance of only about 200 miles. The little trading that the Somalis require is conducted almost exclusively with the neighboring Somali territories across international frontiers. Even provi-

* Some Somalis believe that in addition to the educational purpose, the government's sending of chiefs' children to be educated in Addis Ababa has the political objective of keeping the children as hostages and thus ensuring that the chiefs remain loyal to the government.

sions for the Ethiopian authorities in the Ogaden have ordinarily been purchased through British Somaliland. As long as there are no adequate roads linking the Ogaden with the rest of Ethiopia, no commerce is likely to develop, nor is any significant personal contact or travel likely to occur.

Even those Somalis who have moved outside the Somali-inhabited region do not assimilate easily. Traditional antagonisms between ethnic and religious groups are pronounced. This seems especially the case in Addis Ababa, a city of about 400,000 inhabitants. Unemployment is another problem facing the Somali community there. The government is the largest single employer in Ethiopia; and since the Somalis' loyalty to the state is considered questionable, they have special difficulty in finding jobs.

There is a basic dilemma in the government's policy toward the Somali minority in Ethiopia. It seeks to integrate and assimilate the Somalis; to that end, educational facilities have been provided, and an attempt is being made to place an increasing number of Somalis in civil service jobs in Harar province. Yet the Somalis are not trusted and therefore are not placed in responsible positions. Outside the Somali-populated region, they seem to be at considerable disadvantage, both socially and in terms of employment opportunities. Thus, the education provided for the Somali minority, though constituting a step toward their social and economic advancement, may also produce discontent among increasing numbers of young Somalis, and result in their espousal of Somali nationalism as an outlet for their frustrated ambitions. On the other hand, if the development of educational facilities and the Somalization of the civil service are deliberately retarded, the social and economic progress in the Somali Republic across the border may attract comparison and induce nationalist activity.

So the probable results of these alternative policies—to accelerate the spread of education among the Somalis or not to do so—seem equally menacing. The difficulties inherent in the Somali problem seem to be increasing both in magnitude and complexity.

Chapter 12

The Problem of the Kenya Somalis

Somali nationalism constitutes a challenge to the territorial integrity not only of Ethiopia but also of Kenya. The Somali nationalists claim that the eastern portion of the Northern Frontier Province ought to be detached from Kenya and annexed to the Somali Republic. The area in question covers some 45,000 square miles, and comprises approximately one fifth of the total territory of Kenya. It is mostly savanna, though parts can be described as semi-desert. The area's population is sparse—approximately 94,000—almost all of them Somali nomads. Notwithstanding the sparsity of the population and the meagerness of resources in the area, the issue is likely to be intractable. Kenya African nationalists are determined to safeguard the country's territorial integrity and oppose the cession of territory to the Somali Republic.

The area claimed by Somali nationalists is populated by a number of tribal groups belonging to the Ogaden and the Hawiya. In addition, there are two tribes which are sometimes classified as "semi-Somali": the Ajouran and the Gurreh. Both were among the first Somali tribes to reach the area and were much influenced by its Galla inhabitants. Politically the Ajouran and the Gurreh tend to identify themselves with the Somalis, and are therefore included in this discussion.

Two politically active groups of Somalis in Kenya live outside the disputed area. There is a Somali settlement at Isiolo, at the southern edge of the Northern Frontier Province, estimated in 1960 at 1,500 persons. The settlement was formed during the 1920's when Somali ex-servicemen, most of them from British Somaliland, who had been living in the Kenya highlands, were settled there. The second group are the Somalis of Nairobi, and others scattered in townships throughout Kenya. They too are former military personnel (and their descendants) who settled in Kenya after the First World War. According to a government census they numbered 5,428 persons in 1957. A very high proportion of them used to be stock traders, and their number has been declining since the early 1950's, when the establishment of the Kenya Meat Commission, with a monopoly over the marketing of stock for meat, deprived many of them of their livelihood and induced them to migrate to Tanganyika and Uganda.[1]

The Somalis of Kenya have sympathized with the Somali nationalist movement since its inception. In the mid-1940's, branches of the Somali Youth League (S.Y.L.) were formed in the Northern Frontier Province. It is hard to say how much their establishment was due to local initiative and how much inspiration or initiative came from across the border in Somalia. The S.Y.L. in Kenya, like that of Somalia at the time, had objectives that were primarily educational and social. Soon after its formation, however, its activities began to expand. It reportedly set up courts which levied fines upon individuals cooperating with the government, and some of its leaders apparently resorted to intimidation of their opponents. Moreover, rumors were spread that the British government was preparing to relinquish the administration of the Northern Frontier Province and that an S.Y.L. government would take its place. According to the provincial commissioner, the situation had become so bad in some areas, notably in the Garissa district, that "normal administration work had been brought to a standstill"; and consequently in July 1948 the S.Y.L. was proscribed and its branches were closed.[2] A number of leaders were arrested and later exiled to the Turkana district where they lived in restricted residence. They were released in the summer of 1960 at the time of the independence and unification of British Somaliland and Somalia. Simultaneously the S.Y.L. was removed from the list of proscribed organizations.

At this writing the released former leaders have not regained their influence. The apathy of the Somali population toward their long exile and toward the revival of the S.Y.L. indicates that the organization did not have deep roots, and supports the view that the arrested leaders had attempted to use the organization for personal ends.

For almost a decade following the banning of the S.Y.L. in 1948, no significant nationalist activity had taken place among the Kenya Somalis. The only Somali organizations active in Kenya during this period were the United Somali Association and the Ishaqiya Association. Both associations were limited to the urban Somali population outside the Northern Frontier Province. They were essentially pressure groups representing Somali interests, rather than nationalist organizations. The United Somali Association had mainly a Darod membership, while the Ishaqiya, as its name suggests, was the organization of members of the Ishaq tribes. During the 1950's both organizations campaigned for a change in the Somalis' legal status, and for educational and other privileges similar to the ones enjoyed at the time by the Asian community.[3]

In 1959 the organizations merged to form the Somali National Association. The new organization identified itself with Somali nationalist aims. It remained, however, a pressure group concerned mainly with representing various Somali interests and seeking amends for specific grievances, and did not assume the character of a nationalist movement. Its links with the Somalis of the Northern Frontier Province were tenuous. The nomadic Somalis tended to mistrust their urbanized brethren, and seemed to prefer making representations to the authorities independently.

In the Northern Frontier Province, there was no organized political activity among the Somalis for almost twelve years after the banning of the S.Y.L. in 1948. A revival of nationalist activity was prompted in 1960 by the imminent independence and unification of British Somaliland and Somalia, and by the growing concern among the Somalis that Kenya's constitutional progress might frustrate their hopes for ultimate unification with the Somali Republic. This concern is coupled with a reluctance to become subject to an African government when Kenya attains independence. The Somalis of the province appear to be still much influenced by traditional Somali prejudices against Negro Africans.

On these matters the urban Somalis of Kenya differ somewhat from the nomads to the north. In particular, the educated younger generation, born in Kenya and reared in the nationalist-charged atmosphere in the towns, are more favorably disposed toward the nationalist aspirations of the Kenya Africans. They are sensitive to events elsewhere in Africa, and share the Pan-Africanist sentiments of the urban African elite. Yet they also support the goals of Somali nationalism. With respect to the Somali claims on portions of northern Kenya, their attitude is ambivalent: they support the principle of a "Greater Somalia," but would be greatly troubled if attempts to realize this aspiration led to a conflict between the Somalis and the Kenya Africans.

The reappearance of nationalist sentiments among the Somali nomads prompted a number of petitions to the British authorities, requesting that the Somali-inhabited territory be detached from Kenya and be incorporated in the Somali Republic. An attempt to calm the atmosphere was made by the governor, Sir Patrick Rennison, during a visit to the Northern Frontier Province in the spring of 1960, when he assured the Somalis that they would be consulted on any change in the administration of the area.

That same year saw the creation of a political party, the Northern Province People's Progressive Party (N.P.P.P.P.). It had branches in the main centers of the Somali-populated eastern half of the province. Its active core consisted of young people who had attended schools and had settled in the administrative centers: Isiolo, Wajir, Garissa,

Moyale, and Mandera. The party took up a number of Somali grievances concerning educational facilities and the operation of the African Livestock Marketing Organization (A.L.M.O.).* Yet the party's main objectives were nationalist; it demanded that the Somali-inhabited region be detached from Kenya and united with the Somali Republic.

The Somalis' participation in the political life of Kenya has been very limited. Until 1961, Somalis did not participate in elections to the Legislative Council. The majority of those living outside the Northern Frontier Province were classified as aliens, with no right to vote. As for the province, the commissioner appointed to consider the question of African representation on the Legislative Council reported in 1955 "that the tribesmen had expressed a wish that until such time as the Province could be represented by its own Member their interests should continue to be cared for by the Government through the Provincial Commissioner." [4] In 1959 a Somali, Ahmed Farah Eleya, a trader from Moyale, was nominated for the first time to represent the province in the Legislative Council, and he served until the Council was dissolved in preparation for the elections of February 1961.

In these elections the Somalis were given the right to vote for the first time. Outside the Northern Frontier Province, they were not a political factor. Somalis participated in the elections as individuals and usually voted in conformity to the preferences of the African community.

In these elections the Northern Frontier Province was divided into two constituencies—east and west. The electorate of the constituency of Northern Province West consisted mainly of Turkana and Boran-Galla tribesmen, along with a small number of Somalis (mainly

* The A.L.M.O. had a monopoly over the marketing of livestock in the province. The Somalis complained that they were thus left with no choice but to sell to the A.L.M.O. at prices that this organization fixed. They believed they could get better prices for their livestock if they were permitted to sell it at a free competitive market. The A.L.M.O.'s principal contributions were veterinary supervision and the establishment of cattle-purchasing stations in remote tribal areas.

around Isiolo), Asians, and Arabs. The constituency of Northern Province East comprised the essentially Somali districts of Garissa, Wajir, Mandera, and Moyale. The elections caused some controversy among the Somalis of the province. Most of them feared that their participation in the elections might be interpreted as tacit acceptance of their status as Kenyans. Consequently, electoral registration was generally boycotted by the Somalis, and only 1,622 of them (mainly in Mandera and Garissa) registered. Even these did not actually vote, because, in the constituency of Northern Province East, only a single candidate presented himself, and was thus elected unopposed.

This man was Ali Aden Lord, a 41-year-old Somali, born and educated in Nairobi, who lived in Wajir in the Northern Frontier Province for twenty years, and was engaged there in commerce and transport. Ali Aden Lord was the first president of the Northern Province People's Progressive Party, but later resigned from the party, and was elected to the Legislative Council as an independent. At that time he was secretary of the Wajir Muslim Association.[5] He died a few months after the election, and his place in the Legislative Council was taken by A. R. Khalef.

The elections brought home to many African political leaders the existence of a Somali secessionist movement. Commercial, social, and political contacts between the Northern Frontier Province and the rest of Kenya have been quite limited. Commerce is largely in the hands of Asians. The marketing of livestock is carried out through the African Livestock Marketing Organization and does not afford opportunities for personal relations. Social and political ties are almost nonexistent. The province is physically remote. There are administrative restrictions upon travel in the area. Consequently, few Africans in Kenya have any knowledge of the province, its peoples, its problems, or its administration. In the autumn of 1960, in preparation for the elections, the major political parties, the Kenya African National Union (K.A.N.U.) and the Kenya African Democratic Union (K.A.D.U.), became interested in winning support among the Somalis of the Northern Frontier Province. In this they failed, as neither party was even able to present a candidate in the predominantly Somali constituency. But the African politicians did become aware of the problem presented by Somali nationalism.

The vehemence of Somali feelings regarding secession was again demonstrated during the constitutional conference in Nairobi in September 1961. The Somali representatives came to the conference to present their claims for the right to secede. When their claims were not accepted, they walked out of the conference.[6]

Somali secessionist aims were restated at the Kenya constitutional conference held in London in the spring of 1962. In response to Somali representations the conference authorized the setting up of a commission to investigate the state of public opinion in the Northern Frontier Province. The commission's findings confirmed that the Somali population wished to secede from Kenya and join the Somali Republic, but the commission, by its terms of reference, was precluded from making any recommendations on the subject. On March 8, 1963 (just before this book went to press), Duncan Sandys, the British Colonial and Commonwealth Secretary, announced that the Somali-inhabited portion of the Northern Frontier Province would become one of seven regions into which Kenya is being divided. The Somali population of Kenya thus would gain a wide measure of autonomy. The announcement evoked sharp protests from the Somali Republic, as it seemed to signify Britain's intention of handing Kenya intact to its African government, without meeting the Somali demand for secession.

In the face of Somali insistence upon secession and the ignorance of non-Somali Africans concerning the Northern Frontier Province, the administration of this huge territory will pose many problems to an independent Kenya. Unrest among the Somalis may make the task even more formidable. Yet the alternative, the cession of the Somali-populated portions to the Somali Republic, is unacceptable to Kenya nationalist leaders. The preservation of territorial integrity is a cause that no Kenya nationalist leader can disregard.

Chapter 13

A Question of Boundary Lines

THE Horn of Africa, besides facing the problem of a Greater Somalia, is plagued by disputes of a more limited scope concerning the border between Ethiopia and the Somali Republic. These disputes are formally held to be separate issues, unconnected with the aspirations of Somali nationalism. In reality, it is impossible to make a clean separation. The Somalis' approach to the border problem is conditioned by their commitment to the principle that all Somali-inhabited territories ought to be placed under Somali government. The Ethiopians tend to view the disputes not as isolated cases of unfortunate misunderstandings, but as manifestations of Somali expansionist ambitions. With the broader and more fundamental conflict regarding the establishment of a Greater Somalia looming in the background, the solution of the border disputes tends to become greatly complicated.

There are two major disputes in the area. One concerns the border between Ethiopia and the former British Somaliland, the other the border between Ethiopia and the former trust territory of Somalia. There is also a dispute over the Kenya-Ethiopia boundary, stemming from different interpretations of a 1947 Anglo-Ethiopian agreement which amended the 1907 border agreement. The question is the ownership of the Gaddaduma wells. That area is frequented by Somali tribes, among others, but the quarrel does not directly involve

Somali nationalism.[1] And this chapter will be confined to the two major disputes that have unmistakable relevance to the Somali nationalist movement.

The two cases are in part the legacy of the colonial era, when boundary agreements seem to have been influenced more by the rivalries among the European powers than by local conditions in the Horn. Therefore, to review the cases, one must begin by looking briefly again at the nineteenth century.

Between Ethiopia and British Somaliland

At the time of the establishment of the British Protectorate in the 1880's, the boundary with Ethiopia was left undefined. British protection was accorded to the tribes, and, theoretically, it extended over the territory occupied by them. In the early 1890's, when the Ethiopians began to expand in that direction and establish their authority in an area with no defined international boundary, they frequently clashed with Somali tribes, some of which were nominally under British protection.[2]

The first attempt to define the border of the Protectorate was made in the Anglo-Italian agreement on spheres of influence, signed in Rome on May 5, 1894. The British dealt with the Italians on this occasion, recognizing the Italian claim of a protectorate over Ethiopia and responsibility for that country's foreign affairs. As will be recalled, the Ethiopian emperor refused to acknowledge the Italian claim. Consequently, Ethiopia did not consider itself bound by the Anglo-Italian agreement, and moreover, the emperor denied that any communication on the boundary definition had ever reached him.[3]

After the Italian defeat at Adowa and the failure of the Italian attempt to establish a protectorate over Ethiopia, the British government decided to make a direct approach to Emperor Menelik and try to improve relations. British prestige was low among the Ethiopians, who regarded Britain as the ally of the defeated Italians. Moreover, the French, who were quite active in Ethiopia, were doing their best to weaken the British position there. Indeed, Anglo-French rivalry in the Sudan made it especially important for Britain to win Ethiopia's good will at that time. The Somaliland border question, though regarded as of only secondary importance, was another matter the British hoped to see settled.[4]

The British mission to Emperor Menelik, headed by James Rennel Rodd, who was chief secretary at the British Agency in Cairo at the time, arrived in Addis Ababa in April 1897 after an arduous overland trip from Zeila. The negotiations resulted in the conclusion of a treaty followed by an exchange of notes delimiting the border between the British Somaliland Protectorate and Ethiopia. The treaty included also commercial clauses and assured Britain of Ethiopia's friendly neutrality in the war against the Mahdists in the Sudan.[5]

The settlement of the Somaliland frontier question represented concessions on both sides. The Ethiopians gave up some of their claims, which amounted to about half of the Protectorate's territory. The British, on the other hand, did not insist on recognition of the frontier agreed upon with Italy in 1894, and ceded to Ethiopia some 25,000 square miles of territory they thought they had acquired in the treaty with Italy. The willingness of the British to compromise on this question was motivated chiefly by their desire to obtain Menelik's good will during the crucial period of the reconquest of the Sudan and the competition with France over the sources of the Nile.

The agreement was much criticized in Britain at the time on account of the territorial concessions made to Ethiopia.[6] It was not foreseen, however, that the main weakness of the agreement lay in the practical implementation of its provisions, which were bound to generate friction. The border line cut across customary grazing areas of Somali tribes; therefore an annex to the treaty provided that the tribes "occupying either side of the line shall have the right to use the grazing grounds on the other side."[7] Periodical clashes between British-protected tribes and Ethiopian tribes over grazing areas and wells, and occasional jurisdictional disputes between British and

Ethiopian officials, became a considerable irritant to both sides. In an attempt to eliminate at least that part of the friction caused by uncertainty about the location of the frontier, an Anglo-Ethiopian commission demarcated the border between 1932 and 1934.[8]

The placing of huge chunks of Ethiopia under British Military Administration during the Second World War was provided for by the Anglo-Ethiopian agreements of 1942 and 1944.[9] Article 7 of the 1944 agreement said:

> In order as an Ally to contribute to the effective prosecution of the war, and without prejudice to their underlying sovereignty, the Imperial Ethiopian Government hereby agrees that, for the duration of this Agreement, the territories designated as the Reserved Area and the Ogaden, shall be under British Military Administration.

The "Reserved Area" was a continuous belt of Ethiopian territory touching French and British Somalilands, as well as all land within Ethiopia occupied by the Franco-Ethiopian Railway. The railway was returned to the Franco-Ethiopian Railway Company in 1946, but not the rest of the Reserved Area—that is, the Haud—and not the Ogaden either at that time.

Article 7 had given "the effective prosecution of the war" as the reason for placing these areas under British Military Administration, but it seems that military necessity was not the only consideration in the minds of the British. The arrangement was apparently connected with their plans for unifying the Somali territories and placing them under British trusteeship after the war. After this plan failed to win the support of the "Big Four" Council of Foreign Ministers, the Ogaden was returned to Ethiopian administration in 1948. Even then the Haud grazing areas south of the British Somaliland border were retained under British administration. Since approximately half the population of British Somaliland cross annually to the Haud for seasonal grazing, the return of the territory to Ethiopia was bound to cause administrative difficulties. Most probably, the British government also feared that the return might arouse political unrest in the Protectorate.

Ethiopian requests for the Haud led to protracted exchanges between the two governments. It seems that the British tried to induce the Ethiopians to agree to a revision of the border. At one stage Britain proposed an exchange of territory whereby Ethiopia would have received an outlet to the sea at Zeila in return for the Haud. Failing in this, Britain offered to administer the Haud on a lease from Ethiopia. But this too was unacceptable and Ethiopia continued to press for its return to Ethiopian administration.[10]

The negotiations led finally to the new Anglo-Ethiopian agreement in 1954, and the consequent return of the Haud to Ethiopia in February 1955. The new agreement reaffirmed the 1897 treaty regarding the boundary and grazing rights. It also included additional provisions for the regulation and administration of the seasonal migrations of the British-protected tribes into the Haud. Among them was an ambiguous provision for the continued functioning on Ethiopian territory of tribal authorities, including tribal police, "as set up and recognized by the Government of the Somaliland Protectorate." This authority was to be exercised "without prejudice to the jurisdiction of the Imperial Ethiopian Government."[11] Differences regarding the interpretation of these provisions soon developed and the British government formally expressed its view that "many of the actions of the Ethiopian authorities . . . proved to be neither in accord with the letter nor the spirit of the Agreement . . ."[12] A British mission headed by A. D. Dodds-Parker, then Parliamentary Under-Secretary of State for Foreign Affairs, visited Addis Ababa in 1956 in an effort to resolve the different interpretations of the 1954 treaty, but apparently met with little success.[13]

As we have seen, the resentment caused by the return of the Haud to Ethiopia was of major importance in awakening political interest in the Protectorate and stimulating the growth of the nationalist movement. The Somali nationalists declared that they did not recognize the boundary established by the 1897 Anglo-Ethiopian agreement, and contended that Britain was not authorized to enter into any agreements affecting the boundary without consulting the population. They further accused the British of breach of faith, and of violating the trust placed in them by the treaties signed between 1884 and 1886 whereby the Somali tribes accepted British protection. The charge of breach of faith, together with reports about the "decline of British prestige" in the Protectorate, received considerable publicity in Britain. The British government, striving to preserve Somali good will, assumed an apologetic attitude and seemed to be eager to placate the Somalis. The Secretary of State for the Colonies declared in the House of Commons that he "regretted" the 1897 Treaty, but that it was "impossible to undo it." [14] Somali delegations visiting London were accorded a cordial welcome. But the British government did not support Somali moves to have the issue placed before the United Nations or referred to the International Court of Justice for an advisory opinion.[15]

With the termination of the British Protectorate over Somaliland in 1960, the Somali position on the Anglo-Ethiopian treaties assumed crucial importance. The 1897 Anglo-Ethiopian agreement so heartily disliked by the nationalists contained two major provisions: first, it defined the border, and, second, it established grazing rights for the Protectorate tribes in Ethiopian territory. An official repudiation of the 1897 treaty as not binding upon the Somali Republic would have undermined the legal basis of the tribes' trans-border grazing rights. A repudiation might conceivably have prompted the Ethiopian government to bar the former Protectorate tribes from access to the Haud. This would have been a disaster to about half the population of the former Protectorate.

These possibilities were probably considered by the British government and the Somali leaders prior to the termination of the Protectorate. During the constitutional conference in May 1960, the British government expressed the view that

> the Anglo-Ethiopian treaty of 1897, which, *inter alia,* provided the legal basis for trans-frontier grazing rights, should be regarded as remaining in force as between Ethiopia and the successor State following the termination of the Protectorate; but the main provisions of the Anglo-Ethiopian Agreement of 1954, which accorded the Protectorate certain facilities and powers concerning the exercise of these grazing rights, would lapse.[16]

The Somali authorities seem to have tacitly accepted the same position. At this writing, they have refrained from officially adopting the views expressed by nationalist leaders prior to independence, namely that they did not recognize the validity of the 1897 treaty. The caution of the Somali government indicated that it was concerned about the possible consequences of repudiating the treaty. There was no certainty, though, that internal pressures would not eventually induce the government to take a strong stand on the border issue. If and when this happens, a major crisis will ensue.

Between Ethiopia and Somalia

The other major dispute is legally more complicated, though politically perhaps less explosive. The trust territory of Somalia became independent on July 1, 1960, without a legal international boundary with Ethiopia. The border line currently observed by both sides is the "provisional administrative" line established by the British authorities in consultation with the Italian and Ethiopian governments at the time of the transfer of Somalia to Italian trust administration in 1950.

The legal history is long and complicated. It commenced in the 1890's when the Italians, expanding inland from their coastal possessions, encountered Ethiopian forces establishing their emperor's authority in the southern Ogaden. The contact between the two forces necessarily raised the question: just where was the boundary between Italian Somaliland and Ethiopia? The first attempt to regulate the frontier question by agreement between the two countries was connected with Major Nerazzini's peace negotiations in the autumn of 1896, following the Italian defeat at Adowa in March of the same year. In 1897 an agreement was supposedly reached between an Italian mission and the Ethiopian emperor on a provisional border, running parallel to the coast at a distance of 180 miles from it. However, the precise terms of the agreement are not known because no documents have been preserved.[17]

The only boundary agreement of which records are available is the Italian-Ethiopian convention of 1908.[18] This treaty was supposed to provide the basis for the demarcation of the border. But differences soon developed regarding its interpretation, and the demarcation was never carried out on the ground. The difficulty stemmed partly from the reliance of the 1908 treaty upon "the line accepted by the Italian government in 1897," of which no authentic record was available. Another defect of the 1908 treaty was its attempt to define the international border as coinciding with the boundary between tribes. The signers apparently did not take into account that some of the tribes migrate and do not afford a suitable reference point.

As we have seen, during the Fascist era the absence of a clearly defined border served Italian expansionist aims. The Italians encouraged Somali tribes to move northward, and Italian posts were established in the Ogaden. This policy led to continuous friction with Ethiopia, culminating in the Wal-Wal incident of 1934.

The vexing border question was temporarily eliminated during the period between 1935 and 1948, when the Ogaden was administratively merged with Italian Somaliland, first under the Italians, then under the British.

After the establishment of the United Nations trust territory of Somalia, under Italian administration, the U.N. General Assembly recommended in 1950 that direct negotiations be undertaken between Italy and Ethiopia with the object of reaching an agreement on the exact location of the frontier.[19] Negotiations were delayed at first by the absence of diplomatic relations between the two countries; but, even after relations were restored late in 1951, no progress was achieved. In 1954, the General Assembly reiterated its recommendation that the two parties arrive at a solution by direct negotiation. It recommended that if no agreement were reached by July 1955 they resort to mediation.[20] No attempt was made to submit the issue to mediation. Direct negotiations were carried on intermittently, but failed to bring results. Italy claimed that the international border lay west of the "provisional administrative" line, and that certain areas administered by Ethiopia properly belonged to Somalia. Ethiopia argued the reverse, namely that the boundary lay east of that line and that areas administered as part of Somalia actually belonged to Ethiopia. At one stage of the negotiations, Ethiopia indicated willingness to withdraw its claims and compromise on the provisional administrative line as the permanent boundary. No concession appeared to be forthcoming from the other side; so Ethiopia reverted to its former claim.[21]

Next the General Assembly in 1957 recommended arbitration.[22] During the following year progress was limited to the establishment of an arbitration tribunal consisting of three jurists. The parties were unable to agree on an "independent person" to assist in drawing up the tribunal's terms of reference. The General Assembly therefore recommended in 1958 that the "independent person" be nominated by the King of Norway.[23] The King nominated the former Secretary General of the United Nations, Trygve Lie, who attempted to obtain an agreement between the parties on a *compromis d'arbitrage,* defining the terms of reference of the arbitration tribunal. A draft *compromis* submitted by Lie to the Ethiopian and Italian governments was accepted by them late in 1959 as a basis for discussions; but both governments presented amendments to it which were mutually unacceptable.[24] The negotiations reached a deadlock. During the General Assembly's 1959 session its Fourth Committee debated the issue but made no progress and submitted no recommendations.[25]

The principal obstacle was a fundamental disagreement between the Italian and Ethiopian governments on the proper approach to the problem. The Ethiopian government insisted that the dispute was strictly a legal one, concerning the interpretation of the 1908 treaty. The Italian government contended that the problem was not strictly legal, and that questions of equity ought to be taken into account as well. Throughout the different stages of negotiations, progress was hindered by the insistence of the parties upon these radically different approaches.[26]

The Ethiopian government's insistence on a strictly legal approach probably stemmed from the fear that if principles of equity were admitted as a basis for solution, considerations involving the ethnic composition of the population would be brought to bear on the decision. Any decision based upon ethnic composition would have created a precedent, providing a basis for future territorial claims. Moreover, a strong undercurrent of Ethiopian distrust toward Italy greatly influenced the talks. Italy's insistence that the arbitration tribunal be empowered to consider international agreements other than the 1908 treaty amounted to a contention that agreements between Italy and European powers on spheres of influence in Ethiopia be admitted as relevant. It is not surprising, therefore, that the Italian approach failed to elicit much good will from the Ethiopian side.

As no solution seemed in prospect prior to Somalia's becoming independent, the parties informally agreed in December 1959 that the provisional administrative line should remain in force until a final settlement was made.[27]

It was hoped that the negotiations would be resumed when Somalia became independent, and that direct negotiations between the Somalis and Ethiopians, without the presence of Italian representatives, might proceed more smoothly. After independence, however, the reopening of the negotiations was postponed pending the accreditation of a Somali Republic diplomatic mission in Addis Ababa. Budgetary difficulties, but perhaps political reasons as well, delayed for a while the establishment of such a mission, and, even after the mission was accredited, negotiations did not begin immediately. As this is written, negotiations have not begun.

The negotiations are likely to be difficult. Somali aspirations for national unification and for the establishment of a Greater Somalia would require far greater territorial concessions on the part of Ethiopia than were claimed in connection with the border. To isolate the legal dispute over the boundary from the fundamental political problems raised by these Somali aspirations will probably be impossible. Indeed, so long as the fundamental conflict between Somali nationalism and Ethiopia persists, the border question is likely to remain open.

Chapter 14

The International Environment

THE conflict between Somali nationalism and the interests of the neighboring peoples is by itself dangerous for the peace of the Horn of Africa. This danger is greatly increased by the involvement of a number of more distant foreign countries in the affairs of the region. Britain, France, Italy, the United States, the Soviet Union, China, and Egypt have all displayed considerable interest in the Horn, and appear to be involved in its politics. This involvement compounds the dangers to peace in two ways. First, foreign support tends to encourage the contending parties to pursue militant policies and thus increases the likelihood of war. Secondly, if and when a local conflict erupts into violence, the foreign powers may be drawn into it.

Some of the factors that pulled Britain, France, and Italy to the Horn of Africa in the nineteenth century have ceased to play a role in international politics. Britain and France are no longer competing for the control of the upper reaches of the Nile. Colonies have lost their prestige value; indeed they are now regarded as a liability. Of the interests which played a role in the original establishment of European authority in the region, only the defense of sea communications remains significant.

To be sure, the element of competition has not disappeared, but now it is different in kind. At the turn of the century, the chief rivals were Britain, France, Germany, and Italy, and the object of the competition was the establishment of colonies. Today, the competitors are two power blocs, seeking influence among the uncommitted nations. The mode of the competition has changed, and increasing emphasis is put today on indirect influence over countries and peoples, rather than the establishment of direct control. Yet strategic considerations continue to play a role in the power contest, each side striving to acquire positions which might be of value in case of war, or at least deny these positions to its adversary.

A glance at the map is sufficient to realize the strategic importance of the area. The Horn of Africa flanks the approaches between the Red Sea and the Indian Ocean. The Somali coast could serve as a base for interference with vessels using the Suez route between Europe and Asia, and for harassment of shipping in the Indian Ocean. The area has potential importance for air communications as well. There are numerous airfields, although at this writing none has been developed as a stopover on intercontinental trunk routes. With the extension of the range of aircraft the potential importance of these airfields is likely to decline, though overflight rights will remain of some consequence. The safety and unhindered use of these sea and air communication routes is not merely a European interest, but the interest of south Asian countries as well.[1]

The efforts of the various powers to make themselves felt in this strategically important region are greatly facilitated by the weaknesses of the various territories in the area and their dependence on foreign assistance. They require aid to overcome internal economic difficulties. Furthermore, the contending internal forces in the Horn seek external political and military support against each other.

All the external powers, in their policies toward the Horn, have been influenced by these general considerations regarding the strategic significance of the area and its inner weaknesses; and, in addition, each outside nation has been affected by factors having special application to itself.

Britain and the Horn

Britain's interest in the Horn stems, probably more than that of any other power, from concern for the safety of its sea communications through the Red Sea and the Indian Ocean. The sea lanes, in addition to their economic importance, are regarded as essential "for the intercommunications of ideas, and possibly for the movement of military and economic assistance" between members of the Commonwealth.[2]

British policy has consistently sought to prevent the establishment in the Horn of Africa of a hostile power which might interfere with these communications. In the nineteenth century the potential threat to the sea communications emanated mainly from Britain's European rivals. Today these communications would be threatened if the Soviet Union, or any extremist anti-Western power, gained influence over the area.

In the nineteenth century the most effective means to safeguard imperial communications was to take possession of strategically important areas in the Horn and on the Arabian peninsula. Now that the continued possession of territories in Africa or Asia has ceased to be practicable in the era of nationalist awakening on these two continents, the British have sought to retain their influence in the region through the cultivation of good relations with Somali nationalism.

At the conclusion of the Second World War, Great Britain apparently did not foresee the rapid pace of Somali progress toward independence, and sought to secure a firmer hold over the area through the placing of the entire Horn under British administration. This attempt did not bring the British into conflict with Somali nationalism; on the contrary, it received some support from nationalist quarters. The nationalists did not consider immediate independence attainable at that time. Thus, their objective of the unification of Somali territories coincided essentially with British aims.

During the period of British Military Administration over Italian Somaliland, the British authorities maintained close and friendly relations with the Somali Youth League. Indeed, as indicated earlier, the British Military Administration was apparently associated with the League's establishment. In British Somaliland, as well, the government maintained generally friendly relations with the nationalists. Somali complaints over the transfer of the Haud to Ethiopian administration met with an apologetic response on the part of the British government. Official statements about British support for closer association between British Somaliland and Somalia were another manifestation of British policy. However qualified, the statements were nevertheless in harmony with Somali nationalist aspirations.[3]

British relations with Ethiopia have been marred by several vexatious episodes. In 1923, Britain opposed Ethiopia's admission to the League of Nations. Two years later, in an exchange of notes, it confirmed Italian claims to a sphere of influence in Ethiopia. The abandonment of Ethiopia by the League of Nations in 1935 and the British attitude at that time are remembered by the Ethiopians. Later, at the time of the liberation of the country, there was considerable skepticism in British government circles about the emperor's ability to reestablish his authority. This skepticism was reflected in the terms of the 1942 Anglo-Ethiopian agreement, and apparently affected the attitude of the British military authorities toward the Ethiopian government. Both the 1942 agreement and the 1944 agreement which superseded it included clauses which were repugnant to Ethiopia and were accepted by it only with the greatest reluctance.[4]

Anglo-Ethiopian relations were further disturbed by the aforementioned British proposal to place certain Somali-populated areas, including the Ethiopian territories of the Ogaden and the Haud, under British administration. The delay in restoring the Ogaden to Ethiopian administration until 1948, more than three years after the end of the war, and the subsequent delay in the return of the Haud, did not help to allay Ethiopian suspicions regarding British intentions. The British reputation for sympathizing with Somali nationalism tended to augment Ethiopian misgivings. Anglo-Ethiopian disagreements came into the open again in February 1959 in connection with the declaration by the Secretary of State for the Colonies, Mr. Lennox-Boyd, that under certain conditions Britain would be ready to help arrange negotiations between Somali representatives concerning closer association between Somalia and British Somaliland.[5] The declaration was apparently followed by some sharp diplomatic exchanges.

As long as Somaliland remained a British protectorate, the strong pro-Somali attitudes of the colonial administration tended to differ from the views held in the Foreign Office about the region's problems. The termination of British responsibility for the territory will probably enable the British government to take a more detached view of these problems. This is not to say that Britain ceased to be interested in Somali friendship. On the contrary, as pointed out earlier, the decision to withdraw was prompted by the desire to maintain and strengthen this friendship. Evidence of continued British interest in the region and the desire to maintain a measure of influence upon events there is the provision of assistance to the independent Somali Republic. The British government promised financial assistance to its former protectorate amounting to 1.5 million pounds in the first year of independence, and a smaller sum as assistance to the former trust territory of Somalia.* In addition, Britain provided an aid mission to staff certain civil service posts, and a military mission to remain with the Somaliland Scouts for a transition period of six months. In cooperation with Italy, Britain also undertook to provide military assistance to the Somali Republic.[6]

Currently, British policy is up against the difficult task of pre-

* Some disagreements have developed between the British and Somali governments regarding the distribution and administration of these funds. The British government maintained that its assistance should be apportioned between the Northern and Southern Regions in the manner envisaged prior to independence. The Somali government, on the other hand, assumed the position that it, rather than the regions, is the recipient of this aid, and that the manner in which British assistance is to be apportioned between the regions is its own concern—not to be determined by the British government.

serving friendly relations with Somali nationalists while at the same time encouraging the maintenance of peace and stability in the region. Somali nationalism is not a stabilizing factor; on the contrary, it is committed to the revision of the *status quo*. Unrest may develop in the area either as a consequence of the frustration of Somali nationalism or as a result of its success—that is, its success in undermining the Ethiopian position in the Ogaden and in preventing an independent Kenya from establishing its authority in the Northern Frontier Province. In either case, unrest might open the way for the rise of local extremist movements or to outside intervention.

French Policy

France's involvement in the Horn stems from its position in French Somaliland. As mentioned above, France, though its interest in the region has been modified since the nineteenth century, appears determined to preserve its position in strategic Jibuti. In this, French policy conflicts with Somali nationalism.

French and Ethiopian interests coincide in opposing Somali nationalist ambitions in French Somaliland. France and Ethiopia have traditionally maintained good relations, though marred to an extent by the abandonment of Ethiopia to Italy in 1935. A border dispute between French Somaliland and Ethiopia has been settled amicably, and never seriously disturbed relations between them. The question of Ethiopian dissatisfaction with the operation of the Jibuti-Addis Ababa railroad has also been resolved, and an agreement for the transfer of the railway from French to Ethiopian administration was signed in 1959. The visit of Emperor Haile Selassie to Paris in July 1959 afforded an additional opportunity for cementing friendly relations and perhaps discussing the political problems of the Horn.[7]

It is difficult to speculate as to whether the conflict between France and Somali nationalism will become violent, and as to whether Franco-Ethiopian cooperation will be lasting. Though Somali nationalism does not appear to be strong in French Somaliland, its challenge to the *status quo* is being taken seriously. As long as the challenge persists, the coalition of the forces opposing it (the Danakils, Ethiopia, and France) is likely to hold together. However, Ethiopia's dependence upon Jibuti, its periodic claims for the coastal regions, and its aversion to foreign influence along its borders, point to the possibility that at some future date Ethiopia may wish to annex Jibuti. The French response to this likely move and its effect upon French policy toward the region's problems are difficult to predict.

Italy and the Horn

Italy's loss of its African colonies as a result of the Second World War greatly facilitated its adjustment to the new postwar spirit on the colonial question.

In the peace treaty, Italy formally renounced "all right and title to the Italian territorial possessions in Africa." [8] In fact, however, before as well as after the signing of the treaty, the Italian government persistently pressed for the return of the territories. Considerations of domestic politics probably played the largest part in the Italian government's claim. An additional factor seems to have been the ambition to regain the status of an influential world power, and still another was probably the desire to afford protection to Italian economic investments.[9]

In any event, Italy's efforts to regain its formerly influential position in Africa have generally been adjusted to the new postwar conditions there. The Italian administration in the United Nations trust territory of Somalia strove to demonstrate to the world, and particularly to African and Asian nations, Italy's desire and ability to play a constructive role in Africa. From their own prewar experience, and from the experience of other nations after the war, the Italians apparently concluded that the mere possession of an African territory would not afford them the influence to which they aspired. It was necessary to win the good will of the local population, and indeed of other emerging nations in Asia and Africa. Italian policy in Somalia during the ten-year period of trusteeship was strongly motivated by the desire to win this good will. Italy seems to have been largely successful in its policy. The strong anti-Italian sentiments displayed by Somali nationalists prior to the Italian return to the territory have given way to understanding and good will.

After Somalia's attainment of independence in 1960, Italy retained its interest in the territory. Italy takes pride in the way it advanced the country's readiness for independence, and considers itself as bearing a special responsibility for the future of the territory. The continued Italian interest in the Somali Republic is reflected in the provision of financial and technical assistance to the territory, in the continued purchase of the country's banana crop under specially favorable conditions, and in extensive technical training and scholarship aids. This interest may be in part the result of a sentimental attachment to a territory which has been so long an Italian possession. But it probably stems in large measure from the traditional Italian policy of seeking to play the role of a major power. Before the Second World War the reasoning behind the aspiration for such a role was purely nationalistic, but the emphasis has since shifted to considerations of European interests. Italy seems to see itself particularly well suited to act as a bridge, or mediator, between Europe on the one hand and Africa and Asia on the other. Italy's policy in the Horn should be viewed in the general context of the Italian efforts in this sphere.

The unification of Somalia and British Somaliland, of course, occasioned some set-back to Italian influence. This is most noticeable in the cultural field, and in the prospect of the replacement of Italian by English as the principal European language taught in schools. It is possible to discern a slight sensitivity on the Italians' part concerning the decline of their influence in the territory formerly administered by them, while British influence increases. Yet, as this is written, their sensitivity has not developed into overt competition with Britain for influence in the area.

The United States

American involvement in the Horn of Africa was motivated by the same concern which has been the principal preoccupation of

American foreign policy since the Second World War—the containment of Russian and Chinese influence.

Along with Britain, France, and the Soviet Union, the United States participated after the war in the deliberations on the future of the former Italian colonies. In these discussions the Western powers were agreed on the desirability of excluding Soviet influence from the territories in question, but otherwise maintained at various times divergent views about the territories' future. France consistently supported the return of the former colonies to Italy, probably on the assumption that the alternative might be their placement under British administration. The British sought to acquire trusteeship over Somalia, and were willing to change the status of British Somaliland from protectorate to United Nations trusteeship provided the Ogaden were added to this grouping. The United States at first proposed the establishment of an international administration responsible to the U.N. Trusteeship Council. However, in 1948, concern over the domestic political situation in Italy induced the Western Big Three to propose the return of Somalia to Italian administration under United Nations trusteeship.[10]

The United States, in its attitude toward the Somali nationalists, was consistently friendly. This attitude was clearly reflected in the late 1940's in the general tenor of the remarks of the United States representative on the Four Power Commission of Investigation for the former Italian colonies.[11] Subsequently, during the ten-year period when Somalia was under trusteeship, American good will showed itself in the provision of various assistance programs. American aid was increased after the attainment of independence and the creation of the Somali Republic.

While developing friendly relations with the Somalis, the United States has also maintained close relations with Ethiopia. By 1960, however, American policy seemed to have evoked some displeasure on the part of Ethiopia. Total American assistance over the 1953–1959 period amounted to $107 million, not an impressive figure compared to the loan of $100 million which Ethiopia received in

1959 from the Soviet Union. Ethiopians apparently felt that their country had not been accorded sufficient recognition for its contributions to Western causes, such as its participation in the Korean War and the provision of facilities for an American military communications station within their territory.[12] Ethiopian irritation reached a climax as a result of American participation in unspecified diplomatic representations to Ethiopia connected with the abovementioned Lennox-Boyd declaration of February 1959.[13]

On the other hand, the Somalis in the Somali Republic have exhibited resentment over the reluctance of the United States to support their efforts at establishing an army. Like most newly independent states, the Somali Republic views a national army as a symbol of its sovereignty. It is concerned about its military weakness relative to its principal adversary—Ethiopia. The Somalis' appeals for American assistance in establishing and equipping an army did not bear the expected fruit; and their disappointment was greatly augmented by the knowledge that Ethiopia had received substantial American military assistance. The anti-American demonstrations that followed a clash between Somali tribesmen and Ethiopian forces in which the Ethiopians allegedly used equipment furnished by the United States reflected Somali feelings in this respect.[14]

Thus, American interest in the Horn, motivated by the desire to prevent the extension of Russian and Chinese influence there, brought increasing involvement in local regional quarrels. The United States, and indeed the Western powers, found it more difficult to remain dissociated from such quarrels. One of the problems of being a major world power is that both its actions and its abstention from acting are likely to affect regional politics.

The Soviet Union

Thus far, Soviet involvement in the affairs of the Horn has been limited. The Soviet Union participated after the war in the deliberations on the future of the Italian colonies. Its position during the protracted negotiations in the Council of Foreign Ministers and the United Nations was not wholly a consistent one. In 1945, it proposed the principle of individual trusteeship over the Italian colonies by the great powers. The Soviet Union demanded to be assigned trusteeship over Tripolitania and was apparently ready to concede to Great Britain the trusteeship over the former Italian Somaliland. But in 1946 it proposed that the former colonies be placed under joint administration by Italy and one of the Big Four powers. At the same time it expressed strong opposition to the "Bevin Plan" which envisaged the unification, under British administration, of the former Italian colony, British Somaliland, and Ethiopia's Ogaden. Later, during the same session of the Foreign Ministers, probably with an eye to the forthcoming elections in Italy, Foreign Minister Molotov proposed that the former colonies be returned to Italy under trusteeship. Finally, in September 1948 (after the Four Power Commission had made its report) the Russians shifted their position and proposed collective trusteeship by the United Nations.[15]

During these negotiations the Russians did not display particular ambitions with respect to Somaliland, as they had with regard to Tripolitania. Their maneuvering was motivated largely by their desire for the Tripolitania trusteeship and by their interest in the Italian elections. Their 1948 proposal for a collective United Nations trusteeship was probably a last-ditch attempt to win a role in the administration of the territories. It marked also the new trend in Soviet policy of supporting the Asian-Arab anticolonial bloc, which at the time opposed Italian trusteeship.

Still another consideration which may have played a role in changing Soviet policy was the bitter opposition of Ethiopia to the return of Somaliland to Italy. Traditionally, from Tsarist times, the Russians had felt particular sympathy for Ethiopia. In the late nineteenth century there was considerable discussion in Russia about the supposed affinity between the Orthodox Church and Ethiopian Christianity. Russian adventurers, along with those of other nations, were active in Ethiopia, and one of them played a prominent part in the battle of Adowa. Furthermore, the first hospital in Addis Ababa was established by the Russian Red Cross. After the Second World War the interest in Ethiopia was reaffirmed with the dispatch of a Soviet medical team to staff a new hospital. The loan granted to Ethiopia during the emperor's visit to Moscow in 1959 and the renewed contacts between the Ethiopian and Russian churches are other manifestations of continuing Russian interest.[16]

Soviet attitudes toward Somali nationalism were at first not marked by friendliness. In the report of the Four Power Commission in 1948, the Soviet representative inserted a reservation stating that "the programme prepared by the Somali Youth League is a primitive document, has many contradictions and cannot be considered serious."[17] At that time, the Soviet Union still favored the return of the colonies to Italy, while the Somali Youth League opposed it and demanded Four Power trusteeship instead. Russia's critical attitude toward the S.Y.L. was not, however, long lasting, and changed in 1949.

After that the Russians were friendly toward the Somalis but made no special effort to court Somali nationalism. On the question of the Somali-Ethiopian border disputes the Russians have maintained complete neutrality. The Russian attitude in the United Nations during the discussions on the problem might even be described as one of detachment. The training of Somalis in the Soviet Union did not turn out particularly well; some of the Somalis who had been studying in Moscow returned in 1960 prior to the completion of their projected programs, dissatisfied with the treatment they were accorded.

An intensification of Soviet interest in the Somalis was signified in April 1961 when a Soviet governmental delegation visited the Somali Republic. In the following month the Somali Prime Minister traveled to Russia, accompanied by several members of the cabinet and senior officials; the result was an agreement whereby the Somali

Republic was to receive loans and credits amounting to $50 million, and agreements concerning Soviet technical assistance, commercial relations, and cultural cooperation.[18]

At the time of writing it is still unclear whether the Soviet Union has decided to support Somali aspirations for a "Greater Somalia" or whether it is delaying further involvement until it can better assess Somali claims—their effects upon African alignments and their implications for Soviet policy.

The Appearance of China

There have been growing indications since the late 1950's that Communist China is becoming a factor in the politics of the Horn of Africa. There is nothing extraordinary about the establishment of diplomatic relations and the opening of a Chinese embassy in Mogadishu; but Chinese support of certain Somali political groups and the granting of dozens of scholarships to Somali students indicate that China looks at the area with interest.[19]

The Somali political groups supported by China were generally regarded as extremist, and were in opposition to the government of the Somali Republic. As related earlier, Haji Mohamed Hussein, president of the Greater Somalia League, visited Peiping and reportedly received financial support from Chinese sources. So did Abubakr Socorro, the leader of the Somali National Union, and Mahmoud Harbi, the late nationalist leader from French Somaliland. Scholarship grants for study in China have been made available to leaders of the Greater Somalia League and the Somali National Union and have been distributed among the supporters of these parties. In 1961 there were reportedly forty to fifty Somali students in China, a high proportion of them teen-agers because the number of secondary-school graduates qualified to attend universities is still small. The attention directed at the opposition parties has not been viewed favorably by the Somali government. Nevertheless, diplomatic relations between the two countries appeared to be normal.

The indications of Chinese interest, which are conspicuous because

China is a newcomer to the region, raise the question of Chinese motives. The motives are somewhat obscure, and in any case a detailed analysis of Chinese foreign policy is impossible here, but a few aspects of interest can be mentioned.

First it should be pointed out that the Somali Republic is not the only African country to attract Chinese attention. For example, China aided Guinea, offered assistance to the Algerian nationalists, and was reported active in the Congo. Moreover, China has assumed a leading role in promoting the Afro-Asian Solidarity movement. Its activities in the Horn of Africa are to be seen in this context.

Yet the political climate in the Somali Republic is quite different from the political atmosphere in Guinea, Algeria, and the Congo. The bitterness against the West that was so common among the nationalist leaders in those territories is not characteristic of the Somali Republic. As of this writing, relations between the Somalis and the former colonial powers are friendly. The Western powers may be blamed for the problems of French Somaliland, but elsewhere Somali nationalism is not in conflict with Western powers. The Somalis' main adversaries are their African neighbors, the Danakils, Ethiopians, and Kenyans. Therefore, China's gestures in the Horn do not readily fall into the general pattern of its encouragement of political movements inimical to the West.

It is unlikely that China's support for the opposition parties was motivated by any dislike for the policies of the Somali government, which may have a slight pro-Western bias but is essentially neutralist in its orientation. China may consider its replacement as desirable; yet the replacement of neutralist governments by pro-Chinese regimes does not appear to be a major Chinese preoccupation elsewhere in Africa at this time.

Pending further developments of the 1960's, the most plausible explanation for China's interest in the Horn may lie in the region's geographic location. It could be that the interest is the reflection of a tendency to view the shores of the Indian Ocean as being of special importance for China. Whatever the motives of Chinese policy, one would hardly like to suggest that China's increasing involvement in the politics of the Horn of Africa is lacking in significance.

The Voice of Egypt

Egypt has been the most persistent supporter of Somali nationalism. In the early 1960's, radio broadcasts from Cairo were carrying the nationalist message to all parts of the Horn, attacking Britain, France, and Ethiopia as "imperialist powers" engaged in suppression of Somali nationalism. Egypt has served as host to Somali political leaders who for various reasons wished to live abroad. Among the influential politicians who lived in Cairo were Haji Mohamed Hussein, president of the Greater Somalia League, and the late nationalist leader from French Somaliland, Mahmoud Harbi. Egypt has furnished extensive aid to the Somali Republic in a number of fields. Egypt has granted credits for development purposes, has promised to increase its purchases of Somali export goods, and has operated an elaborate educational assistance program consisting of a network of "Egyptian assisted schools" and hundreds of Egyptian teachers. Moreover, hundreds of Somali students have received scholarships to study in Egypt. Perhaps most significant of all, politically, was the military assistance furnished by Egypt for the equipping and training of the new Somali army.[20]

Egyptian involvement stems in part from religious solidarity; but the principal reason behind it is political. Dependence on the Nile has led Egypt throughout its long history to view the sources of the river and its upper reaches as vital to Egyptian security. Most of the Nile waters which reach Egypt originate in the Ethiopian highlands. Egypt has always feared interference with the flow of the river by Ethiopia or other powers controlling its headwaters.

A protagonist of the idea of an Anglo-Egyptian empire over the Nile basin wrote at the end of the last century that "Egypt must always, as matter of self-defence, be in a position to dominate Abyssinia, either directly or indirectly."[21] Similar appreciations of Egyptian interests have marked Egyptian policy toward Ethiopia from time to time, throughout history. In the 1870's, as we have seen, Egypt under the Khedive Ismail sent expeditions to occupy portions of the East African coast, and Egyptian forces penetrated inland as far as Harar. The same Egyptian ruler also made war on Ethiopia. He suffered a costly defeat, but nevertheless retained possession of the coast.[22]

The fear that the Ethiopian government could unilaterally interfere with the flow of the Nile, disregarding Egyptian interests, is probably unjustified. Nevertheless, it appears that Egyptian policy in East Africa continues to be guided by Egypt's traditional concern with the Nile. During the last decade or so, under the leadership of President Nasser, a vigorous policy aimed at increasing Egyptian influence in the countries containing the headwaters of the Nile has been followed.[23] A convenient lever to exert pressure upon the Ethiopian government seems to be the encouragement of Somali nationalism and of the self-consciousness of other Moslem minorities in Ethiopia. Such pressure, though it might not necessarily ensure Ethiopian subservience to the wishes of the Egyptian government, is likely to induce them to give full consideration to Egyptian views on any project which could affect the flow of the Nile.

Egypt's desire to extend its influence in the Horn is probably motivated not only by its interest in the Nile but also by its realization of the area's strategic importance with respect to sea communications between the Red Sea and the Indian Ocean. Possession of the Suez Canal assures control over access to the Red Sea from the north, and it is likely that Egypt is mindful of the possibilities of extending its influence at the southern end of the Red Sea as well.

The Somalis' need for support for the promotion of nationalist goals, as well as the religious connection, render them receptive to Egyptian influence. On the other hand the Somalis have certain traditional antagonisms toward Egypt; they also have their pride and their dislike of foreign interference in their affairs. Those factors are likely to be obstacles to the extension of Egyptian influence.

The Somali ambivalence toward Egypt was reflected in the

assassination of the Egyptian member of the United Nations Advisory Council in 1957, an incident reportedly connected with Egyptian interference in Somali internal politics.[24] Another event illustrating the difficulties inherent in the Somali-Egyptian relationship was the detection of a clandestine shipment of arms reportedly unloaded near Berbera in the Northern Region of the Somali Republic in October 1960. The bulk of the shipment was destined for the supporters of the late Mahmoud Harbi in French Somaliland, but a portion of it found its way to the hands of the Habr Yunis tribe who live in the Northern Region. Egypt was believed to have been involved in the operation, and the incident reportedly irritated the Somali government.

Yet the intractable nature of the issues raised by Somali nationalism, and Egyptian interests in the Nile basin and at the Straits of Bab al Mandab seem to presage continued Egyptian involvement in the affairs of the region.

* * *

Thus, the present involvement of external powers in the Horn of Africa is motivated by their varying interests and also has been encouraged by the weaknesses of the territories in the region and their need for political and economic support. The involvement of foreign powers in the Horn should not be surprising. Yet it is not conducive to peace. It aggravates regional tensions. It may well result in the serious extension of the cold war to the Horn. In such an event, the local struggle in this remote elbow of the continent may make its contribution to the instability of the world.

Chapter 15

Possibilities

NATIONALISM as the frame of reference guiding political behavior coexists in Africa with two alternative frameworks—tribalism and Pan-Africanism. They can be pictured as three concentric circles to which the individual's loyalty may extend—tribalism being the innermost circle, nationalism the intermediate, and Pan-Africanism the outermost. Until recently, the prevalent pattern of political behavior in the Horn was the one circumscribed by the innermost circle of tribal loyalties. We have seen how nationalism now has become the most dynamic factor influencing political behavior in the area. A telling example of this is the readiness with which the political leaders in British Somaliland and the trust territory of Somalia relinquished their dominant positions within their respective territories, and agreed upon unification under conditions bound to bring about a diminution of their political influence.

A further change to Pan-Africanism as the dominant ideology guiding political behavior cannot be precluded. To be sure, there are formidable obstacles to the spread of Pan-Africanism in the Horn. The traditional antagonisms between the Somalis and their neighbors are deeply engrained. Yet gradual change is taking place. Nationalism and Pan-Africanism are allied in the Horn. Political leaders from the Somali Republic, Ethiopia, and Kenya take an active part in Pan-African conferences. In Ethiopia and the Somali Republic, where traditional attitudes of racial superiority over Negro Africans still exist, political leaders are continually propounding Pan-African themes, and are endeavoring to inculcate their followers with an African consciousness. In the long run, the vague Pan-Africanist theories and slogans may affect political behavior as well.

This could help alleviate some of the tensions in the region. But, to expect that the spread of Pan-Africanism would solve the region's problems seems overly optimistic.

Pan-Africanism represents, in a sense, an attempt to anticipate political problems such as have emerged in the Horn. The All African People's Conference held in Accra, Ghana, in December 1958 called for the adjustment of "artificial frontiers drawn by imperialist powers to divide the peoples of Africa, particularly those which cut across ethnic groups and divide people of the same stock." The same conference also declared that "its ultimate objective is the evolution of a Commonwealth of Free African States" and that "as a first step towards the attainment of the broad objective of an African Commonwealth, the independent states of Africa should amalgamate themselves on the basis of geographical contiguity, economic inter-dependence, linguistic and cultural affinity." [1]

When applied to the problems of the Horn, a Pan-Africanist solution would necessitate a three-cornered union (federal or otherwise), encompassing the Somali Republic, Ethiopia, and Kenya. French Somaliland would easily fit into such a union if it took place. But conditions for a union are not favorable. There is a link between the Somali populations of the various territories, but there are no bonds that unite the Somali Republic with the neighboring states. The links that are supposed to form the basis for such a union, enumerated in the resolution cited above—geographic, economic, linguistic, and cultural—are at best tenuous. Geographic contiguity does not necessarily constitute a bond between peoples. It facilitates contacts, but in the Horn of Africa these have produced conflict rather than harmony. A good case for a union could probably be made in reference to large-scale economic development possibilities. But, at present, the territories are not interdependent economically; on the contrary, economic intercourse among them is very limited (the close link between Ethiopia and Jibuti excepted). There is considerable linguistic and cultural affinity among Somalis, Gallas, and Danakils, but not between the Somalis and the dominant elements in Ethiopia and Kenya. On the contrary, the antagonism between the Somalis and their neighbors stems to a considerable extent from their varying cultural backgrounds: Islamic contrasted with Christian, and nomadic pastoralist contrasted with sedentary agricultural. These antagonisms have been intensified by conflicting political aspirations. It is difficult, therefore, to envisage a wide federation in the Horn of Africa.

The obstacles to a more limited federation involving the Somali Republic and Kenya do not seem as formidable. True, there are no special bonds between the two territories. But there is no deep antagonism either. Thus far the question of the Northern Frontier Province of Kenya has not generated much bitterness. Indeed, political leaders in the Somali Republic have indicated on various occasions their interest in joining an East African federation.[2] If such a federation took place, it would help resolve the conflict with respect to the Northern Frontier Province. Yet the more bitter, and politically more explosive, conflict between the Somali nationalists and Ethiopia, and the problem of French Somaliland, would continue to threaten the peace of the region.

Perhaps a better hope for the avoidance of an explosion than Pan-Africanism lies in the political realism of the leaders in the region. They may have to accept the necessity of learning "to live with" the problem unsolved. This is not a satisfactory situation. But the alternative leads to the introduction of the cold war into the region. That would be even less satisfactory, and would carry with it grave dangers to African independence.

Party Abbreviations

G.F.S. — Giovani Fiqarini Somali (Somali Fiqarini Youth)
G.S.L. — Greater Somalia League
H.D.M. — Hizbia Dighil e Mirifle (Party of the Dighil and Mirifle)
H.D.M.S. — Hizbia Dastur Mustaqil Somali (Somali Independent Constitutional Party)
N.P.P.P.P. — Northern Province People's Progressive Party
N.U.F. — National United Front
P.L.G.S. — Partito Liberale Giovani Somali (Liberal Somali Youth Party)
S.D.P. — Somali Democratic Party
S.N.L. — Somali National League
S.N.L.U.S.P. — Somali National League United Somali Party
S.N.S. — Somali National Society
S.N.U. — Somali National Union
S.Y.L. — Somali Youth League
U.A.S. — Unione Africani Somali (Somali African Union)
U.G.B. — Unione Giovani Benadir (Benadir Youth Union)
U.S.P. — United Somali Party

Notes

SHORT TITLES USED OFTEN IN NOTES

Four Power Commission. Council of Foreign Ministers, Four Power Commission of Investigation for the Former Italian Colonies, *Report on Somaliland* (London, 1948).

Lewis, *Peoples.* I. M. Lewis, *Peoples of the Horn of Africa: Somali, Afar, and Saho* (London: International African Institute, 1955).

Lewis, "Political Movements." I. M. Lewis, "Modern Political Movements in Somaliland," *Africa* (London), a two-part article in vol. XXVIII (July 1958, pp. 244–261; October 1958, pp. 344–363).

Lewis, "Somali Lineage." I. M. Lewis, "The Somali Lineage System and the Total Genealogy: An Introduction to Basic Principles of Somali Political Institutions" (Hargeisa, British Somaliland, 1957, mimeographed).

Rapport sur la Somalie (followed by date). Italy, Ministry of Foreign Affairs, *Rapport du Gouvernement Italien à l'Assemblée Générale des Nations Unies sur l'Administration de Tutelle de la Somalie.* These reports were issued annually in Rome during the 1950's. The dates given in the notes refer to the year covered, rather than to the year published.

Somaliland Protectorate (followed by date). Great Britain, Colonial Office, *Somaliland Protectorate,* issued in London, annually until 1950, every two years in the 1950's. The dates given in the notes refer to the years covered, rather than to the year published.

U.N. Advisory Council (followed by date and U.N. document number). *Report of the United Nations Advisory Council for the Trust Territory of Somaliland under Italian Administration,* issued annually in the 1950's.

Chapter 2: The Land and the People

1. This section of the chapter is based mainly on the following sources: *Somaliland Protectorate 1956–1957,* pp. 46–49.

H. Deschamps, *Côte des Somalis* (Paris: Berger-Levrault, 1948), pp. 3–16.

Rapport sur la Somalie 1959, pp. 4–5.

Lewis, *Peoples,* pp. 56–58, 61–62.

2. Rainfall figures, taken mainly from the above sources, are for various periods and for imprecisely defined areas, and are mentioned here only as rough indications of conditions. The Kenya figures, which are four-year averages (1949–1952), are from [R. G. Turnbull], "Annual Report by the Provincial Commissioner on the Northern Province, 1952."

3. *Somaliland Protectorate 1958–1959,* pp. 47–48. For a comprehensive study, see J. D. Clark, *Prehistoric Cultures of the Horn of Africa* (Cambridge: Cambridge University Press, 1954).

4. For the Biblical references to Ophir see I Kings 9:26–28; II Chron. 8:18–19; Job 28. See also A. Gasparro, *La Somalia Italiana nell' Antichita Classica* (Palermo: Tipografia Francesco Lugaro, 1910), pp. 5–15, 19–31, 35–53; and *The Periplus of the Erythraean Sea,* ed. Wilfred H. Schoff (New York: Longmans, Green & Co., 1912), pp. 26, 83–86.

5. For a study of some of these chronicles, see E. Cerulli, *Somalia:* Scritti vari editi ed inediti, vol. I (Rome: A.F.I.S., 1957).

6. *Ibid.,* p. 46; *Somaliland Protectorate 1954–1955,* p. 39; Italy, Ministry of War, *Somalia,* vol. I (Rome, 1938), pp. 31–32.

7. On the history of Mogadishu see Cerulli, vol. I, pp. 115–121, 135–137, 169–170, and on Merca, pp. 91–100. See also Gasparro, pp. 58–72.

8. J. S. Trimingham, *Islam in Ethiopia* (London: Oxford University Press, 1952), p. 209*n*1; Lewis, *Peoples,* p. 13.

9. Lewis, *Peoples,* pp. 13–14; C. Johnston, *Travels in Southern Abyssinia* (London: J. Madden & Co., 1844), vol. I, p. 13; and (on "Zumal") R. E. Drake-Brockman, *British Somaliland* (London: Hurst & Blackett, 1912), p. 71.

10. The term Hamitic is primarily a linguistic one. Its application to racial classification has been subject to some controversy. See C. G. Seligman, *Races of Africa,* third edition (London: Oxford University Press, 1957), pp. 85–112, 140–141; and J. H. Greenberg, "Studies in African Linguistic Classification: IV. Hamito-Semitic," *Southwestern Journal of Anthropology,* vol. 6 (1950), pp. 55–58.

11. I. M. Lewis, "The Galla in Northern Somaliland," *Rassegna di Studi Etiopici* (Rome), vol. XV (1959), pp. 21–38.

12. On the historic tribal migrations see Trimingham, pp. 5–9, 209–210; Lewis, *Peoples,* pp. 45–48; Lewis, "Political Movements," p. 356. For recent examples of the southward movements see: Great Britain, *Correspondence Respecting Abyssinian Raids and Incursions into British Territory* (Cmd. 2553, 1924–1925), pp. 14–15, 24.

13. Lewis, "Political Movements," pp. 344–346; *Rapport sur la Somalie 1959,* p. 5. In the Somali portions of northern Kenya there were 653 Arabs in 1952.

14. *Four Power Commission,* p. 5.

15. Lewis, *Peoples,* pp. 41–42, 126–127 (the quotation is from p. 41); Trimingham, pp. 220–221; Cerulli, vol. II (1959), pp. 115–121.

16. Lewis, *Peoples,* pp. 42–43.

17. *Rapport sur la Somalie 1959,* p. 5. There were 95 Indians and Pakistanis in the Somali portions of northern Kenya in 1952.

18. On the Italians, see *Rapport sur la Somalie 1959,* pp. 5, 211, 221. Most of the British are in the Northern Region of the Somali Republic. In the Somali-inhabited portions of northern Kenya in 1952 there were 21 Europeans, probably all of them government employees.

19. Sources of population figures: *Somaliland Protectorate 1956–1957,* p. 7; *Rapport sur la Somalie 1959,* p. 213; *The Statesman's Yearbook,* 1959 (London: Macmillan & Co., 1959), p. 339. Some urbanization rates in other African territories are: South Africa 23.6 percent (African population only), Northern Rhodesia 18.4 percent, Southern Rhodesia 12.8, Ghana 12.0, Nigeria 9.4, Congo (former Belgian) 8.0. These figures are from G. A. Almond and J. S. Coleman, *The Politics of the Developing Areas* (Princeton: Princeton University Press, 1960), p. 271. The relatively high urbanization rate of the Somalis is difficult to explain. The data are probably misleading to some extent since the population of most of the towns fluctuates seasonally. This, however, is at best only a partial explanation.

20. Lewis, *Peoples,* pp. 15, 17; Lewis, "Political Movements," p. 244; Trimingham, p. 211. These traditions are discussed in some detail in Lewis, "Somali Lineage," pp. 78–89.

21. On the use of the term "tribe," compare J. S. Coleman, *Nigeria, Background to Nationalism* (Berkeley and Los Angeles: University of California Press, 1958), pp. 427–428. On the Children of Israel see Genesis 46:8–27, 49:1–28. For a systematic definition of Somali kinship groups, see I. M. Lewis, "Clanship and Contract in Northern Somaliland," *Africa* (London), July 1959.

22. Lewis, "Political Movements," pp. 245–250. For further details, see Lewis, *Peoples,* pp. 15–18, 31–50.

23. Lewis, "Political Movements," pp. 245–250; Lewis, "Somali Lineage," pp. 15–36. For further information on the different Samaale tribes, see Lewis, *Peoples,* pp. 115–131.

24. Lewis, "Somali Lineage," p. 41.

25. Lewis, *Peoples,* pp. 51–55; Cerulli (our note 5, above), vol. II (1959), pp. 95–99.

26. On the Sab, see Lewis, "Somali Lineage," pp. 25–28, 39–41. On the Samaale, *ibid.,* pp. 30–41; and Lewis, "Political Movements," p. 248.

27. Drake-Brockman (our note 9, above), p. 102.

28. Maj. H. G. C. Swayne, *Seventeen Trips Through Somaliland* (London: Rowland Ward, Ltd., 1900), pp. 16–18; J. Jennings and C. Addison, *With the Abyssinians in Somaliland* (London: Hodder & Stoughton, 1905), pp. 225–230; Drake-Brockman, pp. 86–107; D. Jardine, *The Mad Mullah of Somaliland*

(London: Herbert Jenkins, Ltd., 1923), pp. 23–24; Deschamps (our note 1, above), pp. 35–37.

29. Lewis, *Peoples,* pp. 131–132.

30. Trimingham, *passim;* Lewis, *Peoples,* pp. 172–173.

31. Trimingham, pp. 214–216; Lewis, *Peoples,* pp. 140–154. On the Sufi orders, and on saint worship, see Trimingham, pp. 233–256; I. M. Lewis, "Sufism in Somaliland: A Study in Tribal Islam," *Bulletin of the School of Oriental and African Studies* (London), vol. XVII (1955), part 3, pp. 581–602, and vol. XVIII (1956), part 1, pp. 145–160. On the Mullah, see our Chapter 5.

32. Lewis, *Peoples,* pp. 11–12; Cerulli, vol. II, pp. 171–175; C. R. V. Bell, *The Somali Language* (London: Longmans, Green & Co., 1953), p. 1; A. N. Tucker and M. A. Bryan, *The Non-Bantu Languages of North-Eastern Africa* (London: Oxford University Press for the International African Institute, 1956), pp. 125–126.

33. *Rapport sur la Somalie 1955,* pp. 131–132. On Osmaniya see M. Maino, "L'Alphabeto 'Osmania' in Somalia," *Rassegna di Studi Etiopici* (Rome), vol. X (1951), pp. 108–121; and I. M. Lewis, "The Gadabursi Somali Script," *Bulletin of the School of Oriental and African Studies,* vol. XXI (February 1958). See also Martino M. Moreno, *Il Somalo della Somalia* (Rome: Istituto Poligrafico dello Stato, 1955), pp. 290–297; United Nations Visiting Mission to Trust Territories in East Africa, 1957, *Report on Somaliland under Italian Administration* (U.N. Doc. T/1344), p. 78; A. A. Castagno, "Somalia," *International Conciliation,* no. 522 (March 1959), pp. 370–372.

Chapter 3: The Somali Nation

1. See Rupert Emerson, *From Empire to Nation* (Cambridge: Harvard University Press, 1960), pp. 89–187. See also *Nationalism,* report by a study group of the Royal Institute for International Affairs (London: Oxford University Press, 1939), p. xx.

2. Lewis, *Peoples,* pp. 127–128; E. S. Pankhurst, *Ex-Italian Somaliland* (New York: Philosophical Library, 1951), pp. 72–81.

3. Lieut. Col. H. Moyse-Bartlett, *The King's African Rifles* (Aldershot: Gale & Polden, 1956), pp. 577–578; Lewis, "Political Movements," p. 254.

4. For a systematic study of the role of communications in the formation of communities and nations, see K. W. Deutsch, *Nationalism and Social Communication* (Cambridge, Mass., and New York: M.I.T. and John Wiley & Sons, 1953).

5. See J. A. Hunt, *A General Survey of the Somaliland Protectorate 1944–1950* (London: Crown Agents for the Colonies, 1951), pp. 156–158.

6. A particularly serious clash occurred in December 1957. See *U.N. Advisory Council 1957–58* (U.N. Doc. T/1372), par. 32–33. One of the basic aims of the Somali Youth League (S.Y.L.) was to put an end to tribal feuds; see *Four Power Commission,* sec. II, chap. 4, app. P.

CHAPTER 4: THE PARTITION OF THE HORN

1. F. L. James, *The Unknown Horn of Africa* (London: George Philip & Son, 1888), pp. 2–3; R. F. Burton, *First Footsteps in East Africa* (London: Longman, Brown, Green & Longmans, 1856), pp. xxxiv–xxxv.

2. The British explorations are reported in the *Journal of the Royal Geographical Society* (London), as follows. Vol. XII (1842): W. C. Barker, "Extract Report on the Probable Geographical Position of Harar; with Some Information Relative to the Various Tribes in the Vicinity." Vol. XIV (1844): "Extract from a Journal by Lieut. W. Christopher, Commanding the H. C. Brig of War 'Tigris,' on the East Coast of Africa." Vol. XVIII (1848): W. C. Barker, "On Eastern Africa," and C. J. Cruttenden, "On Eastern Africa" (two articles with the same title). Vol. XIX (1849): C. J. Cruttenden, "Memoir on the Western or Edoor Tribes, Inhabiting the Somali Coast of Northeast Africa." Further accounts of these early explorations are in *Transactions of the Bombay Geographical Society,* vols. I–XIX, 1836–1873, *passim.*

3. G. Révoil, *Voyages au Cap des Aromates* (Paris: E. Dentu, 1880), pp. vii–viii.

4. Quotation is from Burton's *First Footsteps,* pp. xxv–xxvi. For the Berbera adventure see pp. 441–458. For the Harar trip see not only this book but also Burton's "Narrative on a Trip to Harar," *Journal of the Royal Geographical Society,* vol. XXV (1855).

5. For Speke's diary see Burton, *First Footsteps,* pp. 461–507.

6. G. Révoil, *La Vallée du Darror, Voyage aux Pays Çomalis* (Paris: Challamel aîné, 1882). For an account of an earlier expedition by Révoil, to the Indian Ocean Coast, see his *Voyages au Cap,* cited above. On Paulitschke's expedition, see P. Paulitschke, *Harar: Forschungsreise nach den Somal- und Galla-Ländern Ost-Afrikas* (Leipzig: F. A. Brockhaus, 1888).

7. James, pp. 5–7.

8. *A Complete Collection of the Treaties and Conventions at the Present Subsisting between Great Britain and Foreign Powers,* ed. Sir Edward Hertslet, vol. XIII (London: Butterworths, 1877), pp. 5–6.

9. Treaty with the Sultan of Tajura, *ibid.,* pp. 6–8; with the Governor of Zeila, pp. 8–9; on the slave trade, pp. 9–10; and with the Habr Awal, pp. 10–12. On the punitive measures taken in the Berbera affair, see Burton, *First Footsteps,* pp. xxxvi–xxxvii.

10. W. L. Langer, *The Diplomacy of Imperialism,* second edition (New York: Alfred A. Knopf, 1956), p. 102.

11. *The Map of Africa by Treaty,* third edition, ed. Sir Edward Hertslet (London: H.M.S.O., 1909), vol. II, pp. 614–617; M. F. Shukry, *Equatoria under Egyptian Rule, the Unpublished Correspondence of Col. (afterwards Maj. Gen.) C. G. Gordon with Ismail the Khedive of Egypt and the Sudan during 1874–1876* (Cairo: Cairo University Press, 1953), pp. 69–72; G. Douin, *Histoire du Règne du Khédive Ismail,* vol. III, part 3 (Cairo: Société Royale de Géographie d'Egypte, 1941), pp. 547–602.

12. Hertslet, *Complete Collection of Treaties,* vol. XVIII (London: Butterworths, 1893), pp. 359–361; Shukry, just cited, pp. 87–93.

13. See R. Coupland, *The Exploitation of East Africa, 1856–1890, The Slave Trade and the Scramble* (London: Faber & Faber, 1939), pp. 271–299; Shukry, pp. 63–93, 300–302.

14. Douin, as cited, pp. 602–627; The Earl of Cromer, *Modern Egypt,* vol. II (London: Macmillan & Co., 1908), pp. 49–53. See also P. Paulitschke, "Le Harrar sous l'administration égyptienne," *Bulletin de la Société Khédiviale de Géographie,* IIe serie, no. 10 (Cairo, 1887), pp. 575–576.

15. *British and Foreign State Papers,* vol. 76, 1884–1885 (London: William Ridgway, 1892), pp. 674–677, 681.

16. *Ibid.,* pp. 678–684. Italy, besides expanding its holdings around Assab, tried unsuccessfully to obtain British consent for the dispatch of an Italian garrison to Zeila in order to establish joint Anglo-Italian occupation. See F. Salata, *Il Nodo di Gibuti* (Milan: Istituto per gli studi di Politica Internazionale, 1939), pp. 12–16.

17. *British and Foreign State Papers,* vol. 76, pp. 101–107. The treaties also contained provisions regarding commerce and the slave trade. In addition, the treaties with the Habr Toljala and Habr Gerhajis also provided for the protection of wrecks of vessels.

18. *Ibid.,* vol. 77, 1885–1886 (London: William Ridgway, 1893), pp. 1263–1269.

19. *Ibid.,* vol. 81, 1888–1889 (London: H.M.S.O., no date), p. 936.

20. C. E. X. Rochet d'Hericourt, *Second Voyage sur les deux rives de la mer Rouge dans les pays des Adels et le Royaume de Choa* (Paris: Arthus Bertrand, 1846); for the text of the treaty, signed on June 17, 1843, see pp. 375–378. See also Alexandre de Clercq, *Recueil des Traités de la France,* vol. XV (Paris: A. Durand et Pedone-Lauriel, 1888), pp. 340–341; and G. Hantoux and A. Martineau, *Histoire des Colonies Françaises,* tome IV (Paris: Plon, 1931), p. 581. Shoa, formerly a semi-independent kingdom, now is a province of Ethiopia.

21. Hantoux and Martineau, p. 581; G. Angoulvant and S. Vigneras, *Djibouti, Mer Rouge, Abyssinie* (Paris: J. Andre, 1902), pp. 9–11; E. Rouard de Card, *Les Possessions Françaises de la Côte Orientale d'Afrique,* Extrait de la *Revue Générale de Droit International Public* (Paris: A. Pedone, 1899), pp. 2, 3–5; Comte Stanislas Russel, *Une Mission en Abyssinie et dans la Mer Rouge* (Paris: E. Plon, Nourrit et Cie., 1884), pp. 196, 216–218, 263–266, 281.

22. Alexandre de Clercq, vol. XIV, part 2 (Paris, 1886), pp. 513–516; Hertslet, *Map of Africa by Treaty* (our note 11, above), vol. II, pp. 628–629.

23. For details about de Rivoyre's activity, see the pamphlet published by the Société des Etudes Coloniales et Maritimes, *Les Comptoirs Français de l'Afrique Orientale* (Paris: Morris Père et Fils, 1879). For a French official announcement dated Dec. 25, 1880, about the great risks involved in undertaking any private activity at Obock, see Hertslet, *Map of Africa by Treaty,*

vol. II, pp. 629–630. See also Hantoux and Martineau, vol. IV, p. 582; H. Deschamps, *Côte des Somalis* (Paris: Berger-Levrault, 1948), p. 43; Angoulvant and Vigneras, pp. 16–18.

24. For the text of the treaties, see Hertslet, *Map of Africa by Treaty,* vol. II, pp. 630–633, 726–728. See also Alexandre de Clercq, vol. XIV, pp. 348–349, 418–419, 423, 429–430; E. Rouard de Card, *Les Traités de Protectorat Conclus par la France en Afrique, 1870–1895* (Paris: A. Durand et Pedone-Lauriel, 1897), pp. 38–43, 162–164; Deschamps, just cited, pp. 45–46.

25. Italy, Ministry of War, *Somalia* (Rome, 1938), pp. 15–28, 183–188; Raffaele Ciasca, *Storia coloniale dell' Italia contemporanea* (Milan: Ulrico Hoepli, 1938), pp. 232–233. See also C. Negri, *La grandezza italiana* (Turin: Tip. Paravia e comp., 1864); Italy, Ministry of Foreign Affairs, *l'Italia in Africa,* vol. II (Rome: Istituto Poligrafico dello Stato, 1955), pp. 35–38.

26. Ciasca, just cited, p. 235; Italy, Ministry of War, *Somalia,* pp. 47–48, 200–201; C. Cesari, *La Somalia Italiana* (Rome: Fratelli Palombi, 1934), pp. 39–56.

27. On the Cecchi mission and subsequent events, see Ciasca, pp. 235–237; Coupland (our note 13, above), pp. 444–445; Italy, Ministry of War, *Somalia,* pp. 49–50, 52–54, and (for text of Cecchi's reports on the 1885 treaty negotiations) 203–216. For text of treaty see *British and Foreign State Papers,* vol. 76, pp. 269–273. For text of Anglo-German agreement see Hertslet, *Map of Africa by Treaty,* vol. III, pp. 874–876, 882–887. On the 1888 incident see also G. Hamilton, *Princes of Zinj* (London: Hutchinson, 1957), pp. 191–192.

28. Ciasca, pp. 237–238; Italy, Ministry of War, *Somalia,* p. 54; Hertslet, *Map of Africa by Treaty,* vol. I, pp. 362–364, vol. III, pp. 1088–1093, 1125.

29. For treaties with Obbia and Mijertain, see *British and Foreign State Papers,* vol. 81, pp. 132–134. After the treaty with the Sultan of Mijertain, the boundaries of the protectorate were amended and the powers notified on May 20, 1889. See Hertslet, *Map of Africa by Treaty,* vol. III, pp. 1123–1124. Also: Italy, Ministry of War, *Somalia,* pp. 54–56; and Ciasca, pp. 238–239.

30. Hertslet, *Map of Africa by Treaty,* vol. III, pp. 954–960, 1094–1100.

31. For details on the administrations of the territory in these early years, mentioned in the last four paragraphs, see Italy, Ministry of Foreign Affairs, *l'Italia in Africa,* vol. II, appendix, table IV. On the Filonardi company, see Italy, Ministry of War, *Somalia,* pp. 63–91; the same book, *passim,* discusses later developments. On the period of the Commercial Company of Benadir, see Cesari (our note 26, above), pp. 74–86. For the commission of inquiry's report, see *Le Questioni del Benadir: Atti e Relazione dei Commissari della Societa Signori Gustavo Chiesi e Avv. Ernesto Travelli* (Milan: P. B. Bellini, 1904). For text of convention between Italian government and Commercial Company of Benadir, and for later developments, see Hertslet, *Map of Africa by Treaty,* vol. III, pp. 1104–1107, 1214. On the unrest, see Ciasca, pp. 275–283. Considerable information, though presented with a strong anti-Italian bias, can be found in E. Sylvia Pankhurst's *Ex-Italian Somaliland* (New York:

Philosophical Library, 1951), pp. 38–76. For the story of the Mullah, see our Chapter 5.

32. P. L. McDermott, *British East Africa or IBEA: A History of the Formation and Work of the Imperial British East Africa Company,* second edition (London: Chapman & Hall, 1895), p. 3.

33. *Ibid.,* pp. 10–12; Hertslet, *Map of Africa by Treaty,* vol. I, pp. 339–362. For the treaty dividing the region into British and German spheres of influence see *British and Foreign State Papers,* vol. 77, p. 1130.

34. Hertslet, *Map of Africa by Treaty,* vol. I, pp. 380–381.

35. See F. D. Lugard, *The Rise of Our East African Empire,* vol. II (Edinburgh and London: William Blackwood & Sons, 1893), pp. 563–594, 610–611.

36. On the Juba border, see Hertslet, *Map of Africa by Treaty,* vol. III, p. 948. The border was subsequently amended with the cession of Jubaland to Italy in 1924 (see Cmd. 2194 and 2427). On the border with Ethiopia see Cmd. 4318.

37. See Menelik's circular note to the European sovereigns dated April 1891, reproduced in Clement de la Jonquière, *Les Italiens en Erythrée* (Paris: Henri Charles-Lavauzelle, 1897), pp. 145–146.

38. For an exposition of Ethiopian objectives by Ras Makonnen, see H. G. C. Swayne, *Seventeen Trips Through Somaliland,* second edition (London: Rowland Ward, Ltd., 1900), pp. 172–173.

39. D. Mathew, *Ethiopia: The Study of a Polity 1540–1935* (London: Eyre & Spottiswoode, 1947), pp. 242–243; Guebre Selassie, *Chronique de Menelik II, Roi des Rois d'Ethiopie,* vol. I (Paris: Maisonneuve frères, 1930), pp. 242–245, 307*n*3. For contemporary accounts, see Swayne, *passim;* and P. Paulitschke, *Harar: Forschungsreise nach den Somal- und Galla-Ländern Ost-Afrikas* (Leipzig: F. A. Brockhaus, 1888).

40. Swayne, pp. 115–176, 214–215, and *passim.*

Chapter 5: Two Heroes of Somali Nationalism

1. On the foregoing Ethiopian-versus-Moslem campaigns, see J. S. Trimingham, *Islam in Ethiopia* (London: Oxford University Press, 1952), pp. 79–81, 85–86, 88–89. See also A. H. M. Jones and E. Monroe, *A History of Ethiopia* (Oxford: Clarendon Press, 1955), pp. 55–56, 81–85. For contemporary chroniclers' accounts see Sahab ad-din Ahmad, trans. by P. Paulitschke, *Futuh el Habacha, des Conquêtes faites en Abyssinie au XVI*[e] *siècle par L'Imam Mohammed Ahmad dit Gragne* (Paris: Librairie Emile Bouillon, 1898) and W. E. Conzeleman, *Chronique de Galawdewos* (Paris: Librairie Emile Bouillon, 1895).

2. Lewis, "Political Movements," p. 359; R. L. Hess, "Italian Colonial Policy in Somalia" (diss., Yale University, 1958), pp. 28, 287; H. Jenny, *Äthiopien, Land im Aufbruch* (Stuttgart: Deutsche Verlags-Anstalt, 1957), pp. 34–35.

3. D. Jardine, *The Mad Mullah of Somaliland* (London: Herbert Jenkins, Ltd., 1923), pp. 36–38. See also R. E. Drake-Brockman, *British Somaliland*

(London: Hurst & Blackett, 1912), pp. 175–178; Angus Hamilton, *Somaliland* (London: Hutchinson & Co., 1911), pp. 48–49. On the mystic orders in Islam see Trimingham, pp. 233–256, and I. M. Lewis, "Sufism in Somaliland: A Study in Tribal Islam," *Bulletin of the School of Oriental and African Studies* (London), vol. XVII (1955), pp. 581–602, and vol. XVIII (1956), pp. 145–160.

4. Jardine, pp. 38–40; Great Britain, War Office, *Official History of the Operations in Somaliland, 1901–04* (London: H.M.S.O., 1907), vol. I, pp. 48–49 (hereafter cited as *Official History*); Hamilton, pp. 49–50.

5. Jardine, pp. 40–47; *Official History,* vol. I, pp. 49–51; Hamilton, pp. 50–53.

6. Jardine, pp. 81–86; Hamilton, pp. 89–101; *Official History,* vol. I, pp. 104–108.

7. Jardine, pp. 57–155; *Official History,* vol. I, pp. 49–265; Lieut. Col. H. Moyse-Bartlett, *The King's African Rifles* (Aldershot: Gale & Polden, 1956), pp. 160–190. Angus Hamilton was the Reuter correspondent at the scene during these operations. For his account, see Hamilton, pp. 68–343. For an account of the Ethiopian expedition cooperating with the fourth British expedition, see Maj. J. W. Jennings and C. Addison, *With the Abyssinians in Somaliland* (London: Hodder & Stoughton, 1905).

8. For text of treaty see Jardine, pp. 156–158.

9. Jardine, pp. 156–196; and *Somaliland Protectorate 1956–57,* p. 52.

10. Jardine, pp. 197–229; Moyse-Bartlett, pp. 190–194. See also H. F. P. Battersby, *Richard Corfield of Somaliland* (London: Edward Arnold, 1914).

11. Jardine, pp. 230–308; Moyse-Bartlett, pp. 419–433.

12. Jardine (for Eidagalla appeal, p. 48; Burao declaration, p. 42).

13. Jardine (the Mullah's statement, p. 211; for a translation of Salih's epistle repudiating the Mullah, pp. 184–185).

14. For the 1912 letter see Jardine, p. 209; the same is stated more apologetically in other letters (see *ibid.,* pp. 169–170, 211). On the Dervishes' behavior and motives, see Jardine, pp. 50, 52–53, 71; *Official History,* vol. I, p. 106; and Trimingham, p. 215.

15. Jardine, pp. 48–49.

16. For an example of the modern nationalists' attitude on tribalism, see the 1947 constitution of the Somali Youth League, reproduced in *Four Power Commission,* part II, chap. 4, app. 4. See also Lewis, "Political Movements," pp. 358–359; and Trimingham, p. 134.

17. Jardine, pp. 165–166. In other letters the term Somali is used disparagingly (see *ibid.,* pp. 213–215).

18. See Italy, Ministry of War, *Somalia,* vol. I (Rome, 1938), pp. 94–179; and C. Cesari, *La Somalia Italiana* (Rome: Fratelli Palombi, 1935), pp. 94–145. For a detailed account of the effect of the rebellion on Italian Somaliland, see F. S. Caroselli, *Ferro e Fuoco in Somalia* (Rome: Sindicato Italiano Arti Grafichi, 1931).

19. Jardine, p. 313.

Chapter 6: The Development of National Consciousness

1. See P. Rondot, *Les Forces Religieuses et la Vie Politique: l'Islam* (Paris: Université de Paris, Institute d'Etudes Politiques, 1957), p. 243 and *passim.*

2. Lord Hailey, *An African Survey,* revised 1956 (London: Oxford University Press, 1957), pp. 499–500.

3. For text of agreement see *The Map of Africa by Treaty,* ed. Sir Edward Hertslet, third edition (London: H.M.S.O., 1909), vol. II, pp. 423–429. The grazing rights of the British Somaliland tribes were reaffirmed in 1938, after the Italian occupation of Ethiopia. See Great Britain, *Papers Concerning Grazing Rights and Transit Traffic in British Somaliland* (London: H.M.S.O., 1938), Cmd. 5775.

4. Lieut.-Col. E. H. M. Clifford, "The British Somaliland-Ethiopia Boundary," *The Geographical Journal* (London), vol. 87 (1936), p. 296.

5. *Parliamentary Debates,* House of Commons, fifth series, vol. 289, cols. 488–489 (May 3, 1934).

6. Somaliland Protectorate, *Education Department Triennial Survey, 1955–1957,* pp. 2–4.

7. The British government maintained that Haji Farah Omar's right to speak on behalf of the Somali population had been repudiated by "responsible leaders." See *Parliamentary Debates,* House of Commons, fifth series, vol. 293, cols. 1019–1020 (Nov. 7, 1934).

8. For much of the information contained in the preceding paragraphs, I am indebted to the Hon. Michael Mariano.

9. Lieut.-Col. H. Moyse-Bartlett, *The King's African Rifles* (Aldershot: Gale & Polden, 1956), p. 434.

10. For detailed accounts of the Jubaland disturbances, 1893–1925, see *ibid.,* pp. 111–120, 215–227, 434–439; and W. Lloyd-Jones, *K.A.R.* (London: Arrowsmith, 1926), pp. 72–74, 122–124, 215–220.

11. The foremost authority on this subject is Sir Richard Turnbull. It is to be hoped that the valuable information he gathered during the many years he spent administering Somali areas will be published. For an illuminating attempt to reconstruct the history of Somali expansion, see I. M. Lewis, "The Somali Conquest of the Horn of Africa," *Journal of African History* (London), vol. I, no. 2 (1960). See also British Colonial Office, *Kenya Land Commission, Evidence and Memoranda* (London: H.S.M.O., 1934), vol. II, pp. 1649–1652.

12. Quoted in Lloyd-Jones, *K.A.R.,* p. 123*n*1. The advice was given, presumably in 1919, by an unnamed senior K.A.R. officer to another British officer.

13. H. Deschamps, *Côte des Somalis* (Paris: Berger-Levrault, 1948), p. 47.

14. *Ibid.,* pp. 49, 81–82.

15. For detailed accounts see Italy, Ministry of War, *Somalia,* vol. I (Rome, 1938); C. Cesari, *La Somalia Italiana* (Rome: Fratelli Palombi, 1935), pp. 87–178.

16. For details on the formation of local forces, see Cesari, pp. 197–207.

17. R. Lefevre, *Politica Somala* (Bologna: Licinio Capelli, 1933), pp. 31–32;

and M. Perham, *The Government of Ethiopia* (New York: Oxford University Press, 1948), p. 233. Forced labor was a common practice in Africa. See Hailey (our note 2, above), pp. 1357–1358, 1362–1364. Bitter memories of prewar Italian practices still linger on; see J. Buchholzer, *The Horn of Africa* (London: Angus and Robertson, 1959), pp. 183–184.

18. *Four Power Commission,* p. 106. For Somali comments on the subject see the testimony of the Somali Youth League in *ibid.,* sec. II, chap. 4, app. A, p. 9.

19. For an account of this competition by Italian Foreign Minister Tittoni, see C. Rossetti, *Storia Diplomatica dell' Etiopia* (Turin: S.T.E.N., 1910), pp. 409–410.

20. Italy, Comando della forze armate della Somalia, *La Guerra Italo-Etiopica: Fronte Sud* (Addis Ababa: Governo Generale dell' A.O.I., 1937), vol. I, pp. 106–113 and *passim.* See also Marshal Emilio de Bono, *Anno XIIII: The Conquest of an Empire* (London: Cresset Press, 1937); and Marshal R. Graziani, *Il Fronte Sud* (Milan: A. Mondadori, 1938).

For information about the Italian penetration of the Ogaden and the Wal-Wal incident see: Maj. R. Cimmaruta, *Ual-Ual* (Milan: A. Mondadori, 1936). Cimmaruta was in command of the Italian forces at Wal-Wal at the time of the incident. Abundant information is available also in A. de la Pradelle, *Le Conflit Italo-Ethiopien* (Paris: Les Editions Internationales, 1936), pp. 147–610. Professor de la Pradelle was the Ethiopian Representative on the Conciliation and Arbitration Commission created after the incident.

For an account of the Ogaden fighting, see H. de Monfreid, *Les Guerriers de l'Ogaden* (Paris: Gallimard, 1936). That author was a French adventurer who lived many years in French Somaliland and Ethiopia, and covered the campaign from the Italian side for the *Paris Soir.* An excellent book by a journalist covering the campaign from the Ethiopian side was written by George Steer, correspondent for *The Times* (London); see his *Caesar in Abyssinia* (Boston: Little, Brown, 1937).

21. A. A. Castagno, "Somalia," *International Conciliation,* no. 522 (March 1959), p. 343.

22. *Four Power Commission,* sec. III, appendices. Although some of the data supplied by the Chamber of Commerce to the Four Power Commission tended to exaggerate Italian achievements, it nevertheless indicated a higher degree of economic development than elsewhere in the Horn, with the possible exception of Jibuti. See also Lefevre, pp. 165–221.

23. *Four Power Commission,* p. 96 and sec. IV, chap. 3, appendix.

24. Maj. H. G. C. Swayne, *Seventeen Trips Through Somaliland,* third edition (London: Rowland Ward, Ltd., 1903), pp. vii–viii and *passim.* See also Capt. J. C. Francis, *Three Months Leave in Somali Land* (London: R. H. Porter, 1895), pp. 36, 37, 65, 86.

25. W. J. Jennings and C. Addison, *With the Abyssinians in Somaliland*

(London: Hodder & Stoughton, 1905), pp. 162–163, 190–191, 231–232, 254–255.

26. A. H. M. Jones and E. Monroe, *A History of Ethiopia* (Oxford: Clarendon Press, 1955), pp. 153–159; Perham, pp. 60–62; J. S. Trimingham, *Islam in Ethiopia* (London: Oxford University Press, 1952), pp. 129–131; C. Sanford, *The Lion of Judah Hath Prevailed* (New York: Macmillan & Co., 1955), pp. 37–40. Lij Yasu was captured in 1921, and died in 1935.

27. Steer, pp. 16–18, 87, 109, and *passim;* Perham, pp. 336–338. See also de la Pradelle, Cimmaruta, de Monfreid, Graziani, all cited in our note 20, above.

28. For further details on these operations, see Great Britain, Ministry of Information, *The Abyssinian Campaigns* (London: H.M.S.O., 1942). A number of good books were written by war correspondents and others who participated in the fighting. See: C. Birkby, *It's a Long Way to Addis* (London: Frederick Muller, Ltd., 1942); K. Gandar Dower, *Abyssinian Patchwork* (London: Frederick Muller, Ltd., 1949); J. F. MacDonald, *Abyssinian Adventure* (London: Cassel & Co., 1957).

29. For further details on the Somalis' participation in the military operations, see Moyse-Bartlett (our note 9, above), pp. 492, 494–503, 522*n*1, 577–578, 663–672, 682. On their mass desertion from the Italian army, see K. Gandar Dower, just cited, pp. 249–253.

30. On the Reserved Area see Lord Rennell of Rodd, *British Military Administration of Occupied Territories in Africa, 1941–1947* (London: H.M.S.O., 1948), pp. 194–207, 493–497; and *Four Power Commission,* sec. II, chap. 6, app. A, p. 8. See also our Chapter 13, including notes 9–11.

31. Quotation is from the Atlantic Charter, Aug. 14, 1941.

32. *Parliamentary Debates,* House of Commons, fifth series, vol. 423, cols. 1840–1841.

33. *Four Power Commission,* sec. II, chap. 4, app. A, p. 15. See also Douglas Collins, *A Tear for Somalia* (London: Jarrolds, 1960), p. 164.

34. See "Treaty of Peace with Italy," annex XI, *United Nations Treaty Series,* vol. 49, I, no. 747, pp. 214–215 in English text.

35. *Four Power Commission,* sec. II, chap. 4, app. A, pp. 10–18.

36. *Somaliland Protectorate 1949,* p. 3.

37. On the dissemination of information about the United Nations, see United Nations Visiting Mission to Trust Territories in East Africa, 1951, *Report on Somaliland under Italian Administration* (U.N. Doc. T/1033), pars. 325–333; U.N. Visiting Mission, 1954, *Report* (U.N. Doc. T/1200), pars. 445–447; and annual reports of the United Nations Advisory Council in Mogadishu.

38. Lewis, "Political Movements," pp. 348, 356*n*1, 360–361. See also the articles by S. Apolonio and A. A. Castagno in the periodical *Africa Special Report,* December 1958, pp. 10, 14; and an article in *New York Times,* June 13, 1956, p. 1.

39. Earlier figures from *Four Power Commission* (as last cited), pp. 96–97;

and *Somaliland Protectorate 1948,* p. 14. Later figures from *Rapport sur la Somalie 1956,* p. 258; and *Somaliland Protectorate 1956–1957,* p. 23.

40. Lewis, "Political Movements," pp. 359–360.

CHAPTER 7: NATIONALISM AND POLITICS IN THE TRUST TERRITORY OF SOMALIA

1. For example, the quotas allocated to provinces of the trust territory of Somalia for the 1960 recruitment into the police force were filled without difficulty in all provinces except in Upper Juba (predominantly Rahanwein). For some figures on tribal proportions in government service, see Lewis, "Political Movements," p. 355*n*3. See also A. A. Castagno, "The Republic of Somalia," *Africa Special Report,* July 1960, p. 9.

2. The British Military Administration's role was referred to recently by F. M. Thomas, who had served with the Administration in Somalia during the war, during a discussion at the Thirteenth Conference of the Rhodes-Livingstone Institute for Social Research. Commenting on an observation by Dr. I. M. Lewis that "there had been real political progress in Somalia and that there was a growing national consciousness," Thomas said that "if that were so, then it had been worth starting the Youth Club even though this had called down on him the wrath of many other administrators including the late Governor of British Somaliland, Sir Gerald Reece." See *From Tribal Rule to Modern Government,* the Thirteenth Conference proceedings of the Rhodes-Livingstone Institute for Social Research, ed. Raymond Apthorpe (Lusaka, 1959), pp. 169–170. For some additional information see I. M. Lewis, *A Pastoral Democracy* (London: Oxford University Press, 1961), pp. 305–306.

3. See *Four Power Commission,* report and appendices.

4. For further details on the constitutional progress see *Rapport sur la Somalie 1959,* pp. 22–30; also United Nations Visiting Mission to Trust Territories in East Africa, 1951, *Report on Somaliland under Italian Administration* (U.N. Doc. T/1033), pars. 64–88; *U.N. Advisory Council 1956–57* (U.N. Doc. T/1311), pars. 52–64.

On the municipal elections see U.N. Visiting Mission, 1954, *Report,* pars. 31–33; and *U.N. Advisory Council 1958–59* (U.N. Doc. T/1444), pars. 82–96 and annex I.

For details of the general elections see *U.N. Advisory Council 1955–56* (U.N. Doc. T/1245), pars. 25–26; *U.N. Advisory Council 1958–59* (U.N. Doc. T/1444), pars. 103–142 and annexes II–V. See also A. A. Castagno, "Somalia," *International Conciliation,* no. 522 (March 1959), p. 358. See also notes to our Table 3.

5. See articles 15 and 19 of the "Law on Political Elections," in *U.N. Advisory Council 1958–59* (U.N. Doc. T/1444), annex III.

6. The group's point of view was ably presented at the United Nations Trusteeship Council by Abdirazaq Haji Hussein. See the Council's *Official Records,* 24th session, 1022nd meeting, July 22, 1959. See also U.N. Docs. T/1473 and T/PET.11/L.43.

7. *Four Power Commission,* sec. II, chap. 4, app. P, p. 3. For Haji Mohamed Hussein's testimony, see *ibid.,* app. A, p. 15.

8. *Ibid.,* app. R.

9. *Ibid.,* app. N, p. 9. The same is reflected also in other parts of the testimony.

10. Quoted by Castagno (our note 4, above), p. 359. See also U.N. Doc. T/PET.11/583 and *U.N. Advisory Council 1957–58* (U.N. Doc. T/1372), par. 61.

11. *Rapport sur la Somalie 1959,* p. 168.

12. *Ibid.,* p. 167.

13. *Rapport sur la Somalie 1955,* pp. 131–132. On Osmaniya see M. Maino, "L'Alphabeto 'Osmania' in Somalia," *Rassegna di Studi Etiopici* (Rome), vol. X (1951), pp. 108–121. See also Martino M. Moreno, *Il Somalo della Somalia* (Rome: Istituto Poligrafico dello Stato, 1955), pp. 290–297.

14. The most recent committee was appointed in October 1960, and was supposed to submit its report by March 1961. See *Corriere della Somalia* (Mogadishu), Oct. 27, 1960. See also Castagno (our note 4, above), pp. 370–372.

Chapter 8: Nationalism and Politics in British Somaliland

1. For a vivid though fictional account of policy considerations regarding Somaliland, see Margery Perham's novel, *Major Dane's Garden* (Boston: Houghton Mifflin, 1926).

2. Lewis, "Political Movements," pp. 348–349.

3. *Somaliland Protectorate 1949,* p. 3; *Somaliland Protectorate 1950–1951,* p. 3.

4. Quoted in *Africa Digest* (London), vol. III, no. 7 (March–April 1956), p. 11. On the spread of political interest, see Lewis, "Political Movements," p. 351*n*.

5. Lewis, "Political Movements," p. 255.

6. *Somaliland Protectorate 1948,* p. 32.

7. *Parliamentary Debates,* House of Commons, fifth series, vol. 596, col. 532 (Nov. 27, 1958); *Commonwealth Survey* (London), vol. 5, no. 8 (April 14, 1959), pp. 355–356; *Somaliland Protectorate 1958–1959,* p. 6. See also *Report of the Commission of Inquiry into Unofficial Representation on the Legislative Council,* Hargeisa, June 1958 (mimeo.).

8. *Commonwealth Survey,* vol. 5, no. 16 (Aug. 4, 1959), pp. 702–703; vol. 6, no. 6 (March 15, 1960), pp. 271–273; vol. 6, no. 9 (April 26, 1960), pp. 402–404; British Colonial Office, *Report of the Somaliland Protectorate Constitutional Conference* (London: H.M.S.O., 1960), Cmd. 1044.

Chapter 9: The Problems and Politics of Unification

1. Policy statement issued by the Secretary of State for the Colonies, Alan

Lennox-Boyd, at Hargeisa, Feb. 9, 1959. For text see *Commonwealth Survey* (London), vol. 5, no. 4 (Feb. 17, 1959), pp. 178–179.

2. Quoted in *Somaliland Protectorate 1958–1959* (issued at London in 1960), p. 4. On the political atmosphere at the time see Sir Douglas Hall, "Somaliland's Last Year as a Protectorate," *African Affairs* (London), January 1961.

3. For the communiqué issued at Mogadishu on April 16, 1960, see *The Times* (London), April 18.

4. *Corriere della Somalia* (Mogadishu), July 2, 1960.

5. For details on the different legal systems, see *Somaliland Protectorate 1957–1958*, pp. 29–32; and *Rapport sur la Somalie 1956*, pp. 25–28.

6. Great Britain, *Agreements and Exchanges of Letters between the Government of the United Kingdom of Great Britain and Northern Ireland and the Government of Somaliland in Connexion with the Attainment of Independence by Somaliland* (London: H.M.S.O., 1960), Cmd. 1101.

7. All these figures are percentages of total value, annual averages, 1958 and 1959. From *Rapport sur la Somalie 1959*, pp. 238–245, 250–255; and *Somaliland Protectorate 1958–1959*, pp. 19–20.

8. Banana export data from *Rapport sur la Somalie 1959*, pp. 256–257. Also, on the banana trade and Italian subsidies, see M. Karp, *The Economics of Trusteeship in Somalia* (Boston: Boston University Press, 1960), pp. 154–159.

9. For details on British Somaliland's foreign trade see *Somaliland Protectorate 1956–1957*, pp. 15–17; and *Somaliland Protectorate 1958–1959*, pp. 17–21.

10. Rupert Emerson, *From Empire to Nation* (Cambridge: Harvard University Press, 1960), p. 95.

11. *Somaliland News* (Hargeisa), Oct. 3, 1960.

Chapter 10: The Politics of French Somaliland

1. Figures based on *Guide Annuaire de la Côte Française des Somalis, 1959* (Jibuti), p. 36.

2. See *L'Afrique Française* (Paris), May–June 1956, p. 114; *Ethiopian Economic Review* (Addis Ababa), June 1960, p. 79; *Guide Annuaire de la Côte Française des Somalis, 1959*, pp. 141–145.

3. H. Deschamps, *Côte des Somalis* (Paris: Berger-Levrault, 1948), pp. 61–62; J. Chatelain, "L'Application des dispositions constitutionelles relatives à l'Union française," *Revue Juridique et Politique de l'Union Française* (Paris), vol. I (1947), p. 401.

4. Lewis, "Political Movements," pp. 345–346; A. A. Castagno in *Africa Special Report*, December 1958, pp. 11–12; *Africa Digest* (London), vol. 5 (1958), pp. 183–184.

5. Sources of figures in this paragraph: *Chroniques d'Outre-Mer* (Paris), November 1958, p. 40; *Chroniques de la Communauté* (Paris), May 1960, p. 30.

6. Lewis, "Political Movements," p. 345.

CHAPTER 11: THE PROBLEM OF THE ETHIOPIAN SOMALIS

1. For an example of this migration see Lord Rennell of Rodd, *British Military Administration of Occupied Territories in Africa, 1941–1947* (London: H.M.S.O., 1948), pp. 488–489.

2. Chamber of Commerce, *Guide Book of Ethiopia* (Addis Ababa, 1954), pp. 169, 174–185; D. A. Talbot, *Contemporary Ethiopia* (New York: Philosophical Library, 1952), p. 15; E. W. Luther, *Ethiopia Today* (Stanford: Stanford University Press, 1958), pp. 69, 136. For a journalistic account of the oil explorations, see H. Jenny, *Äthiopien, Land im Aufbruch* (Stuttgart: Deutsche Verlags-Anstalt, 1957), pp. 141–143.

3. On the Ethiopian peoples and languages, see Luther, pp. 24–25, and E. Ullendorff, *The Ethiopians* (London: Oxford University Press, 1960), chaps. III, IV.

4. On the Moslems, and on minorities in general, a very instructive book is J. S. Trimingham, *Islam in Ethiopia* (London: Oxford University Press, 1952).

5. See G. K. N. Trevaskis, *Eritrea, A Colony in Transition: 1941–52* (London: Oxford University Press, 1960), chaps. III, IV.

6. For some interesting illustrations see E. Cerulli, "The Folk-Literature of the Galla of Southern Abyssinia," *Harvard African Studies*, vol. III (1922).

7. No meaningful population figures on the Gallas are available. According to one estimate, as many as 40 percent of the inhabitants of Ethiopia (excluding Eritrea) are Galla or of Galla origin; see G. W. B. Huntingford, *The Galla of Ethiopia* (London: International African Institute, 1955), p. 23 and *passim*. See also Trimingham, pp. 187–209 and *passim*. On the 1915–1917 constitutional crisis, see A. H. M. Jones and E. Monroe, *A History of Ethiopia* (Oxford: Clarendon Press, 1955), pp. 153–159; Trimingham, pp. 129–131; and M. Perham, *The Government of Ethiopia* (New York: Oxford University Press, 1948), pp. 60–62. On the Gallas during the Italian-Ethiopian war, see G. Steer, *Caesar in Abyssinia* (Boston: Little, Brown, 1937), *passim*.

8. For a frank expression of concern by the emperor see *New York Times*, Feb. 16, 1957. On Egyptian policy see Chapter 14 below.

9. For echoes of the diplomatic exchanges which took place at the time see *The Times* (London), Feb. 19, 1959.

10. Menelik's circular is quoted in Clement de la Jonquière, *Les Italiens en Erythrée* (Paris: Henri Charles-Lavauzelle, 1897), pp. 145–146. On subsequent territorial claims see Ethiopia, Ministry of Foreign Affairs, *Digest of Memoranda Presented by the Imperial Ethiopian Government to the Council of Foreign Ministers, in London, September 1945* (revised edition, April 1946), pp. 3–11; N. Bentwich, *Ethiopia at the Paris Peace Conference* (London: Abyssinia [Ethiopia] Association, 1946), p. 4. See also U.N. Docs. A/C.1/429, A/991, A/1191. The claim that the Horn of Africa once formed a part of the Ethiopian empire would be difficult to substantiate historically.

11. Quoted in *Ethiopia Observer*, vol. I, no. 1 (December 1956), p. 8. In Somalia and British Somaliland the speech was described as "imperialistic,"

because of its call upon all Somalis to join Ethiopia. The Somalia Legislative Council issued an official reply. See *U.N. Advisory Council 1956–57* (U.N. Doc. T/1311), par. 56; and Lewis, "Political Movements," pp. 348, 355.

12. *Ethiopia Observer,* vol. I, no. 1 (December 1956), pp. 5–6. For further expression of the emperor's interest in the development of the Ogaden see his speech from the throne at the opening of Parliament on November 2, 1957, in *Ethiopia Observer,* vol. II, no. 2 (January 1958), p. 92.

Chapter 12: The Problem of the Kenya Somalis

1. J. M. L. Elliot, "Report on the Census of the Somali Population of Kenya Colony," Nairobi, 1957 (unpublished). On the origins of the Somali settlement at Isiolo see British Colonial Office, *Kenya Land Commission,* Evidence and Memoranda (London: H.M.S.O., 1934), pp. 1643–1649.

2. Kenya, *African Affairs Department Annual Report, 1948* (Nairobi: Government Printer, 1950), pp. 4–5.

3. Lewis, "Political Movements," p. 254; A. A. Castagno in *Africa Special Report,* December 1958, p. 12.

4. [W. F. Coutts], *Report of the Commission Appointed to Enquire into Methods for the Selection of African Representatives to the Legislative Council* (Nairobi: Government Printer, 1955), p. 28.

5. For the election results, see the *East African Standard* (Nairobi), March 3, 1961. For the biographical information on Ali Aden Lord, I am indebted to the Ministry of Information and Broadcasting, Nairobi.

6. *East African Standard,* Aug. 27 and 29, Sept. 13, 14, 15, 18, 1961. See also *The Observer* (London), Sept. 10, 1961. The Kenya Africans may also face difficulties with the Boran-Galla tribes of the Northern Frontier Province. Some of them apparently sympathize with the idea of joining Ethiopia (where the majority of Gallas live) when Kenya becomes independent. The Gallas and associated groups in the province number close to 50,000.

Chapter 13: A Question of Boundary Lines

1. On the Kenya-Ethiopian border dispute see *British and Foreign State Papers,* vol. 100, 1906–1907 (London: H.M.S.O., 1911), pp. 459–460; and vol. 147, 1947, part I (London: H.M.S.O., 1955), pp. 791–795.

2. H. G. C. Swayne, *Seventeen Trips Through Somaliland,* third edition (London: Rowland Ward, Ltd., 1903), *passim.*

3. On the 1894 agreement see *The Map of Africa by Treaty,* third edition, ed. Sir Edward Hertslet (London: H.M.S.O., 1909), vol. III, p. 951. On Ethiopia's reaction see Sir James Rennell Rodd, *Social and Diplomatic Memoirs,* second series, 1894–1901 (London: Edward Arnold & Co., 1923), pp. 164–165.

4. Rodd, pp. 109–114; W. L. Langer, *The Diplomacy of Imperialism,* second edition (New York: Alfred A. Knopf, 1956), pp. 546–547. On the Anglo-

French rivalry over the sources of the Nile and the French use of Ethiopia as a base for some of their expeditions, see Langer, pp. 537–577.

5. Rodd, pp. 162–188. For the text of the treaty, see Hertslet, *Map of Africa by Treaty,* vol. II, pp. 423–429. For an account of the mission see Count Albert E. W. Gleichen, *With the Mission to Menelik, 1897* (London: Edward Arnold, 1897). See also Swayne, pp. 268–292. The questions of the Ethiopia-Sudan border and the border between Ethiopia and British East Africa could not be resolved and were deferred for subsequent negotiations.

6. *Parliamentary Debates,* House of Commons, fourth series, vol. 53, cols. 1527–1528, 1579–1605 (1898).

7. Hertslet, *Map of Africa by Treaty,* vol. II, p. 428; Rodd, pp. 167–169, 181–183.

8. Lieut.-Col. E. H. M. Clifford, "The British Somaliland Ethiopia Boundary," *The Geographical Journal* (London), vol. 87 (1936), p. 296.

9. *Agreement and Military Convention between the United Kingdom and Ethiopia,* Addis Ababa, 31st January 1942 (Cmd. 6334); *Agreement between His Majesty in respect of the United Kingdom and His Imperial Majesty the Emperor of Ethiopia,* Addis Ababa, 19th December 1944 (Cmd. 6584). For a comprehensive discussion of British Military Administration over the area see Lord Rennell of Rodd, *British Military Administration of Occupied Territories in Africa, 1941–1947* (London: H.M.S.O., 1948).

10. See *Exchanges of Notes between His Majesty's Government in the United Kingdom and the French Government regarding a Proposed Cession of Territory in the Zeila Area to Ethiopia* (Cmd. 7758, May 10, 1949); *Parliamentary Debates,* House of Commons, fifth series, vol. 537, col. 1684 (Feb. 25, 1955). See also M. Perham, *The Government of Ethiopia* (New York: Oxford University Press, 1948), pp. 388–400; D. J. Latham Brown, "The Ethiopia-Somaliland Frontier Dispute," *International and Comparative Law Quarterly* (London), April 1956, pp. 245–264.

11. *Agreement . . . relating to certain Matters connected with the Withdrawal of British Military Administration from the Territories designated as the Reserved Area and the Ogaden* (Cmd. 9348, Nov. 29, 1954).

12. H. Hopkinson, Minister of State for Colonial Affairs, *Parliamentary Debates,* House of Commons, fifth series, vol. 546, col. 907 (Nov. 17, 1955).

13. *The Times* (London), April 14 and 26, 1956.

14. *Parliamentary Debates,* House of Commons, fifth series, vol. 537, col. 1285 (Feb. 23, 1955).

15. *The Times* (London), May 5, 6, 10, 13, Oct. 18, 1955; *Africa Digest* (London), January–February 1956, p. 12. It is interesting to recall that the issue of whether the Protectorate population ought to be consulted was raised in 1935 in connection with the British offer to transfer to Ethiopia a portion of British Somaliland territory with an outlet to the sea—as an inducement to Ethiopia to make concessions to Italy and thus avert war. The British compromise proposal was rejected by Mussolini. See *Parliamentary Debates,* House

of Commons, fifth series, vol. 303, cols. 2004–2008 (July 4, 1935), and vol. 304, cols. 5–7 (July 8, 1935).

16. Great Britain, Colonial Office, *Report of the Somaliland Protectorate Constitutional Conference* (London: H.M.S.O., 1960), Cmd. 1044. See also the Prime Minister's statement expressing this view in *Parliamentary Debates,* House of Commons, fifth series, vol. 621, col. 105 (April 11, 1960). For a detailed discussion of the legal aspects of the problem see D. J. Latham Brown, "Recent Developments in the Ethiopia-Somaliland Dispute," *International and Comparative Law Quarterly,* January 1961, pp. 167–178.

17. C. Rossetti, *Storia Diplomatica dell' Etiopia* (Turin: S.T.E.N., 1910), pp. 404–416; M. Magini, *Variazioni territoriali nell' A.O.I. dal 1880 al 1938* (Florence: Carlo Cya, 1939), pp. 47–48.

18. For text of convention see Hertslet, *Map of Africa by Treaty,* vol. III, pp. 1223–1224.

19. General Assembly Resolution 392 (V), Dec. 15, 1950.

20. G.A. Res. 854 (IX), Dec. 14, 1954.

21. See U.N. Docs. A/3753, A/3754.

22. G.A. Res. 1213 (XII), Dec. 14, 1957.

23. G.A. Res. 1345 (XIII), Dec. 13, 1958.

24. For the draft and the proposed amendments see U.N. Doc. A/4325 (Dec. 3, 1959).

25. U.N. Doc. A/4350. For the discussion in the Fourth Committee see U.N. Docs. A/C.4/SR. 986, 990, 991, 997–1001.

26. Besides the documents just cited, see U.N. Docs. A/3753, A/3754, A/4030, A/4031, and A/C.4/SR. 779, 782–786, 789, 797.

27. U.N. Doc. A/C.4/SR. 1001.

Chapter 14: The International Environment

1. See *Defence and Security in the Indian Ocean Area,* a report by a study group of the Indian Council of World Affairs (London: Asia Publishing House, 1958), pp. 5–25; *British Interests in the Mediterranean and the Middle East,* a report by a Chatham House study group (London: Oxford University Press, 1958), pp. 25–27, 32–34; Adm. R. L. Conolly, "Africa's Strategic Significance," in *Africa Today,* ed. C. G. Haines (Baltimore: Johns Hopkins Press, 1955), p. 61.

2. *British Interests,* just cited, p. 33. Other relevant discussion is on pp. 25–27 and 32–34 of that report.

3. See statement by the Parliamentary Under Secretary of State for the Colonies, Lord Lloyd, May 29, 1956, quoted in *Somaliland Protectorate 1956–1957,* pp. 58–59; and statement on Feb. 9, 1959, by the Secretary of State for the Colonies, A. T. Lennox-Boyd, quoted in *Commonwealth Survey* (London), vol. 5, no. 4 (Feb. 17, 1959), pp. 178–179. For an official expression of sympathy for nationalist grievances regarding the Haud issue see *Parliamentary Debates,* House of Commons, vol. 537, col. 1285 (Feb. 23, 1955).

4. M. Perham, *The Government of Ethiopia* (New York: Oxford University Press, 1948), pp. 63, 93–94, 345, 357, 390–396.

5. See our note 3, above.

6. See Great Britain, Colonial Office, *Report of the Somaliland Constitutional Conference* (London: H.M.S.O., 1960), Cmd. 1044; and Great Britain, *Agreements and Exchanges of Letters in Connexion with the Attainment of Independence by Somaliland* (London: H.M.S.O., 1960), Cmd. 1101. Also *Africa Digest* (London), August 1962.

7. On the border settlement see *The Times* (London), Sept. 10, 1945. On the railway see *Journal Officiel de la République Française,* Lois et Décrets, 92nd year, no. 114, May 15, 1960. On the Emperor's visit see *New York Times,* July 21 and 22, 1959.

8. Article 23 of "Treaty of Peace with Italy," *United Nations Treaty Series,* vol. 49 (1950.I.no. 747), p. 139.

9. See *Italy and the United Nations,* report of a study group set up by the Italian Society for International Organization, prepared for the Carnegie Endowment for International Peace (New York: Manhattan Publishing Co., 1959), pp. 54–58; and B. Rivlin, *The United Nations and the Italian Colonies* (New York: Carnegie Endowment for International Peace, 1950), pp. 42–43.

10. They could not agree, however, on a joint proposal with respect to Eritrea and Libya. Rivlin, pp. 9–12, 24–25.

11. *Four Power Commission,* report and appendices, *passim,* and particularly pp. 15–16 and 117–119 of the report. The text is interspersed with separate comments and reservations by the representatives.

12. *New York Times,* July 5, 1959. See also *New York Times,* Jan. 31, 1960, and *Christian Science Monitor,* April 7, 1960. For the agreement granting facilities for defense installations, see *United States Treaties and Other International Agreements,* vol. 5, part 1, 1954, pp. 750–761.

13. *The Times* (London), Feb. 11 and 19, 1959.

14. *New York Times,* Jan. 3 and 4, 1961.

15. Rivlin, pp. 11–13, 24.

16. W. L. Langer, *The Diplomacy of Imperialism,* second edition (New York: Alfred A. Knopf, 1956), pp. 274, 280, 291. For a detailed study, see C. Jesman, *The Russians in Ethiopia* (London: Chatto & Windus, 1958). See also Perham (our note 4, above), pp. 238, 394; *Ethiopia Observer* (Addis Ababa), vol. I (1957), pp. 131–132; *New York Times,* July 13 and Aug. 24, 1959; and Y. Tomilin, "Soviet-Ethiopian Friendship," *International Affairs* (Moscow), July 1959, pp. 91–93.

17. *Four Power Commission,* p. 11*n*1.

18. *New York Times,* June 18, 1961.

19. For a recent account of Chinese activity, see Robert Counts, "Chinese Footprints in Somalia," *The Reporter,* Feb. 2, 1961.

20. *U.N. Advisory Council 1957–58* (U.N. Doc. T/1372), par. 261 and annex

VI; *U.N. Advisory Council 1958–59* (U.N. Doc. T/1444), pars. 247, 258; *Le Monde* (Paris), April 7, 1961.

21. A. Silva White, *The Expansion of Egypt under Anglo-Egyptian Condominium* (London: Methuen & Co., 1899), p. 29.

22. For a summary of these developments see Langer, pp. 102–107. See also Chapter 4 above. For a thorough study of Egyptian policy under Ismail see G. Douin, *Histoire du Règne du Khédive Ismail,* vol. III, part 3 (Cairo: Société Royale de Géographie d'Egypte, 1941).

23. For Nasser's reflections on Egypt, the Nile, and Africa, see G. Abdul Nasser, *Egypt's Liberation* (Washington: Public Affairs Press, 1955), pp. 109–111.

24. A. A. Castagno, "Somalia," *International Conciliation,* March 1959, pp. 396–397. See also Castagno's article in *Africa Special Report,* December 1958, p. 14.

Chapter 15: Possibilities

1. The resolutions are reprinted in *Current History,* vol. 37 (July 1959), pp. 41–46. For the three quotations given here, see pp. 45, 46.

2. The question was raised by Somali leaders in discussions with Julius Nyerere and other members of the Tanganyika delegation to Somali independence celebrations in July 1960. An explicit call for federation was included in the resolutions adopted by the Third National Congress of the National United Front in Hargeisa in October 1960. For some interesting exchanges on this subject between the Kenya nationalist leader Jomo Kenyatta and the Somali prime minister, see *Africa Digest* (London), October 1962.

Index

Abdi Hassan Boni, 113
Abdinur Mohamed Hussein, 92
Abdirashid Ali Shermarke, 90, 113
Abdirazaq Haji Hussein, 90, 113
Abdullah, Sheikh, 96
Abdullahi Ali, Amir, 35
Abdullahi Issa, 90, 91, 97, 98, 113
Abdulqadir Mohamed Aden, 93
Abgal tribe: lineage, 17; and P.L.G.S., 92, 93
Absame tribe, 17, 133
Abubakr Hamud Socorro, 100, 176
Abu-Bekr. *See* Ibrahim Abu-Bekr
Adal, 9, 49–51
Addis Ababa, 77
Addurrahman Mursaal, 67
Aden: occupied by British (*1839*), 31, 33; treaty with Habr Toljala tribe, 33; and British Somaliland, 103
Aden Abdulla Osman, vii, 112, 122
Adowa, Italian defeat at, 48, 155, 160, 175
African Livestock Marketing Organization (A.L.M.O.), 151, 152
Ahmadiyah, 21
Ahmed Dini, 127
Ahmed Farah Eleya, 151
Ahmed Gran, 49–51
Ahmed ibn Ibrahim al Ghazi, the Imam, 49–51
Ajouran tribe: lineage, 17; in Ethiopia, 134; in Kenya, 147
Ali Aden Lord, 152
Ali Aref Bourhan, 127
Ali Giumale, Sheikh, 122
All African People's Conference, 141, 182
Amaranis, 13
Amharas, 22, 50–51, 74, 132–133, 137
Ancestry, belief in common, 15, 17, 24–25
Anglo-Ethiopian agreements, 63, 157–160, 167
Arab, 17
Arabs, 9, 12, 15, 72
Assab, 36, 40, 124
Aubad, 33
Aulihan tribe, 17, 66–67

Ba Gheri, 17
Bajunis, 13
Barghash, Sultan, 41
Barker, Lt. W. C., 31
Benadir: and Italy, 41, 42, 43–44; Commercial Company of, 44; elections, 93, 94
Benadir Youth Union, 93, 94, 184. *See also* Somali National Union
Berbera, 14–15, 34, 52–53
Bevin Plan, 78–80, 139, 140, 174
Bimal tribe: lineage, 17; and P.L.G.S., 92
Border problems: between Ethiopia and British Somaliland, 63, 154–160; between Ethiopia and Somalia, 154, 160–163; between Ethiopia and Kenya, 154
Brava, 42
Bremer, Capt., 32–33
British East Africa, 45–47
British East Africa Company: aids Italy, 41–42, 43; its start, 46
British Military Administration: its start, 78, 102; and S.Y.L., 86, 166–167; and Ethiopia, 103, 134, 139, 157
British Somaliland, 2; established, 32–37; the Mullah in, 52–55, 62; rising nationalism in, 62–66, 101–108; in-

vaded by Italy, 77; liberated by Allies, 78; and Bevin Plan, 79; and S.Y.L., 95; unites with Somalia, 109–122, 134, 167, 168, 181; border dispute with Ethiopia, 154–160. *See also* Somali Republic
Burao, 52, 65
Burton, Richard F., 31–32, 33

Cecchi, Capt. Antonio, 41, 45
Chiesi, Gustavo, 44
China: and Somali Republic, 3; and Haji Mohamed, 91, 100; and Ethiopia, 140–141; current role in area, 164, 176–178; and United States, 172, 173
Christopher, Lt. W., 31
Civil Service: in British Somaliland, 65–66; and tribalism, 86; in Somali Republic, 114–115
Cold war, 3, 140–141, 180
Commerce: a consideration in colonization, 37, 38, 40; and nationalism, 82
Communication difficulties: lack of written language, 21, 26, 98–99, 114; lack of transportation facilities, 25–28, 114
Compagnie Franco-Ethiopienne, 39
Corfield, Richard, 54–55
Crittenden, Lt. C. J., 31
Currency, 117–118

Da Gama, Cristovão, 50
Danakils: in French Somaliland, 2, 38, 123–131; and religion, 20, 183; characteristics, 22; in Adal, 49
Darod tribe: migrations of, 11, lineage, 17; rivalry with Hawiya, 28; and the Mullah, 59; and civil service, 86; and S.Y.L., 89–90, 93, 104; and G.S.L., 91, 93; and U.S.P., 105; in Somali Republic, 120; in Ethiopia, 133, 134; in Kenya, 149
De Gaulle, Charles, 130–131
De Langle, Capt. Fleuriot, 38
De Rivoyre, Denis, 39
Dervishes, 56–57, 58–59
D'Hericourt, C. E. X. Rochet, 38
Dighil tribe, 17, 86
Digodia, 134
Dir tribe, 17, 59
Dodds-Parker, A. D., 158
Dolbahanta tribe, 32; lineage, 17; and the Mullah, 52; and parties, 104–106; in Ethiopia, 133–134
Donbira, 17
Drake-Brockman, R. E., 19

East India Company, 33
Economic aid, 3; from United States, 172–173; from Soviet Union, 173, 175, 176; from Egypt, 178
Economic factors in nationalism: in Italian Somaliland, 72–73; in Somalia, 97; and unification, 109–110, 116–118, 119; in French Somaliland, 124; in Ethiopia, 145–146; and Pan-Africanism, 182–183
Education: in British Somaliland, 64–65, 82, 102; in Italian Somaliland, 73, 82; role in nationalist movement, 83–84; in Ethiopia, 144–145, 146; Egyptian assistance to, 178
Egypt: supports Somali nationalism, 3, 81–82, 139, 164, 178–180; ancient relation to Horn, 8; and nineteenth-century expansionism, 33–36; and Great Britain, 46, 48; and G.S.L., 91
Eidagalla tribe, 17, 56
Eritrea, 40, 79, 138
Ethiopia: Somali territorial claims, 2; and Soviet Union, 3, 174–175; and United States, 3, 140, 172–173; Somali population in, 12, 132–146; religion, 20; under Menelik II, 30, 47–48; and Egypt, 33–34, 178–179; conquers Harar, 35; and Italy, 40–41, 70, 71–72, 77; holy war with Somalis, 49–51; and the Mullah, 55; Anglo-Ethiopian relations, 63, 157–160, 167–168; rise of nationalism, 73–76; Reserved Area, 78; and Bevin Plan, 79; and the Haud, 103, 104, 106–107; and French Somaliland, 124, 130, 131, 169–170; border dispute with British Somaliland, 154–160; border dispute with Somalia, 154, 160–163; border dispute with Kenya, 154; and Pan-Africanism, 181–183

Etymology of "Somali," 9–10
Exploration, 30–32, 41

Farah Omar, Haji, 65
Filonardi, Vincenzo, 41, 42–43
Four Power Commission of Investigation: its establishment, 80–81; and S.Y.L., 86–87, 95; and H.D.M.S., 92, 96; and United States, 173; and Soviet Union, 174, 175
France: current role in area, 3, 164, 169–170, 172; early exploration by, 30–32; takes possession of Tajura, 36; founding of French Somaliland, 37–40; rising nationalism in French Somaliland, 69–70; on Four Power Commission, 80; constitutional progress of French Somaliland, 124–125, 129–131
Franco-Ethiopian Railway, 157
French Somaliland, 2, 3; Somali population in, 12; founding of, 37–40; rising nationalism in, 69–70; surrenders to Allies, 77; constitutional progress in, 124–125, 129–131; and Ethiopia, 169–170; and Pan-Africanism, 182
Futuh al Habasha, 9

G.F.S. *See* Somali Fiqarini Youth
G.S.L. *See* Greater Somalia League
Gadabursi tribe: lineage, 17; treaty with Great Britain, 36–37; and parties, 105, 106; in Ethiopia, 133
Gaddaduma wells, 154
Galawdewos, 50
Gallas, 10, 11, 183; religion, 20; characteristics, 22; in Adal, 49; in Ethiopia, 132, 138–139, 143
Genealogy of Somalis, 15–17
Gerhajis, 17
Germany, 165; exploration, 32; relations with Great Britain in Africa, 41, 42, 45–46; German East Africa Company, 42, 43
Gobad, Sultan of, 40
Gordon College, 64
Gran, Ahmed, 49–51
Great Britain: current role in area, 3, 164, 166–169, 172; early exploration by, 30–32; founding of British Somaliland, 32–37; treaty with France, 40; supports Italy, 41–42; British East Africa, 45–47; and the Mullah, 52–55, 56, 58–59; and rising nationalism in British Somaliland, 62–66; and rising nationalism in Kenya, 66–69, 150; second World War, 77, 78–80; on Four Power Commission, 80; and Ethiopia, 103, 104, 140, 154–160; and unification of British Somaliland and Somalia, 110–112, 167–169
Greater Somalia, 2. *See also* Unification
Greater Somalia League (G.S.L.): and *1954–1959* elections, 88, 93, 94; formation, 89, 90–91; on unification, 97–98; attitude on foreign affairs, 99–100; in Somali Republic, 120, 121, 122
Guillain, Charles, 31
Gurreh tribe: lineage, 17; in Ethiopia, 134; in Kenya, 147

H.D.M. *See* Hizbia Dighil e Mirifle
H.D.M.S. *See* Hizbia Dastur Mustaqil Somali
Habr Awal tribe: lineage, 17; and treaties with Great Britain, 32–33, 36–37
Habr Gedir, 17
Habr Gerhajis tribe, 36–37
Habr Toljala tribe: lineage, 17; and treaties with Great Britain, 33, 36–37; and the Mullah, 52; and parties, 104–106
Habr Yuni tribe, 17, 52, 179
Haile Selassie, Emperor: made regent, 74; regains throne, 77, 79; and cold war, 140; and Italian Somaliland, 142; British attitude to, 167; and French, 169; and Soviet Union, 175
Harar: Burton on, 31; under Egyptian rule, 34, 35, 48; Somali inhabitants, 132
Hargeisa, 14
Harti, 17
Hassan Gouled, 125–127
Haud, the, 103, 104, 106–107, 139, 157–158, 159, 167
Hawiya tribe: migrations, 11; lineage,

17; rivalry with Darod, 28; and civil service, 86; and S.Y.L., 89–90, 91, 93; and P.L.G.S., 92; and Somali Republic, 118, 120; and Ethiopia, 134; and Kenya, 147
Hildebrandt, 32
Hiran province, 94
History of the Horn, early, 8–9
Hizbia Dastur Mustaqil Somali (H.D.M.S.): supported by agricultural tribes, 28; in elections of *1954–1959*, 88, 94; and Sab, 92–93; attitude to unification, 95–97; attitude to foreign affairs, 99; in Somali Republic, 120, 121. *See also* Hizbia Dighil e Mirifle
Hizbia Dighil e Mirifle (H.D.M), 87, 92. *See also* Hizbia Dastur Mustaqil Somali
Horn of Africa, *passim;* defined, 5; map, 7; population table, 12

Ibrahim Abu-Bekr, 38, 127
Imi, 48
Independent African States, Conference of, 141
India, 32, 33, 35
Indochina, 37, 38, 39, 130
Irrir, 17
Ishaq tribe, 11; lineage, 17; and the Mullah, 52, 54, 59; and S.N.L., 104; and Somali Republic, 118, 120; in Ethiopia, 133, 134, 135; in Kenya, 149
Ishaqiya Association, 149
Isiolo, 148
Ismail, Khedive, 33, 34, 35, 179
Issa tribe, 11; lineage, 17; treaty with Great Britain, 36–37; treaty with France, 40; and parties, 105, 106; and separatism, 128–129; in Ethiopia, 133, 135
Issa, Abduallahi. *See* Abdullahi Issa
Issa Mahamoud, 17
Italian-Ethiopian Convention of *1908*, 160–161, 162, 163
Italian Somaliland, 2; established, 40–45; Somalis migrate from, 47; and rising nationalism, 70–73; postwar disposition of, 77, 78–81, 87, 172, 173–174; and Ethiopia, 139, 141–142, 160–161. *See also* Somalia; Somali Republic
Italy: current role in area, 3, 164, 170–171, 172; and coastal towns, 9; early exploration by, 30, 32; extends holdings around Assab, 36; establishment of Italian Somaliland, 40–45; Anglo-Italian agreements, 46, 155–156; Ethiopia and, 47–48, 76, 77, 133, 138–139, 155–156; and the Mullah, 54, 59; its racial policy, 62, 71; rising nationalism in Italian Somaliland, 70–73; second World War, 77; attitude on unification of British Somaliland and Somalia, 110, 168; and border dispute between Ethiopia and Somalia, 160–163; Soviet Union and, 174, 175

Jama Abdullahi Gabib, 113
James, F. L., 32
Jardine, Douglas, 59–60
Jelani Sheikh bin Sheikh, 96–97
Jews, 8
Jibuti, 69; and S.Y.L., 95; Ethiopian dependence on, 124, 169–170
Jidwak tribe, 17, 133
Juba river, 6, 11, 13, 16, 41, 46, 117
Jubaland, 66–67

Kenya: Somali conflict with, 2–3; rainfall, 8; Somali expansion into, 11, 12, 24, 46–47, 67–68; and religion, 20; racial tensions in, 25; and Great Britain, 46; rising nationalism, 66–69; second World War, 77; and S.Y.L., 95; Somali nationalism challenges, 147–153; border dispute with Ethiopia, 154; and Pan-Africanism, 181–183
Kenya African Democratic Union (K.A.D.U.), 152
Kenya African National Union (K.A.N.U.), 152
Kenya Meat Commission, 148
Khalef, A. R., 152
Khalifa, Sultan, 41
King's African Rifles, 53, 55, 67, 68–69
Kismayu, 41, 42
Korean War, 140, 173

Lagarde, Leonce, 39
Lambert, Henri, 38
Language, 21–22; need for script, 21, 26, 98–99, 114; as criterion for nationhood, 24; a complication to unification, 114
League of Nations, 167
Lebna Dengel, Emperor, 50
Lennox-Boyd, Alan Tindal, 168, 173
Lewis, I. M., 7, 17, 18, 185
Liberal Somali Youth Party (P.L.G.S.): in *1954–1959* elections, 88, 94; formation of, 91–92, 93; and foreign affairs, 99
Lie, Trygve, 162
Lij Yasu, 74, 138
Lineage of Somali tribes, 15–17
Lord, Ali Aden. *See* Ali Aden Lord
Lower Juba province, 91, 93, 94, 97

Mackinnon, Sir William, 41, 45
Mad Mullah. *See* Mohamed ibn Abdullah Hassan
Madagascar, 37, 39
Madoba, 17
Mahdist revolt, 35
Mahmoud Harbi, 125–128, 176, 178, 180
Malingur, 17
Marehan tribe: lineage, 17; in Jubaland, 66–67; in Ethiopia, 133, 134, 135
Marehan Union, 88
Mariano, Michael, 103, 104–105
Mecca, 31
Menelik II, Emperor: extends Ethiopian power, 30, 35, 47–48, 73–74, 141; boundary dispute with Italy, 155–156, 160
Merca, 14, 42
Midgan, 18
Mijertain province: rainfall, 8; German claims to, 42, 43; Italian Protectorate, 43; unrest in, 44; election, 94
Mijertain tribe: lineage, 17; and G.S.L., 89–90; in Ethiopia, 133, 134
Minorities in the Horn, 11–13
Mobilen, 17
Mogadishu, 14, 15; Italians control, 42; British capture, 77; and G.S.L., 91; political influence resented, 119, 121
Mohamed, the Prophet, 15, 17
Mohamed Haji Ibrahim Egal, 113
Mohamed Hussein, Haji, 80; forms G.S.L., 89, 90–91; on unification, 95; and China, 99–100, 176; and Egypt, 178
Mohamed ibn Abdullah Hassan (the Mullah), 21, 49; his poems, 24; and Italian Somaliland, 44–45; his career, 51–60; and Ogaden tribe, 74
Mohamed Kamil, 127
Mohamed Zubeir, 17
Molotov, V. M., 79, 174
Moresby, Capt. Robert, 33
Mudugh province, 8, 94
Mullah, the. *See* Mohamed ibn Abdullah Hassan
Muscat, Imam of, 9
Mussa, 33
Mussa Boqor, Haji, 90
Mysticism. *See* Salihiyah; Sufism

N.P.P.P.P. *See* Northern Province People's Progressive Party
N.U.F. *See* National United Front
Nairobi, 148
Nasser, Gamal Abdel, 179. *See also* Egypt
National United Front (N.U.F.): in British Somaliland, 104–108; in Somali Republic
Nationhood, Somali claims to, 23–29
Negri, Cristoforo, 40
Negroes: a minority in the Horn, 12–13; Somalis' attitude to, 13, 25, 150, 182
Negus Yeshaq, 9
Nerazzini, Major, 160
Nile river, 33, 46, 164, 178–180
Nomadism, 14, 24; and Samaale, 16; and religion, 20–21; differences from settled tribes, 22; and communication, 27–28; and difficulties of unification, 109
Northern Province People's Progressive Party (N.P.P.P.P.), 150–151, 152

Obbia, 42–43, 44
Obock, 38–40

Occupational statistics, 14
Ogaden region: early exploration, 32; and Ethiopia, 47, 48, 75–76, 139, 142–146, 160–161; postwar disposition, 78, 102, 157, 167, 169, 172
Ogaden tribe: lineage, 17; and Ethiopia, 75, 133, 134–135; and the Mullah, 74; in Kenya, 147
Olol Dinle, Sultan, 75
Omar Mahamoud, 17
Omar Samantar, 72
Osman, Aden Abdulla. *See* Aden Abdulla Osman
Osmaniya, 21, 99
Osman Mahamoud tribe, 17, 90
Osman, Yusuf Kenadid. *See* Yusuf Kenadid Osman
Ottoman Empire, 9

P.L.G.S. *See* Liberal Somali Youth Party
Pan-Africanism, 4, 181–183
Partito Liberale Giovani Somali. *See* Liberal Somali Youth Party
Paulitschke, P., 32
Phoenicians, 8
Politics: influence of nationalism, 3–4; sophistication of Somalis, 27; organization in British Somaliland, 65, 101–108; tribal basis, 85–86; in Somalia, 86–100; problems in Somali Republic, 118–122; in French Somaliland, 123–131; in Ethiopia, 134–136; in Kenya, 147–153
Porro, Count, 32
Portugal: early exploration by, 9, 30; aids Ethiopia in holy war, 50

Qadiriyah, 21, 53
Quraysh, 15

Racial tensions: between Somalis and Negroes, 13, 25, 150, 182; between Italians and Somalis, 62, 71
Rahanwein tribe: migrations, 11; lineage, 17; and civil service, 86; and S.Y.L., 92
Rainfall, 6–8
Ras Makonnen, 48
Ras Tafari. *See* Haile Selassie, Emperor
Referendum of June *20, 1961,* 120–121
Regional Boundaries Commission, 153
Religion: a factor in expansion, 11; a unifying force among Somalis, 20–21, 25, 62, 63–64, 73, 74–75, 76, 82–83, 84; in Ethiopia, 20, 137–138, 142–143; holy war between Ethiopia and Somalis, 49–51; and the Mullah, 51–60; and Egyptian support of Somalis, 178, 179; and Pan-Africanism, 183
Rennison, Sir Patrick, 150
Rer Abdulla, 17
Rer Ali, 17
Reserved Area, 78, 103, 157–158
Révoil, Georges, 32
Rifaiyah, 21
Rivers, 6
Rodd, James Rennel, 156
Russel, Comte Stanislas, 38

S.D.P. *See* Somali Democratic Party
S.N.L. *See* Somali National League
S.N.L.U.S.P. *See* Somali National League United Somali Party
S.N.U. *See* Somali National Union
S.Y.L. *See* Somali Youth League
Sab: compared to Samaale, 16–18, 28; lineage, 17; political organization, 18; dialect, 21; and Hizbia Dighil e Mirifle, 87, 92, 95
sab, 18
Sahle-Selassie, 38
Salihiyah, 21; influence on the Mullah, 51–52, 56, 57
Samaale: compared to Sab, 16–18, 28; lineage, 17; political organization, 19, 92; dialect, 21
Samarone, 17
Seamen's Union, 70
Separatism: and Issa tribe, 128–129; in Ethiopia, 138, 139; in Kenya, 152–153
Sheikhal, 17
Shermarke. *See* Abdirashid Ali Shermarke
Shoa, Kingdom of, 31, 38
Société Française d'Obock, 39
Society for German Colonization, 45
Somali African Union (U.A.S.), 88
Somali Camel Constabulary, 54–55

Somali Democratic Party (S.D.P.), 88, 92
Somali Fiqarini Youth (G.F.S.), 88, 94
Somali Independent Constitutional Party. *See* Hizbia Dastur Mustaqil Somali
Somali Islamic Association, 65
Somali National Army, 115
Somali National Association, 149
Somali National League (S.N.L.): in British Somaliland, 103–108; in Somali Republic, 113, 119–120
Somali National League United Somali Party (S.N.L.U.S.P.), 119–120, 121
Somali National Society, 103
Somali National Union (S.N.U.): elections of *1954–1959,* 88, 93, 94; attitude to foreign affairs, 99–100
Somali Officials' Union, 65, 104
Somali Republic, 2; a note on the name, *facing 1;* and Soviet Union and China, 3; Somali population in, 12; occupational statistics, 14; formation of, 108, 109–122, 134, 167, 168, 181; Italy's attitude to, 171; Pan-Africanism, 181–182. *See also* British Somaliland; Italian Somaliland; Somalia
Somali Youth Club. *See* Somali Youth League
Somali Youth League (S.Y.L.): in Somalia, 86–99; in British Somaliland, 103–108; in Somali Republic, 112, 113, 120, 122, 166–167; in Ethiopia, 134, 135; in Kenya, 148–150; and Soviet Union, 175
Somalia, 2, 76; a note on the name, *facing 1;* a U.N. trust territory, 76; development of nationalism, 85–100; compared to British Somaliland, 101–102; joins with British Somaliland to form Somali Republic, 108, 109–122, 134, 181; border dispute with Ethiopia, 154, 160–163; and United States, 173. *See also* Italian Somaliland; Somali Republic
Somalia Conference, 96
Somaliland Camel Corps, 25, 55
Somaliland Scouts, 115
Soviet Union: current role in area, 3, 164, 166, 173–176; and Four Power Commission, 80; and Haji Mohamed, 91, 100; and Ethiopia, 140–141; and United States, 172, 173
Speke, John H., 31
Suez Canal: focuses European attention on Africa, 30, 33, 35, 38, 39; and Egypt, 179
Suffrage, 87, 125, 151
Sufism, 21, 25. *See also* Salihiyah

Tajura, 33, 36, 40
Tanganyika, 148
Tariff, 117
Trade, 116–117
Travelli, Ernesto, 44
Tribalism: lineage, 16–19; an obstacle to integration, 28; the Mullah's attitude on, 58–59; in Kenya, 66–67; and nationalism, 84, 85–86; in Somalia, 88–96; in British Somaliland, 102, 104–107; and unification of Somali Republic, 118–120
Tribes, theories of origin of, 10
Tripolitania, 174
Tumal, 18
Turkey, 34–37

U.A.S. *See* Somali African Union
U.G.B. *See* Somali National Union
U.S.P. *See* United Somali Party
Uganda, 46, 148
Unification: attitudes of political parties on, 93–99, 104, 105–108; problems of, 109–122; reactions to, 134, 150
Union of Benadir Youth. *See* Somali National Union
Union Républicaine, 125, 126
Unione Giovani Benadir (U.G.B.). *See* Somali National Union
United Nations: Italian Somaliland placed under trusteeship of, 81, 87, 172; its attitude on unification of British Somaliland and Somalia, 110–111, 113; and border dispute between Ethiopia and Somalia, 161–162; Soviet Union in, 174, 175
United Somali Association, 149

United Somali Party (U.S.P.): in British Somaliland, 105–106; and Somali Republic, 113, 119–120. *See also* Somali National League United Somali Party
United States: current role in area, 3, 164, 171–173; on Four Power Commission, 80; Ethiopia and, 140, 172–173
Upper Juba province, 92, 93, 94, 97
Urbanization, 15, 27

Wajir Muslim Association, 152
Wal-Wal incident, 72, 139, 161
Warsangeli tribe, 32; lineage, 17; treaty with Great Britain, 37; and parties, 104–106
Warsheikh, 42
Webi Shebeli river, 6, 11, 13, 16, 48, 117, 136
World War *I,* 69–70
World War *II:* impact on rising nationalism, 76–84; and border dispute between Ethiopia, British Somaliland, 157

Yemen, 9
Yibir, 18
Yusuf Kenadid Osman, 21, 99

Zanzibar, 9; British support, 35; Italian exploration, 41; British protectorate established, 43, 45
Zauditu, Empress, 74
Zeila, 33, 34, 36, 47

BOOKS PREPARED UNDER THE AUSPICES OF THE CENTER FOR INTERNATIONAL AFFAIRS, HARVARD UNIVERSITY

PUBLISHED BY HARVARD UNIVERSITY PRESS

The Soviet Bloc, by Zbigniew K. Brzezinski, 1960 (sponsored jointly with Russian Research Center).

Rift and Revolt in Hungary, by Ferenc A. Váli, 1961.

The Economy of Cyprus, by A. J. Meyer, with Simos Vassiliou, 1962 (jointly with Center for Middle Eastern Studies).

Entrepreneurs of Lebanon, by Yusif A. Sayigh, 1962 (jointly with Center for Middle Eastern Studies).

Communist China 1955–1959, with a foreword by Robert R. Bowie and John K. Fairbank, 1962 (jointly with East Asian Research Center).

In Search of France, by Stanley Hoffmann, Charles P. Kindleberger, Laurence Wylie, Jesse R. Pitts, Jean-Baptiste Duroselle, and François Goguel, 1963.

Somali Nationalism, by Saadia Touval, 1963.

AVAILABLE FROM OTHER PUBLISHERS

The Necessity for Choice, by Henry A. Kissinger, 1961. Harper & Brothers.

Strategy and Arms Control, by Thomas C. Schelling and Morton H. Halperin, 1961. Twentieth Century Fund.

United States Manufacturing Investment in Brazil, by Lincoln Gordon and Engelbert L. Grommers, 1962. Harvard Business School.

OCCASIONAL PAPERS IN INTERNATIONAL AFFAIRS, PUBLISHED BY CENTER FOR INTERNATIONAL AFFAIRS

1. *A Plan for Planning: The Need for a Better Method of Assisting Underdeveloped Countries on Their Economic Policies,* by Gustav F. Papanek, 1961.
2. *The Flow of Resources from Rich to Poor,* by Alan D. Neale, 1961.
3. *Limited War: An Essay on the Development of the Theory and an Annotated Bibliography,* by Morton H. Halperin, 1962.
4. *Reflections on the Failure of the First West Indian Federation,* by Hugh W. Springer, 1962.
5. *On the Interaction of Opposing Forces under Possible Arms Agreements,* by Colonel Glenn A. Kent, 1963.